QUEER CARNIVAL

Queer Carnival

Festivals and Mardi Gras in the South

Amy L. Stone

NEW YORK UNIVERSITY PRESS
New York

NEW YORK UNIVERSITY PRESS
New York
www.nyupress.org

Library of Congress Cataloging-in-Publication Data
Names: Stone, Amy L., author.
Title: Queer carnival : festivals and mardi gras in the South / Amy L. Stone.
Description: New York : New York University Press, [2022] | Includes bibliographical references and index.
Identifiers: LCCN 2021025477 | ISBN 9781479801961 (hardback ; alk. paper) | ISBN 9781479801985 (paperback ; alk. paper) | ISBN 9781479801992 (ebook) | ISBN 9781479802029 (ebook other)
Subjects: LCSH: Gays—Social life and customs—21st century. | Carnival—Southern States. | Festivals—Southern States. | Gay culture—Southern States. | Multiculturalism—Southern States.
Classification: LCC HQ76.3.U52 S685 2022 | DDC 306.76/60975—dc23
LC record available at https://lccn.loc.gov/2021025477

New York University Press books are printed on acid-free paper, and their binding materials are chosen for strength and durability. We strive to use environmentally responsible suppliers and materials to the greatest extent possible in publishing our books.

Manufactured in the United States of America

10 9 8 7 6 5 4 3 2 1

Also available as an ebook

CONTENTS

Introduction

The first time I attended Cornyation I laughed so hard that my cheeks hurt. From my seat in the large Empire Theatre in downtown San Antonio, Texas, I was fascinated by the show from the start, when the "royalty" of the event, King Anchovy, appeared. King Anchovy was none other than the city manager, Sheryl Sculley. She was decked out in a skintight red bodysuit, floor-length cape, and stiletto boots. Sculley danced around the stage as the Masters of Ceremony announced that it was time to "let the queens be unleashed!" King Anchovy presided over an hour-long show of skits that mocked local and national current events using drag, satire, and an often-vulgar sense of humor. A cast of more than one hundred performed in all manner of costume throughout the night. Many of the cast and show designers were Latinx lesbian, gay, bisexual, transgender, or queer (LGBTQ) people. The audience was full of excited adult spectators wearing colorful hats and sashes or vests covered in medals from Fiesta San Antonio events. Fiesta San Antonio is the annual citywide festival for San Antonio, Texas, that includes almost one hundred events, one of which is Cornyation. Some people carried *cascarones*, eggs filled with confetti, that they tossed at each other during intermission. I learned from the friendly heterosexual couple sitting next to me that the event began in 1951 as a fundraiser for a local theater company, and I wondered if the show had the same gay, campy aesthetic back then. I read in the show's program that Cornyation was attended by more than five thousand people a year and had raised almost $2 million for AIDS service organizations (ASOs) and other charities.[1] That night sparked my fascination with LGBTQ involvement in festivals.

A newspaper article the next day reported, "There is probably nowhere else where the city manager goes by the name King Anchovy, dresses up as Superwoman and shares a stage with drag queens doing raunchy spoofs of everything from an upcoming mayoral election to a raid on a polygamist ranch. Through Thursday, San Antonio—at least

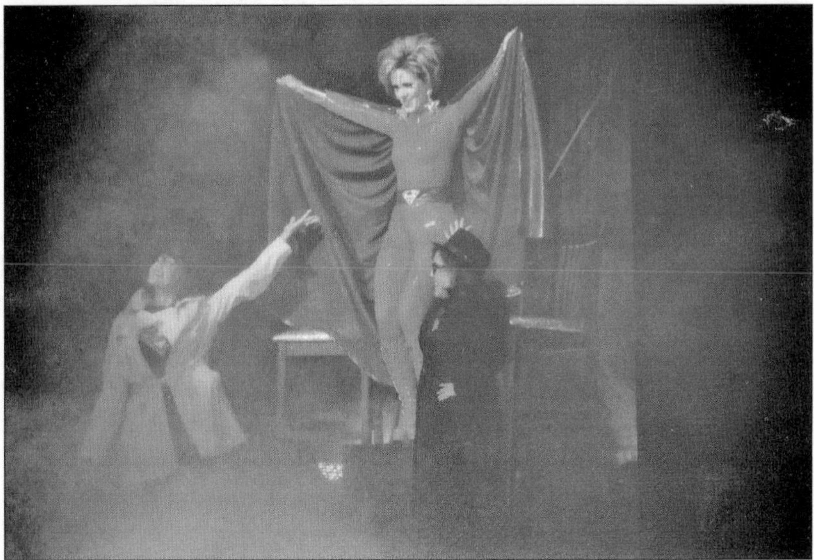

Figure I.1. Sheryl Sculley as King Anchovy

some of San Antonio—is proud to be that place."[2] The cast repeated the show five times over the next two evenings, raising in excess of $120,000 for local charities, most of which went to ASOs.[3] One of the beneficiaries, Michele Durham, the director of Black Effort Against the Threat of AIDS (BEAT AIDS), a small non-profit focused on HIV prevention and testing in the Black community, proclaimed when she received her $35,000 check that "we can't survive without it," as the organization had almost closed its doors the previous month due to lack of funds.[4]

I was filled with questions after watching the show and learning more about it. Cornyation is just one of hundreds of events that take place during the annual citywide festival, Fiesta San Antonio. Are events like this common during Fiesta? How does it affect the city to have a LGBTQ-positive event like Cornyation as a long-standing tradition? Are audience members predominately heterosexual? And, most important, how did the show organizers get the city manager to dance on stage in a provocative outfit?

The show raised bigger questions for me about what it means to be part of a city and community. As LGBTQ people gain more legal rights, it's important to think of more complex ways of being included in society. Legal rights like same-sex marriage or non-discrimination laws are part of what makes LGBTQ people included and recognized in society, but legal change is not enough. Having full citizenship is more than a passport or social security card. The term "second-class citizen" describes someone who is a legal part of society but is otherwise marginalized. This book focuses on the cultural aspects of citizenship, which capture the important elements of belonging and acknowledgment by emphasizing what scholars James Holston and Arjun Appadurai refer to as "the moral and performative dimensions of membership which define meanings and practices of belonging in society."[5] This book locates these questions of belonging and acknowledgment as rooted in place, as something that an individual may feel about where they live. I analyze how this citizenship is about a sense of belonging, including incorporation into community traditions and rituals, that includes valuing LGBTQ people for their cultural difference. I also look at how this citizenship forces scholars to rethink the importance of festivals, the city, and the South and Southwest for LGBTQ people.

This book is not about Pride. Pride events, the annual parades or festivals held in many cities in the summer by the LGBTQ community, are an important part of LGBTQ culture and have been the subject of many studies.[6] Pride events are emblematic of cultural change and defiant visibility. Pride events are ultimately organized by the LGBTQ community and reflect the values of many community members.

Instead, this book approaches LGBTQ belonging and citizenship by analyzing it through urban cultural events. Festivals play an essential role in urban culture, and these events have been neglected by scholars of citizenship and urban life.[7] From the Mardi Gras celebrations in the Deep South to the Mummers Parade in Philadelphia to the Portland Rose Festival, communities across the United States gather to celebrate, participate in parades, encourage tourism, cultivate local traditions, and craft a sense of place. Early sociologists like Émile Durkheim theorized about the importance of celebrations like festivals for developing a sense of collective effervescence or community among participants.[8] I am interested in large public festivals like Fiesta San Antonio, because these festivals are *supposed to be* a time when the city comes together as one to appreciate the diverse contributions of people within the city. Festivals such as Fiesta are understood as an important part of city life and perhaps characteristic of the city itself. In this way, festivals are part of how a sense of place is made in the city.[9] San Antonio is often described as "the Fiesta city," for example. During festivals, *whose* culture gets included and valued, *which* events are allowed, and *how* different communities are represented, become socially significant and fraught with questions. In *Music/City*, a study of music festivals in the United States, sociologist Jonathan Wynn describes festivals as "illuminating some of the key struggles in our modern urban and cultural lives, as they bring some groups together and marginalize others, impose a crafted image of place for locals and visitors, and create unintended opportunities and challenges."[10]

These celebrations also communicate power and social relations.[11] There is a long history of conflict about racial segregation in American urban festivals.[12] Black, Latinx, and indigenous individuals often create what Marvin Dawkins describes as "parallel structures," separate festival organizations for marginalized communities.[13] There is also a history of contention about LGBTQ involvement in public events such as festivals and parades.[14] In 1995, the US Supreme Court heard the case *Hurley v. Irish American Gay, Lesbian, and Bisexual Group of Boston*, in which a LGBTQ organization sued for the right to march in Boston's St. Patrick's Day parade. The Supreme Court ruled that the parade organizers had the right to exclude the group, and all Irish LGBTQ groups were excluded from the parade for two decades, until a veteran's group was permitted to march in 2015. In other words, a decade after same-sex marriage became legal in Massachusetts, gay and lesbian groups were not allowed to march in the St. Patrick's Day parade. In March 2020, when Miss Staten Island came out publicly as bisexual, she was banned by organizers from marching in the same parade.[15] Although there are many examples like these, there is limited research available on the greater context and history of these incidents, and even less is known about LGBTQ involvement in urban festivals in the United States.

For this book I traveled across the Gulf South and American Southwest, interviewing people and attending festival events. Along the way, I learned a lot about how to eat crawfish, wear a tuxedo, make my own festival hat, and catch beads. I studied two types of festivals common in this region: Carnival or Mardi Gras traditions of the Gulf South and the historical pageantry of Southwestern Fiesta celebrations.

I conducted research on Mardi Gras in Mobile, Alabama, and Baton Rouge, Louisiana. Mardi Gras is run by private organizations called krewes that sponsor private masque balls and organize public parades. Except for the New Orleans French Quarter, most Mardi Gras parades are targeted to families and children. I collected data on Fiestas in Santa Fe, New Mexico, and San Antonio, Texas. Fiestas are typically ten-day events that are common throughout Texas, New Mexico, and Southern California. These fiestas tend to include multiple parades, fairs, theatrical events, and the crowning of festival royalty. Many Southwestern festivals rely on pageantry about the Western frontier, romanticized Spanish history, and stories of racist conquest.

In this book, I take the cultural traditions of each festival seriously and examine the way that LGBTQ people fit themselves into these traditions. I build on the approaches of scholars studying citizenship, culture, and symbolic interaction to highlight how the cultural traditions of these festivals impact LGBTQ people's sense of belonging in the city. Two of the festivals in this study—Fiesta de Santa Fe and Mobile Mardi Gras—have a reputation for being more old-fashioned, traditionalistic festivals: religious, controlled by local social elites, or having strict reinforcement of festival traditions. Among these four cities, only one of them, Santa Fe, has a strong reputation for being LGBTQ-friendly. The Santa Fe city website has a section for gay and lesbian visitors and has a large population of gay and lesbian retirees. Yet, Fiesta de Santa Fe was the most religious festival event of the four cities and had the least visible involvement of LGBTQ people in the event.

Throughout this book, I argue that we need to push beyond seeing regions or cities as inherently hostile or welcoming places for LGBTQ people and instead understand citizenship in the city as contingent, relational, and uneven. How LGBTQ people fit into city festival life depends on how they relate to the cultural traditions of the festival and city in question, how they are positioned in relation to other festival participants, and their demographics. But festival participation can be a rich site for LGBTQ participants to be valued for their cultural differences and find a sense of belonging in the city.

The LGBTQ urban residents of the South and Southwest in this book are often *queer citizens*, not because they necessarily identify as queer personally, but because of their defiant push for belonging and recognition within their city traditions and festivities. Some scholars have described queer sensibilities and citizenship as fundamentally at odds with each other, as the respectability required of citizenship cannot be queered.[16] However, the queer citizenship in this study embraces contradictions. LGBTQ people in this study find their place in the city spatially and socially, by both fitting into existing cultural traditions and actively challenging these traditions. They are queer citizens in the ways that they use glitter, satire, and fabulousness to make a place for themselves in the city.

In these cities, LGBTQ participants hold elaborate balls, raise money for HIV/AIDS and other relevant causes, run alternative and innovative events, crown their own festival royalty, push the boundaries of social elites, and critique racist festival practices. I argue in this book that LGBTQ city dwellers are effective at making inclusive collective parties that bring the city together. LGBTQ artistry is at times a spectacle but also can serve as a distinctly LGBTQ contribution to the city's cultural event. Some contributions are more visible than others: Cisgender gay men consistently receive greater recognition for their artistic and cultural contributions to festivals. LGBTQ participants are still excluded from some of the most heteronormative and racially exclusive events of elites. LGBTQ-run festival events can also be a site of reconciliation between parents and their LGBTQ adult children, as parents show up to lend their support. Many scholars have argued that part of marginalized groups becoming accepted in society is whether these groups are valued for their contribution to society *and* recognized for their difference. In this study, LGBTQ participants in festivals often experienced both: a sense of being valued for their cultural contribution to the city and respect for the glitter and fabulousness of LGBTQ culture.

Why Festivals?

I read about the first LGBTQ group to march in the 2015 St. Patrick's Day parade on my phone while waiting for a Mardi Gras men's parade to start in Lafayette, Louisiana. Lafayette is not one of the cities in my study, but I was determined to watch one of the few examples of gay men parading openly downtown for the general public during Mardi Gras in the Gulf South. Lafayette was perhaps a surprising place for this parade to happen, because it is a small city of about 120,000 people in the Acadiana or French Louisiana part of the state. Although separated from Baton Rouge, a city that I did study, by a long causeway bridge over the largest swamp in the United States, there were many connections between the LGBTQ communities in the two cities. That night, I was underdressed for the bitterly cold February evening. I impulsively bought a Hello Kitty hat that had a long scarf and mittens attached to it from one of the vendors that wheeled a cart full of light-up toys and hats through the parade route before things got started. Although Hello Kitty is definitely not my aesthetic, the hat was warm and re-giftable to a friend. I wrapped the scarf and mittens around my cold hands as I continued to read on my phone about the first time an openly LGBTQ group could march in the infamous St. Patrick's Day parade.

A group composed of gay men, the Krewe of Apollo de Lafayette, had two floats at the end of this Carnival parade, which is essentially a parade of white men's festival organizations. I had wandered by the floats while they were lined up that afternoon in front of the Acadian Cultural Center. The floats were rented by all the festival groups to spare them the expense of having to design and store their own floats. The Krewe of Apollo members were busy decorating their float with no fewer than four rainbow Pride flags and the insignia of the club, a topless mythical-looking young white figure of Apollo. They had stashes of regular beads and special rainbow beads to throw. Krewe members were busy putting on masks and various costumes when I came by. Most of the participants were middle-aged or young adult white gay men. The Mardi Gras royalty of the group, a Black gay man dressed in drag with an exuberant wig, fur stole, and sparkling crown as the "queen" and a young white man dressed in a sparkling suit and crown as the "king," were featured on the top of one of the parade floats. I was struck to see that they were the only group parading among a dozen floats that had Black men on their float, and later I discovered that LGBTQ festival organizations in the South have the longest history of commitment to racially integrated festival organizations. I talked to the men for almost an hour while they stapled materials onto the two floats and got ready. Two middle-aged white men filled me in on the history of the krewe's participation in the parade. Although the krewe was established in 1976, the men's parade was more recent. The Krewe of Apollo de Lafayette, known explicitly as a gay men's krewe, had

Figure 1.2. Krewe of Apollo Lafayette parading

been asked to join almost a decade ago by the other men's krewes that organized the parade. "We've had no issues," says Tim, who emphatically stapled on their insignia as he said it. "The crowd is never mean to us, but sometimes they throw the cheap penny beads back at us."

When the parade got going, I stood downtown leaning against the barricades with my Hello Kitty hat on, standing in a crowd of senior citizens, young white men with mullets and disdain for the parade, and young Black woman and white man next to me who screamed the names of the Krewe of Apollo de Lafayette members. They are friends of the krewe members, they tell me, and they shout their friends' names during the parade in hopes of getting coveted special rainbow beads thrown by the krewe members. I was initially concerned that the gay men's krewe was at the end of the parade as a kind of marginalization. But I realized almost immediately that they were the grand finale. I could hear them coming around the corner before I saw them, and the crowd started getting louder and more enthusiastic as they anticipated the krewe's arrival. The krewe float had a DJ playing loud music on a sound system and two searchlights flashing all over the buildings and sky downtown. At the helm of the first float was a krewe member dressed in a Captain America-style costume, including a helmet and shield that was decorated with LED lights. The krewe members threw beads at parade goers. The last float had at least three Pride flags on the back of it. I recorded video of the floats on my phone as they passed, chasing the slow-moving floats down several blocks of the parade route to follow the flow of the parade. Several things about this moment struck me: The gay men in Lafayette had been included in the parade without issue for almost a decade, there was nothing hidden or discreet about their presence, and ultimately being included in the parade is symbolically important.

Power and Inequality During Festivals

Much of the scholarship on festivals is written in the humanities, where attention is focused on the carnivalesque qualities of the events. Theories of the carnivalesque conceptualize festival time as a liminal or "in-between" space where the status quo is partially or completely inverted. Many scholars argue that festivals, by permitting temporary moments of subversion, allow people to blow off steam and then uphold the status quo the rest of the year.[17]

To this end, transgressive displays like irreverence or cross-dressing become part of the way festivals turn the "world upside down." Similarly, events like drag shows or festival performances are quickly dismissed by some people as just a spectacle, as something that allows a heterosexual public to consume yet dehumanize queer people. Although festival events can be a spectacle, sociological research also shows us that even short events like drag shows and trashy talk shows on LGBTQ issues can positively impact heterosexual audiences.[18] Additionally, festival events may be symbolically important for both organizers and attendees.

In this book, I urge readers to consider festivals in more complex ways, as nuanced public events that combine belonging, spectacles, status intensification, commemoration, hierarchies, and resistance. Although these festivals are oriented toward tourism, they are simultaneously about belonging and placemaking by city residents. In a broader sense, festivals are about the negotiation of urban space and place, including what geographer Tim Cresswell describes as the way "ideas about what is right, just and appropriate are transmitted through space and place."[19] For example, parades during festivals can be a way of exerting elite superiority and patriotism but can also be used as a form of democracy without government through the reclamation of public space by marginalized community members.[20]

Central to my approach is the ways that festivals bring to the surface and allow contestation of power dynamics that happen throughout the year. My analysis takes seriously the historical roots of these festivals in relation to processes of settler colonialism and racial segregation. Settler colonialism is a system of displacing, destroying, and appropriating indigenous people and culture to replace it with a new society of settlers.[21] Settler colonialism does not just describe the past but is an ongoing system in which indigenous customs are appropriated and consumed within festivals while indigenous people are displaced and tokenized. The historical pageantry of Southwestern fiestas includes celebration of conquest. Racial segregation includes the creation and defense of white-only organizations that are featured prominently in festival events as the oldest, most high-status events. These roots are enduring parts of such festivals. For example, white high-status krewes in Mobile, Alabama, and other Gulf South cities often still throw large carnival balls that exclude Black participants. The major royalty of Fiesta San Antonio, the Queen of the Order of the Alamo, has never been crowned to a Latina woman, in a city that is majority Latinx.

These systems of power and inequality are reinforced most consistently by local social elites. Festivals are a place where social elites—wealthy and socially powerful residents of the city who often form a tight-knit, racially exclusive group—exert a lot of social power. Social elites are usually the most prominent royalty of the festival and run some of the most prestigious and exclusive events. These events are part of the way that symbolic boundaries enforce social inequalities.[22] Festivals are a site where LGBTQ participants can directly face off against social elites and challenge cultural hierarchies and valuations. LGBTQ festival participants make dresses for elite debutantes, attempt to join elite festival organizations, and openly satirize elite culture in their events.

These power dynamics are embedded within the cultural traditions of each festival in this book. Cultural structures—or institutionalized cultural repertoires—involve "patterned logics" that are repeated annually in festivals.[23] Yearly, the same people are in charge, familiar symbols are deployed, and the overall shape of the festival remains similar. There is a dynamic quality to repetition and invention in these festivals, described by Samuel Kinser, a scholar of Mardi Gras, below:

> Carnival is so ambivalent in nature that it produces its own opposite, which is mechanical, spiritless, drab repetition. If applause greets a Mardi Gras gesture and it feels good, its success encourages its incorporation in a traditional repertory . . . Inevitably, then, Mardi Gras parades exhibit many loads of dead wood, antique traditions blindly repeated from year to year until they are knocked off the float-wagons by the genius of excess and enlargement, which has inspired someone else's inventions and drawn from the crowd bigger yells of glee. The contrast between invention and repetition, between the carnivalesque and traditional, gives a dynamic pattern to Carnival's unfolding qualities over the years.[24]

The cultural structures of festivals are one part of how cities are socially and culturally made. Gerald Suttles astutely described some of these cultural structures in the city as the durability and "cumulative texture of local urban culture," stressing the importance of "sentiments and symbols" in the creation of this local culture.[25] In each of the four cities studied here, there were festival traditions that were considered distinct to that city and its local culture.

In this study, LGBTQ festival participation gains recognition when it fits within the cultural structures of local urban culture. LGBTQ people are often considered at odds with tradition, yet in this study LGBTQ people engage meaningfully with local traditions that are important to them and this engagement enhances their sense of belonging in the city. Some of these festival traditions overlap well with LGBTQ culture. For example, one white lesbian interviewee in Mobile, Alabama, told me that, "Mobile is a party town anyway, so if you put on a good party, everybody respects you for it." And, indeed, some LGBTQ people can put on a good party. But urban festivals are also an opportunity for LGBTQ people to grapple with their feelings about belonging and contributing to cultural traditions—everything from religious ritual to segregated events. Because of this complex relationship between place, tradition, and queerness, I argue these festivals are an excellent site to study recognition and cultural citizenship for LGBTQ people.

Recognition and Cultural Citizenship

Picture this. Two women are romantically involved. They can legally get married but when visiting family, they avoid holding hands or touching each other due to family disapproval. A citywide film festival refuses to include a film about transgender coming-of-age stories because it's too "political" and "controversial." A transgender woman goes to her church, and the pastor rails against the increasing visibility of transgender people in society, proclaiming that transgender rights are really "men trying to use women's bathrooms." The city's history museum includes information about the social history of the city but fails to include information on LGBTQ contributions to city life. At an awards celebration, philanthropists and volunteers across the community are recognized, but none of them are individuals who support ASOs or LGBTQ organizations.

Scholars have long debated what creates full inclusion for groups in society.[26] Most research on citizenship, particularly LGBTQ citizenship, focuses disproportionately on the relations between citizens and the state and the formal rights acquired by citizens, like laws about same-sex marriage or discrimination.[27] What happens in the courtroom or in the statehouse is often the easiest form of progress to observe and study. Yet legal rights do not guarantee that someone is socially or culturally integrated into society.[28] For example, legal rights do not guarantee family acceptance, societal approval, positive media representation, or respect from others.

Marginalized groups are often not recognized for their contributions to society. Scholars like Nancy Fraser have long argued inequality comes not just from the unequal distribution of resources like money but also through difference in recognition, which is less tangible than money.[29] This recognition is about acknowledging the personal dignity in individuals and their place in society, what Margaret Somers refers to as "a moral equal treated by the same standards and values and due the same level of respect and dignity as all other members."[30]

Sociologist Michèle Lamont asserts that one issue faced by marginalized groups in society is a *recognition gap*, that the positive social worth of a group is unacknowledged and unrecognized by others.[31] This recognition gap is multilayered, from the interpersonal to the institutional level. In everyday life, disrespect may be a profound part of this recognition gap. In a multi-nation study of racial marginalization, minoritized people were more likely to mention as problematic being stigmatized, experiencing "assault on worth," and desiring respect than episodes of discrimination.[32] Sometimes this recognition is formal. For example, memorials and statues signify who is considered to have positive social worth. Whose accomplishments get featured in the history museum is a recognition process.

There are some long-standing barriers to this recognition gap in the United States for LGBTQ people, barriers that persist particularly for transgender people. We could easily describe these barriers as homophobia, transphobia, or biphobia, casting the issue of the recognition gap onto the prejudices of individuals. But there is a systemic way that morality politics interferes with the recognition of LGBTQ citizenship, in which religious, scientific, and cultural traditions create a barrier against this citizenship.[33] A history of religious disapproval against LGBTQ sexuality, relationships, and support in public life contributes to the second-class citizenship of LGBTQ people in the United States.[34]

To counter morality politics, there is often pressure for LGBTQ people to reject their culture and conform to mainstream cisgender, heterosexual norms.[35] Historically, citizenship was created in the United States for white, wealthy heterosexual men.[36] Citizenship is conflated with assimilation and the expectation that minority group members will bend and conform to majority culture to be considered full citizens. Marginalized group members may experience pressure to engage in what scholar Evelyn Brooks Higginbotham calls the *politics of respectability*, to prove their moral worth as citizens by crafting respectable social identities and engaging in boundary work to distance themselves from less respectable group members.[37] For LGBTQ individuals, then, these politics of respectability may include diminishing visible same-sex affection, limiting gender-transgressive behavior, and downplaying queer sexual norms.[38] For example, drag and camp—two common forms of queer visibility at festivals—are two gay cultural styles that are rarely associated with citizenship and respectability.[39]

Yet at the same time, part of cultural citizenship is that groups have what anthropologist Renato Rosaldo has called the "right to be different."[40] Difference is often misunderstood as potentially antagonistic and disruptive.[41] However, seeking the respect for cultural difference is an important part of LGBTQ activism. The most common LGBTQ urban events—annual Pride parades and festivals—are focused on advocacy for cultural change through visibility. Early Pride parades in the 1970s had the central purpose of "proclaiming the cultural worth and dignity of gays and lesbians."[42] Early Pride events functioned as an event to publicly celebrate LGBTQ identities, to include the many parts of the LGBTQ community, and to have fun. As Katherine Bruce argues in her book about Pride parades, "just because a public act is fun does not mean that it is unintentional."[43]

Here, I argue that festivals are just one way of looking at this issue of belonging that can give us insight into how the recognition gap may be intensified or narrowed within a particular social context. First, *recognition is about more than being tolerated, it is about being wanted and valued for your difference.* We underestimate the value of being desired. In her book, *The Tolerance Trap*, Suzanna Walters suggests that for marginalized groups to be fully included in society requires more than "tolerance." She states that "to live freely and fully is not to be 'tolerated' but to be included, even sometimes celebrated."[44] In this book, recognition was about similar kinds of access, being treated the same as other groups or organizations by festival organizers, but it was also about being valued and celebrated.

Second, *recognition does not accrue evenly to marginalized group members.* The forms of culture that are the most familiar get the most recognition. Gay male culture is disproportionately recognized. At these festival events, there was more appreciation for camp, drag, and other gay aesthetics—along with an ethos of fabulousness—than any other identifiable part of the LGBTQ community. Like citizenship in general, the LGBTQ community privileges white men at the expense of women, racial minorities, bisexuals, and gender-transgressive individuals within the community.[45] This emphasis on gay male culture alienates other members of the LGBTQ community. There were also some parts of festival life that were more impenetrable by all LGBTQ people—specifically, the events run by entrenched social elites, especially white social elites.

Third, as symbolic interactionists have long understood, *recognition is always contextual*, in this case within the context of local festival cultural structures and city power dynamics. Anthropologist Aihwa Ong describes the process of cultural citizenship as simultaneously one of minority members asserting their cultural difference ("self-making") and the existing cultural structures shaping the possibilities of what can happen ("being made").[46] LGBTQ people are constantly asserting their selves during festivals, but they do so within the existing possibilities. Lamont suggests that sociologists have not thoroughly studied destigmatization, or "the process by which low-status groups gain recognition and worth."[47] Lamont suggests that stigmatized groups draw on cultural repertoires or structures in their environments to get recognition and become less stigmatized.[48] I argue that LGBTQ groups draw on festival cultural structures and situate themselves within local festival culture while simultaneously and actively challenging the elitism and racism of that culture. These challenges are occurring in the urban South and Southwest, the regional focus of this book.

The Queer Citizen in the South and Southwestern City

When I tell people outside of the South that I study LGBTQ life in Texas, I sometimes get the puzzling response that Texas does not seem the kind of place where there would be extensive opportunities to study gay life.[49] Usually I point out that an estimated 600,000 LGBTQ adults live in Texas and that all major cities in Texas have thriving LGBTQ communities.[50] Texas is one of the most populous states, I argue. Of course there are LGBTQ people here! The person making this response invariably disregards the Latinx heritage of the state in favor of stereotypes about cowboy hats, the Alamo, and guns.

But scholars know surprisingly little about urban life in the South and Southwest. Southern cities have had a slower progressive development compared to some of their Northern counterparts, and Southern city life challenges existing theories about race, urban forms, and immigration in the city.[51] The Sun Belt cities of the United States—a region of urban development that spans between Southern California to the southeastern coast of the United States—are some of the fastest growing cities in the country with the most dramatic development taking place since World War II.[52]

Scholars know even less about queer urban life in the South and Southwest. Even though more than 35 percent of LGBTQ people live in the South and Southwest states, scholars know significantly less about the urban LGBTQ experience in these regions.[53] The South is often depicted as inherently hostile to queer life. Yet E. Patrick Johnson asserts that "the South is always already queer."[54] Much research on LGBTQ urban experiences is collected in the big four major cities or the "great cities": San Francisco, New York, Los Angeles, and Chicago.[55] Many theories about how urban queer life works are created studying the same neighborhoods and cities over and over again.[56] It is important to study LGBTQ life everywhere, but it is problematic to develop theories about the social world based on a few, atypical places. These studies rely upon several assumptions: that most LGBTQ life happens in the great cities and that all other LGBTQ urban life is merely a copycat of trends in these major cities.[57] This book challenges many of these assumptions.

Urban research on LGBTQ life disproportionately focuses on a few things—gay neighborhoods (or "gayborhoods"), bars, or activism. Urban scholar Japonica Brown-Saracino queries, "I often wonder what we would know about sexualities and place if our inquiries were more expansive."[58] In this book, I take a page from geographer Gavin Brown, who suggests that we need to expand the range of urban LGBTQ spaces we study, that we need to look beyond "not just the inner-city leisure zones and gentrified neighborhoods" and "consider the spatial organization of sexualities across the whole of urban space, in a way that is attentive to the specific histories and geographies of each city."[59] For example, scholars studying Southern LGBTQ life demonstrate the importance of churches and other Southern cultural forms in the city.[60] Beyond LGBTQ spaces, we need to understand the complex ways that LGBTQ people become citizens of the city.

I studied these four cities—Mobile, Baton Rouge, San Antonio, and Santa Fe—because they are all examples of typical cities that LGBTQ people live in. These cities provide insight into what the experience might be of LGBTQ people living in the urban South and Southwest.

Studies of Southern urban life tends to focus on cities like Austin, New Orleans, or Atlanta, that have a history of LGBTQ supportive legislation and policies. But I believe we need to think in more complex ways about how to study LGBTQ urban life and what it means to be recognized in urban spaces in places more similar to where the majority of LGBTQ people actually live.

Place deeply shapes the texture of LGBTQ community, identity, and subjectivities.[61] In her study of Pride parades across the United States, Katherine Bruce argues that what is defiant visibility in each city depends on the local context.[62] Holding hands in public may be defiantly assertive at one event and completely quotidian at another Pride event. This study focuses on the (often temporary but recurring) spaces that LGBTQ people make in the city during festivals. For example, among the major events that define Mardi Gras season in the Gulf South cities of Mobile and Baton Rouge are private masque balls put on by krewes. I spent time at six masque balls run by LGBTQ krewes in these two cities, and two of these balls had more than one thousand guests in attendance, including many heterosexual attendees and the city mayor. Krewe members—mostly white lesbian women and/or gay men—intentionally transformed major convention ballrooms into intentional LGBTQ spaces for the evening. These spaces were shaped by the cultural traditions of festivals but also frequently challenged them. For example, many private masque balls are racially segregated, while LGBTQ krewes have a long history of being racially integrated for both krewe members and ball attendees.

Studying the Carnival City

I never imagined myself as someone who would study festivals. I am not a fan of parades and crowds, and I rarely drink. I do not enjoy staying up late, and I have a vascular disorder that makes drinking and being on my feet complicated to navigate. Festivals are not a subject I had interest in before I began this project. As an academic, most of my research has been focused on politics and organizations in the LGBTQ community. I have studied questions of how LGBTQ people gain political power, get laws passed, protect those laws from attack, and negotiate all the significant differences within the community. Indeed, I was in the middle of writing a book about anti-gay ballot measures in 2009 when the inspiration for this book struck during a show of Cornyation, as I described at the start of this chapter. I often joke during academic talks that I needed to cleanse my palate of studying anti-LGBTQ activism for more than a decade by studying something that has more glitter and rhinestones. However, some of the same questions about belonging, anti-gay animus, and community that motivated my previous work also drive this study.

I began this research in 2012 with a summer project on the early history of Cornyation, the outrageous Fiesta San Antonio tradition that began in the 1950s. With my summer research assistants Jady and Caitlin, I scoured old archives, interviewed people who were involved in the show back in the 1950s and 1960s, and happened upon old copies of the subversively campy scripts in the closet of the local theater company.[63] The study quickly grew beyond this small project. The next summer I jumped in my car with my student research assistant, Analicia, and drove from San Antonio, Texas, to Mobile, Alabama. I remember the surreal feeling I experienced going over the Atchafalaya Bridge, an 18-mile passage over swampland and waterways to get from Lafayette, Louisiana to Baton Rouge. I had never been in the Deep South before, and the two-week trip was a crash course in the white sand beaches of Mississippi, crawfish, Mardi Gras etiquette, regional food specialties, and the beauty of the region. We toured Carnival museums, met members of Mardi Gras krewes in multiple cities, and got invitations to private balls for the next festival season.

Four years later, I had attended more than one hundred days of festival events across the South and Southwest, conducted 101 interviews, and spent additional weeks in the summer camped out in various cities doing research. I read archival materials about LGBTQ and festival history in museums, public libraries, storage units kept by festival groups, and individuals' living rooms. The ephemera that comes with festivals—special doubloons for balls, homemade and manufactured fiesta pins, and t-shirts from events—piled up in my suitcases next to the formal wear that was required for Carnival balls. I now own two tuxedos, a floor-length ball gown, and more colorful hats and costumes than I know what to do with.

Festivals are diffuse and complicated, so I approached data collection with attention to obtaining diverse perspectives on the individual

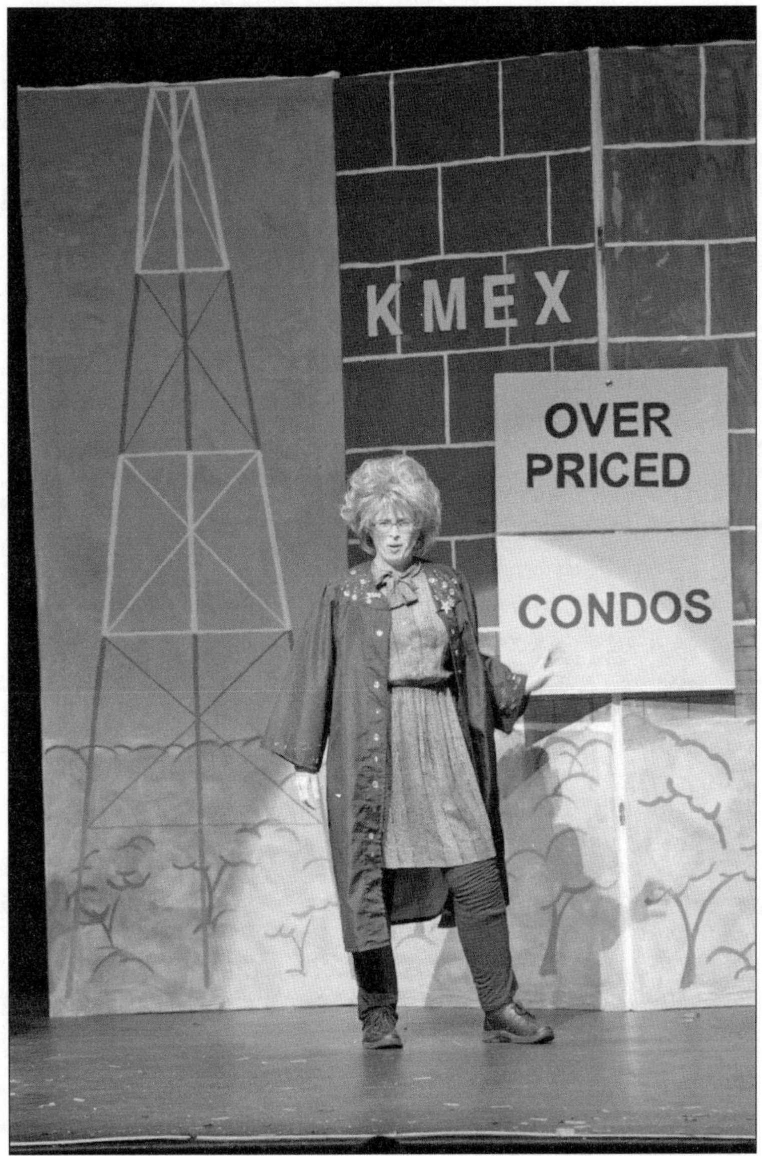

Figure 1.3. Author as Cornyation duchess in skit about gentrification. Credit: Lauryn Farris

events and overall festival experience. I tried to capture events that openly embraced LGBTQ culture and participation, events that evoked more traditional festival culture, and events that were "people's events" and intended to bring the whole city together at one time. I attended multiple examples of each of these types of events in each city, speaking with organizers, participants, guests, and staff members who worked the events. I paid special attention to the largest LGBTQ-run events in each city. These are most likely to be attended by social elites, recognized in museum displays, and written about in the local paper; thus they are critical sites for the acknowledgment of LGBTQ contributions. Santa Fe does not have an explicitly LGBTQ event. I attended the major LGBTQ events in the other three cities—Order of Osiris in Mobile, Krewe of Apollo in Baton Rouge, and Cornyation in San Antonio—multiple times and became more involved. For the two major krewes, I attended dinners with family members, royalty receptions, members' brunches, and ball setup and dress rehearsal. For Cornyation, I worked as stage crew for two years and performed on stage for two additional years. Some of the festivals—those in San Antonio and Mobile—are much larger than those in Santa Fe and Baton Rouge. It is not just that greater numbers of people attend, but there are multiple ways that LGBTQ people can directly or indirectly engage with the event. So, I have conducted more interviews and spent disproportionately more time studying festival life in these two cities.

In each city, I interviewed organizers of explicitly LGBTQ organizations or events (e.g., LGBTQ krewes, events like Cornyation), LGBTQ participants in general festival organizations, along with LGBTQ individuals who participate in the festival as royalty, organizers, and professionals (e.g., hairdressers, artists, seamstresses). I also interviewed people at each site who could provide an overview of festival history, organization, and culture to help ascertain how exclusive the festival culture is. For example, in Mobile, I spoke with the local historian who reenacts major figures from Mardi Gras history, the business organizer at a Mardi Gras supply store who works with all the krewe members, and the curator at the Carnival Museum. I also read about the representation of LGBTQ events and figures in the local media, including a search of newspaper databases, and conducted archival research on the history of the festival and festival events.

In this book, I use the names of the cities and organizations I studied. Information about almost all these organizations and events is widely available online. Transparency about the place of research is an important part of ethnography.[64] However, I do maintain the confidentiality of my interviewees and informants. Almost all names used in this book are pseudonyms, apart from the names of friends, assistants, and colleagues who attended events with me and a few individuals who consented (or insisted) that I use their real name.

Overview of Chapters

In the first two chapters, I provide important background information on this study and each individual case. In chapter 1, I provide an overview of historical understandings of the South and Southwest and the scholarly study of festivals. Chapter 2 will dispel misunderstandings about Mardi Gras and Carnival in the American Gulf South that are based on limited media coverage of the tourist debauchery of the New Orleans French Quarter. I provide a brief overview of the distinctly different ways that Carnival is celebrated in Mobile, Alabama, and Baton Rouge, Louisiana, along with highlighting what these two cities have in common. Chapter 2 also positions Southwestern Fiesta celebrations within the history of settler colonialism, which has most profoundly impacted the way Fiesta de Santa Fe is organized. This chapter highlights three commonalities between Mardi Gras and Fiesta traditions: the control of festival content by social elites, the role of debutante culture, and racist festival histories.

I then take up issues of being wanted, making community, gaining access and acknowledgment, taking care of one's own, and symbolizing progress. Chapter 3, "The Hottest Ticket in Town Is a Gay Ball," focuses on the way that LGBTQ accomplishments during festivals create value and respect for gay culture. In three cities in this project, multiple sources, including interviewees and news coverage of events, describe the largest LGBTQ-sponsored events as the "hottest ticket" during the festival. These events are *the best* fundraisers, *the most* professional performances, *the* "raunchiest and cheapest" events. This chapter is about how creating these large events is fundamentally about being wanted, although this recognition focuses disproportionately on the fabulousness of gay male culture. Chapter 4, “Inclusive Collective Partying,” describes how these LGBTQ events create inclusive collective parties as a way of forging community. I argue that in some cities, LGBTQ festival organizers use these inclusive collective parties as a limited way of resisting racial segregation and settler colonialism during festivals. Conversely, other LGBTQ events struggle to maintain their cultural autonomy or keep the event intentionally small and inclusive to foster community.

In chapter 5, “Social Elites, Glass Closets, and Contested Spaces,” I analyze the ways that LGBTQ individuals gain access and acknowledgment, such as being included as festival royalty, being recognized by festival organizations, and being included in museum exhibits. This push for access and acknowledgment is very much about fitting into cultural traditions and feeling out of place in the city. I argue that in more traditionalistic festivals, LGBTQ people are expected to remain in the glass closet to participate in social elite events. In chapter 6, “Fundraising and Benevolent Aid,” I highlight the role the festival events have played in fundraising for AIDS and ASOs. These fundraisers are more than a politics of respectability but rather a profound way of enacting benevolent aid and taking care of one’s own community members. Chapter 7, “Partying with the Mayor and Your Mom,” is about the symbolic importance of major political figures and family members attending LGBTQ festival events. The mayor and your mom visibly and enthusiastically supporting LGBTQ cultural events symbolized progress and acceptance that was often reconciliatory for LGBTQ participants.

The conclusion returns to broader questions about citizenship, belonging, and the city. In the appendix, I provide an overview of the methods I used for the book with attention to the process of studying ephemeral events and secret societies.

Note on Language

Throughout this book, I am attentive to the language that people use to describe their own race, gender, and sexuality and the way this language reflects their sense of place. For example, I use the term Hispano to discuss Hispanic identifications in New Mexico, a term that is wildly inappropriate to described Latino/Latina/Latinx identities in San Antonio, Texas. Latinx is not used much in the broader San Antonio community but is common in the LGBTQ community. I am also attentive to the terms that individuals use to describe themselves. I do not edit my interviewees when they use outdated language about their own transgender identities, such as describing themselves as "transgenders" or "half and half." These are the ways they speak about themselves. It does not fit neatly into what Jason Orne refers to as queernormativity, the reliance on the right phrases to signal queer virtue.[65] However, this language is authentic to how individuals understand themselves.

I also rarely use the word "queer" to describe the identities of my interviewees, as few of them identified as queer. Instead, I think of the kind of citizenship they are crafting as a queer sort of citizenship. I consistently use the acronym LGBTQ in my project, even though few interviewees openly identified as queer, transgender, or bisexual. Even when people did not explicitly identify as these identities on their interview demographics form, they occasionally gestured toward queer, transgender, or bisexual sentiments or understandings of themselves. Also, these festival events were attended by people across the LGBTQ spectrum, even if the organizers of the events were frequently gay- and lesbian-identified people.

1

Thinking about the South, the Southwest, and Festivals

When I discuss this research project with other people, I get a few typical responses. One response is that these cities are an odd place to study LGBTQ cultural citizenship, as the Deep South and Texas are not known for their accepting ways. "That happens in Texas?!" well-meaning colleagues from outside the state often exclaim. The second, contradictory response is that *of course* a festival like Mardi Gras includes gay visibility, as the event encourages revelry and rule breaking. Amidst all the drunkenness and debauchery of festivals, there must de facto be room for gay culture like drag and same-sex affection. This hypothetical complete acceptance lasts only for a moment, as it disappears after the festival ends. There is an overwhelming assumption that what happens during festivals does not matter the rest of the year.

These responses are at odds with each other, as if the urban South and Southwest is simultaneously irrevocably hostile most of the time and completely accepting once a year. I contend that these images of the South, the Southwest, and festivals rely on limited understandings of all three things. These caricatures obscure our ability to see the complexity of both life in the South and Southwest and the importance of festivals. In this chapter, I provide an overview of conceptions and misconceptions about the urban South and Southwest and festivals.

The South and Southwest

There is a long history of consuming, distancing, and romanticizing the South and Southwest.[1] Many scholars have argued that the South and Southwest operate in a complex way as an "internal other," a contrast to the overcivilized East and progressive West coasts.[2] Both regions are frequently portrayed as developmentally backward or stunted, an "easy repository for all that is backward and hurtful in the United States,"[3] cast before the North in time ("two decades behind") and culturally or geographically distinct. According to historian Donna Jo Smith, "America has long projected its 'Queer Other' onto the South."[4]

The Southerner pictured in Smith's projection is invariably white, rural, straight, attached to the Confederate flag, and bigoted. The images of the South and Southwest are often counter to our images of the city, as a place of freedom, homosexuality, progressiveness, and openness to multiculturalism.[5] Yet, most Black and Hispanic residents of the United States reside in the South and Southwest, along with a large proportion of American Indians. In *Chocolate Cities*, Marcus Anthony Hunter and Zandria Robinson argue that Black American social life occurs mostly in "The South" but also that Black migrants from the South have brought Black Southern customs with them across urban America.[6]

Historians, scholars, and politicians debate the distinctiveness of Southern culture and history.[7] Myths of Southern exceptionalism obscure American history, including histories of northern racism, segregation, and slavery, creating a false dichotomy between "an exceptional, reactionary South and a normative, progressive North."[8] This debate also ignores major differences within the South, from the Deep South to Appalachia. The Gulf South, where most Mardi Gras celebrations take place, is part of the Deep South. Unlike the rest of the Deep South, the Gulf South is shaped more by Catholicism than evangelical religious influence and contains French- and Spanish-colonized port cities that give it a more laissez-faire attitude than other cities in the region.[9] Consideration for which states are part of the South is sometimes based on geography and alternatively on the original Confederate states, which includes Texas.[10] Texas contains elements of both the South and the Southwest. South Texas, which includes San Antonio, is more culturally aligned with the Southwest.[11]

The Southwest is romanticized as mythical, untamed, and magical, often through cultural appropriation of Hispanic and American Indian culture used as a kind of tourist marketing.[12] Marta Weigle described this type of internal Orientalism as "Southwesternism," a discourse dominated by cultural appropriation as a lure for tourists.[13] In this consumption of Hispanic and Indian culture,

> pictures of Plains Indian chiefs are painted on restaurant walls together with promises of free geodes with the purchase of a burger, "sleepy" plaster of Paris sombrero-Mexicans rest against saguaros in garden shops, and curio stores sell mass-manufactured kachina dolls and "Indian" jewelry that was made in Japan.[14]

Southwesternism is a mash-up of tourist advertising, cultural appropriation, and eroticization of the Southwestern landscape.

This internal Othering of both regions impacts how LGBTQ rights are perceived in those regions. The South is framed as uniformly more hostile to LGBTQ rights, ignoring the variations within the region and changes in attitudes over time.[15] The experience of someone who is LGBTQ in Nashville, Tennessee, may be different from the experience in Birmingham, Alabama or Biloxi, Mississippi. In this study, the recognition of LGBTQ participants in urban festivals was more closely related to the traditions and organizations of the festivals themselves than to regional differences in LGBTQ life. And these pockets of citizenship and belonging in the South and Southwest may be more meaningful when compared to other cities or towns nearby.

There are also cultural norms within Southern and Southwestern culture that support LGBTQ lives. Southwestern histories of cowboys and rodeo culture support gay masculinity.[16] In his historical research on Black gay men in the South, E. Patrick Johnson argues that Black gay Southern men "draw upon the performance of 'southernness'—for example, politeness, coded speech, religiosity—to instantiate themselves as 'legitimate' members of southern and Black culture while, at the same time, deploying these very codes to establish and build friendship networks and find life and/or sexual partners."[17] Southern or Southwestern customs like rodeos and pageantry thus may support certain kinds of LGBTQ culture.[18] Work by historian Brock Thompson on queer Arkansas suggests that Southern pageantry supports public visibility of cross-dressing and drag.[19] Indeed, drag is widely supported in the South as an integral part of Southern LGBTQ culture.[20] In *The Lesbian South*, Jaime Harker demonstrates the ways that a network of literary lesbians in the South reworked southernness to include intersectional radicalism and transgressive sexuality.[21] The South and

Southwest are rich culturally, and South and Southwestern festival life is central to placemaking in the region.

Festivals

Similarly, scholars often have simplistic understandings of festivals. Later in this book, I will refer to Mardi Gras festivities as Carnival season, but in the study of festivals, "carnival" describes any kind of popular festival. In anthropology, folklore studies, and other humanities disciplines, studies of festivals are shaped by the most prominent works on this subject, in this case Russian scholar Mikhail Bakhtin's book, *Rabelais and His World*, published in the late 1960s about popular humor and folk culture in the Middle Ages and Renaissance.[22] Additionally, in 1986 American literary scholars Peter Stallybrass and Allon White published *The Politics and Poetics of Transgression*, which was also focused on early European festivals.[23] Anthropological work by scholars like Victor Turner and the body of work on ritual performances coincides with the work done in literary studies.[24] Together these works have focused the study of festivals on questions about the "carnivalesque" or the political tradition of mocking the powerful, a common feature in rituals and festivals.[25] These debates center on questions about whether these carnivalesque practices are a legitimate "bottom-up" challenge to elites or just a way of appeasing the common peasant with bread and circuses. There are long debates in the humanities and social sciences about the liminal space created by festivals that turns the "world upside down" or creates a "time out of time" through inverting or challenging existing social hierarchies, such as through making a peasant the king for a day.[26] This carnivalesque revelry is both romanticized and dismissed by scholars. One consequence of this literature is that festivals have been framed as simultaneously a challenge to power through satire and revelry and also largely inconsequential, as if events that happen in one part of the year have little to no relation to power dynamics throughout the rest of the year.

A lot of theorizing is based on early European festivals. Most of the revelry in the eighteenth- and nineteenth-century European festivals was done by peasants and the urban poor, whose actions were often a source of disdain by European elites similar to their disdain for the colonial "Other."[27] In these early festivals, peasants blew off steam and cavorted, using "low culture" satire and vulgarity to criticize the "high culture" of social elites. This mockery became distinctly political after the Middle Ages, and violent social clashes often occurred during festival season.[28] Some major political revolts and revolutions have emerged from the ends of festivals, when workers refused to quit the festival and return to work.[29]

Nowadays there are lots of opportunities for this carnivalesque abandon and release, but festivals are still an opportunity for organized and symbolic transgression.[30] In contemporary urban festivals in the United States, festivals do involve a lot of revelry. People go on what sociologists refer to as a "moral holiday" at festivals, in which they drink, eat, say, and do things they might not do the rest of the year.[31] Festivals have a lot in common with Halloween and other rituals in this regard.[32] It is undeniably a time when people enjoy themselves, usually in the company of crowds, alcohol, and rowdiness. Sometimes laws like open-carry alcohol laws are temporarily suspended, and police go easy on the drunken crowds. Satire and mockery are abundant in contemporary festivals. All four of the festivals that are part of this study included satirical events that mock politicians, current events, and power dynamics of the city and nation.

I argue that festivals are much more than the carnivalesque. Scholars who study festivals outside of the European context, particularly festivals in colonized or postcolonial spaces, criticize this overwhelming emphasis on revelry and "time out of time" as ignoring the ways that festivals exacerbate existing social inequalities and antagonisms.[33] Gerard Aching, an Africana scholar focusing on the Caribbean festival tradition, challenges the assumption that carnival time is both distinct from modern social life and is a time and space "in which ideologies may be blissfully suspended."[34] These scholars are skeptical of the carnivalesque, as what appears to be free, forbidden, and spontaneous "upon examination proves to occur between the three poles of the permitted, the perpetrated, and the reinstated."[35] In other words, there is a constant tension within festivals between what is allowed, what is challenged, and what is being supported.

Carnival is not separate from everyday life in the city; it is deeply embedded in all the other social processes in the city.[36] My work here responds to the call for the study of festivals and Carnival to include deeper analysis of history, imperialist power relations, and racist power dynamics.[37] In the rest of this chapter, I highlight my understanding of festivals as pluralistic, highly organized, linked to local culture and power dynamics, and a site of cultural citizenship.

Contemporary Festivals Are Highly Organized Affairs

Festivals are managed by organizations and groups that plan events. These organizations engage in intensive advance planning and coordination. Even the smallest Mardi Gras krewe that I spoke with, a "krewe" of a dozen friends who own a float trailer and parade in the Spanish Town Parades in Baton Rouge, start planning months ahead of time for their costumes, decorations, and parade float theme. The festival itself is typically overseen by a major festival organizational body like a council or commission that governs official events.[38] This council or commission has an investment in the festival going smoothly and has rules and policies to govern events that are sponsored by the governing body. These council members and city leaders typically have deep investments in the festival attracting tourists and generating revenue for the city. In this book, I consider the power dynamics within these festival organizing bodies as part of the cultural traditions of the festivals.

This festival organizing is embedded within the social and political organization of a city throughout the year. In his book, *Lords of Misrule*, about race in New Orleans's Mardi Gras, journalist James Gill describes Mardi Gras in New Orleans as "year-round obsessions for many people" and "much of the city's social intercourse centers on krewe get-togethers and the endless planning for the next parade."[39] Most of the organizations in this book that run festival events also operate throughout the rest of the year, holding events and fundraisers outside of festival time. When I performed in the event Cornyation, which takes place on three evenings in mid-April, we began work on costuming and music in early December and attended events both leading up to and after the performances.

Festivals Are Pluralistic

Festivals are pluralistic, meaning that these events have multiple orientations simultaneously. Too easily anthropologists and folklorists have analyzed rituals and festivals as a "uniform expression of a collective consciousness," in which individuals have one collective experience, which ignores history and context.[40] At one contemporary urban festival, there may be nationalist displays during parades, assertions of power and prestige by festival royalty who are social elites, and irreverently named unofficial royalty like King Anchovy. Some events may highlight the culture of Black, Latino, LGBTQ, indigenous or American Indian communities sponsored by those communities. These events operate alongside ones that culturally appropriate the culture of these communities, valorize settler colonialism or racism, or are deeply religious or patriotic celebrations. Within a citywide festival there are events carefully cultivated for a tourist audience, ones that are chaotically and spontaneously organized, and some that are now tourist events that at one time were more authentically local events. Sometimes these events all happen on the same day and place. One event can contain multitudes of individual experiences and power relations.

Contemporary festivals are also pulled in a variety of directions. These festivals are indelibly about tourism.[41] Many of them were created by boosters to support the growth of tourism in an area, to portray an often mythical placemaking. But regardless of the origins of a festival, these events often become part of what makes a city special. San Antonio markets itself as "the Fiesta city," but individual city residents may also embrace Fiesta culture as part of what it means to live in the city, regardless of whether they are born and bred in that city.[42] These contemporary festivals can become a "battlefield of contention" between tourist pressure to make local culture a spectacle and local autonomy.[43] Sociologist Kevin Gotham argues that tourism "disempowers localities at the same time that it creates new pressure for local autonomy and resistance to hegemonic images."[44] Even tourists are not necessarily passive visitors who are clueless about deep meaning and contexts; festivals can be a time of connection for them as well.[45]

Festivals Involve Both Status Intensification and Challenge

I draw on research about Caribbean Carnival to understand the complexity of power dynamics during festivals, how festivals are simultaneously about elites amplifying their existing status (status intensification), and also about the challenge of power dynamics by marginalized groups. In their work in Trinidad Carnival, Milla Cozart Riggio argues that Carnival in Trinidad must be understood within the context of the festival itself, as an event that "actually both critiques official culture and supports it. It is an event both 'of the people' and 'of the nation.'"[46] Riggio describes Trinidad Carnival as simultaneously "bottom up" and "top down."

From the "top down," LGBTQ involvement in urban festivals is entangled in the governance of festival life and the status intensification of social elites. There are many overt displays of power in festival life.[47] Social elites are a critical part of festival life. Even in early festivals, the elite partook in their own traditional rituals during carnival time, along with joining in the melee of peasants.[48] There is a long history of elite festival traditions excluding Black, Latinx, and American Indian individuals.[49] In 1991, a desegregation ordinance requiring parading festival organizations to prove lack of discrimination based on race, gender, and disability sent shock waves through the New Orleans Carnival community. A few of the largest men's krewes ceased parading rather than accept women or Black men into their organizations.[50] Challenges to the racial homogeneity of these organizations is often handled through recognition of what Marvin Dawkins describes as "parallel structures," organizations for marginalized communities that mirror their elite counterparts.[51] So, instead of diversifying white elite organizations, elites instead recognize Black royalty or Hispanic-led organizations during festivals.

The kings of contemporary festivals are often the richest city residents, occupying positions that may bring them power, money, and good marital prospects. This royalty is not a peasant cavorting in the streets with a meatball impaled on a fork for a scepter. In San Antonio, the kings and queens of the festival journey from event to event in black SUVs, with a police escort. These assertions of power amplify the existing power dynamics in the city during festival time. LGBTQ people, particularly gay and bisexual men in the arts, play a role in supporting this "top-down" power, by providing gay creative labor to make it happen through doing makeup, designing sets, and working on costuming.

However, some elements of festivals are "bottom up," created by marginalized groups pushing for change, control, and recognition. Scholars frame the spontaneity and liminality of Carnival as achieving or desiring personal freedom and social visibility.[52] LGBTQ people are involved in this "bottom-up" process of autonomy, creativity, and meaning making. Some of these performances are about satirizing elite practices and traditions, which is linked to festival practices but also to histories of satire within the LGBTQ community such as the Sisters of Perpetual Indulgence.[53] Like the Sisters, LGBTQ festival performances entail serious parody, parody that provides humor and also contests social meanings.[54] Performances by LGBTQ people and members of other marginalized groups allow people to project "images of themselves and their worlds to their audiences."[55] These communities transmit these ideas both to members of their own community and to interested outsiders such as tourists.[56] Tourists may search for authenticity, tradition, and pleasure from these same performances. The combination of top-down and bottom-up processes in festivals makes recognition and cultural citizenship central to festival life for marginalized groups, especially LGBTQ communities.

Festivals Are Often Used as a Site of Recognition and Cultural Citizenship

This bottom-up process during festivals makes festivals a site of recognition and cultural citizenship. Even just visibility and invisibility during festivals are part of strategic relations throughout the rest of the year, and cultural displays during festivals become a "contested arena for competing meanings."[57] During festivals, power relations are more transparent and can be easily contested by marginalized groups that "desire social recognition because they want to belong to and participate in their societies in more satisfactory ways."[58] At times, studies of the power dynamics of festivals hint at LGBTQ festival life. In the *Lords of Misrule*, a book about the history of racial segregation and contestation during Mardi Gras, sexual orientation was dropped from the Carnival desegregation ordinance by city politicians, and Gill notes that "homosexuals had established their own flamboyant parades and were not pushing to be admitted to the ranks of the straight krewes."[59] Like other minority groups in the city, LGBTQ people had formed their own parallel organizations and events rather than pushing for admittance to high-status groups.

What little we know about LGBTQ involvement in citywide festivals is that they are often a site of contestation and visibility. The limited scholarship is about the involvement of gay men in a New Orleans Mardi Gras and Carnival in Rio De Janeiro, and drag and cross-dressing are central to this visibility. Cross-dressing as a kind of normative subversion is common in many festivals and rituals.[60] In James Green's 1999 book, *Beyond Carnival: Male Homosexuality in Twentieth-Century Brazil*, he examines the development of gender and sexual expression for gay men during Carnival in Rio, and the relationship between Carnival time and the rest of the year. The prevailing stereotype when Green did the study was that "apparent permissiveness during Carnival . . . symbolizes a sexual and social regime that unabashedly accepts fluid sexual identity, including male-to-male sexuality."[61] Yet the rise of gay visibility during Carnival coincided with increased violence against gay men, lesbians, and transgender people in Brazil at that time. In the history of New Orleans Mardi Gras in the 1960s, gay men could only cross-dress publicly during Carnival season.[62] This book explores the ways that this contestation and visibility are part of recognition and cultural citizenship for the LGBTQ community.

2

Mardi Gras and Fiesta in the American Gulf South and Southwest

Festivals sometimes reflect both the region and specific place where they occur. The festivals in this book are located within regional culture, part of the way regional differences are enduring in the United States.[1] Mardi Gras is quintessentially linked to Gulf South culture, just as Fiestas are part of Southwestern history. In this chapter I provide background for these regional festivals in general and each individual city's festival in particular.

These festivals are both connected to regional culture and a placemaking practice for each city. Many cities and towns have annual festivals of some kind, such as art, music, or literary festivals. Some of these festivals help define that city or town as a certain kind of place. For example, Austin City Limits in Austin, Texas, is part of how city residents craft a sense of that Texas city as a musical place.[2] In Mobile, Baton Rouge, Santa Fe, and San Antonio, these urban placemaking festivals offer a local flavor of the regional festival style.

Mardi Gras Traditions in the American Gulf South

Mardi Gras is not what you imagine it is. Most people picture Mardi Gras as a long weekend of thousands of half-naked college students in the New Orleans French Quarter engaging in unrestricted debauchery. One of the most iconic aspects of the New Orleans French Quarter Mardi Gras is rituals around "boobs for beads" in which women raise their shirts to get parade beads thrown at them. This celebration of Mardi Gras is in many ways the easiest to study, and sociological studies of "ritual disrobement" and "moral holidays" abound.[3] The fact that our strongest association of Mardi Gras is with the New Orleans French Quarter is due to centuries of successful publicity and public enchantment with images of these festivities. The debauchery of Mardi Gras has become part of how New Orleans is imagined in the American gaze.[4] Cities across the country have tried to imitate the success of this festival, and New Orleans Mardi Gras has become both the template and the standard for judging the success of urban festivals.[5] However, rituals like "boobs for beads" and hordes of college student tourists celebrating Mardi Gras is something that *only* happens in the French Quarter of New Orleans. In this section I provide an overview of American Mardi Gras and then a history of the cultural traditions of Carnival in Mobile and Baton Rouge.

Mardi Gras is celebrated all along the Gulf South, from Galveston, Texas, to Pensacola, Florida, in both cities and rural areas. The festival is a season—the Carnival season—that runs from the day of Epiphany in January to Fat Tuesday. Because the scheduling of Fat Tuesday varies, the timing of Carnival is sometimes just a few weeks but may last up to almost two months. Gulf South Carnival is many things at once: a festival with deep ties to religion, a chance to blow off steam before Lent, a family event, a showcase of city debutantes, a tourist spectacle, and a way of organizing the social life of the city. Carnival is linked to the Lost Cause mythology of the confederacy through the valorization of figures like Old Slac in Mobile (described later in this chapter) who fought back against Yankee occupiers during Restoration. Carnival is simultaneously a site of visibility and social identity by marginalized groups.[6]

In the streets of the cities where it is celebrated, Carnival appears to be unrestrained revelry. Behind the scenes, the festival is an intensely organized affair. American Mardi Gras is run by krewes and social clubs, private non-governmental social organizations that run parades, balls, and other events during Carnival season. Social clubs emerged in the Black community of New Orleans, are oriented toward benevolent aid and community support, and do not always involve royalty.[7] Krewes are modeled after elite white organizations like secretive Masonic societies. Krewes are similar to American fraternities and sororities in that the groups tend to be single-sex, racially homogenous groups of people who are from a similar class background.[8] Some krewes are mystic societies, and the identity of members is secret; they wear masks when they parade publicly and their full name never appears in the newspaper. One becomes a member through family connections or being voted into the group. Many krewes are actively, purposefully segregated by race. The oldest krewes are white, upper-class businessmen who proactively safeguard their organizations and events from racial integration; in New Orleans, these particular krewes "have played a big part in perpetuating the myth that the South sustained a great civilization until it was destroyed by Yankee vandals."[9] A strong Black Carnival tradition in cities of the Gulf South like New Orleans and Mobile includes the debut of Black debutantes, operating as a "parallel structure" to white Carnival events.[10] In New Orleans, legal attempts to racially integrate parading krewes were met with strong opposition and limited success.[11]

The largest, richest krewes have club houses, recruit hundreds of members, and host huge parades with floats they have made themselves. The smallest krewes are groups of a dozen people who have access to a flatbed trailer, a truck big enough to tow it, and their imagination. These smallest krewes often parade in the "people's parades," huge community parades that only require a small entry fee for a float and are composed of many krewes. Krewe members parade, throwing beads, stuffed animals, light-up toys, and sweets at eager parade attendees, many of whom are children. "Throw me something, mister" is one of the catch phrases of Mobile Mardi Gras, shouted by children at costumed, parading figures.[12]

If a trailer is not available, you can join or create a walking krewe. One of the most entertaining walking krewes, for example, is the Krewe of Yazoo in Baton Rouge, a brigade of people in costumes pushing decorated lawn mowers while following choreography. Second line parades are walking parades with high participant involvement and expressive movement that are a historical response from the Black community to a history of racial segregation in parading in New Orleans and other cities.[13]

Not all krewes parade. However, almost all big krewes host a ball or other major private gathering during Carnival season. Masque balls are typically elaborate, costumed affairs that require formal attire for guests, all of whom are invited through krewe member social networks. These krewes host elaborate balls for their family, friends, and neighbors; occasionally, the general public can buy tickets to these events. All of these balls include refreshments, decorations, music, and a tableau or "call outs" of acting, dancing, or displays put on by the krewe members that are related to the theme of the event that year. Each krewe typically crowns their own royalty at their ball, comprised of devoted members who have contributed to the group. In high-status krewes, these balls are used to debut the teenage daughters of krewe members, one of whom is selected to be the krewe queen for that year.

For adults living in the Gulf South, these exclusive balls are an important component of the Carnival season. Scholars rarely study Carnival balls, as they are more challenging to access, and they are mostly studied historically rather than ethnographically.[14] The omission of these events from understanding urban festivals means that scholars focus disproportionately on public drunkenness and celebrations rather than on events that involve status intensification, such as balls.

Since World War II, there has been increasing visibility for LGBTQ people during urban Carnival events. In 1956, scholar Munro Edmunson observed a high incidence of cross-dressing masquerade on the streets of New Orleans and portrayals of fairies and Greek gods by participants.[15] White gay men have organized gay krewes since the 1950s and 1960s in cities throughout the Gulf South.[16] Many of the explicitly LGBTQ krewes are formed by white gay men, and most Louisiana gay krewes still do not allow cisgender women to participate. These early attempts at organizing were not without opposition; early krewes faced police raids and bomb threats. In the 1980s, krewes of lesbians and all-inclusive LGBTQ krewes emerged. All-inclusive krewes are common in Mobile and Pensacola, Florida; these krewes have the least restrictive requirements to join. I have only found three krewes explicitly for LGBTQ women in all of the Gulf South: the Mystic Womyn of Color in Mobile in the 2010s, and the Krewe of Ishtar in New Orleans and Daughters of Gaia in Mobile—both of which were active only in the 1980s. There is also a long history of lesbian, bisexual, and queer women being involved in women's krewes, some of which are known to be more lesbian-friendly than others.[17] Krewes organized by LGBTQ people in the Gulf South have historically been open to Black participants but typically are predominately white organizations. A few krewes, like Mwindo in New Orleans and Mystic Womyn of Color in Mobile, are organized exclusively by Black LGBTQ participants.

For this study, I selected the Carnival traditions of Mobile, Alabama, and Baton Rouge, Louisiana. The two cities have notable things in common. A third of the population of both Baton Rouge and Mobile MSA are Black, according to the 2010 Census. Both cities have established LGBTQ businesses, bars, churches, and other organizations. These two cities are also more typical of LGBTQ rights in the urban South than New Orleans, in that both states lack municipal protections against discrimination in employment, housing, and public accommodations due to sexual orientation and gender identity.[18] They have an important difference: Mobile's Carnival is well known for being more traditionalistic and "old school" in the Gulf South, whereas Baton Rouge Mardi Gras is mostly a post–World War II phenomenon that is not institutionalized or controlled by social elites in the same way as Mobile. This contrast between the two cases is important for understanding how both the type of festival and local festival traditions impact LGBTQ involvement.

Mobile, "The Birthplace of Mardi Gras"

Mobile, Alabama (pronounced moh-BEEL), is a small port city of approximately 190,000 people situated at the Mobile Bay. Mobile is on the land of the Chahta Yakni or Chocktaw tribe. At one time, Mobile was a colony of France, Britain, and Spain before becoming annexed into the United States, creating a city that to this day remains rich in architectural and cultural influences from its colorful history. The city has a walkable downtown filled with street art, statues, museums, and regional food specialties. Demographically, half of Mobile residents identify as Black or African American on the Census, and about 45 percent of the city population is non-Hispanic White. The greater Mobile County, which includes the outlying suburbs, is majority white. The median income is low and the poverty rate is higher than the national average, at 22.4% of the population.

The City of Mobile website touts the festival as "the original Mardi Gras." The Mobile Carnival Museum proclaims that the city is the "birthplace of Mardi Gras."[19] My fieldnotes are full of conversations with people about whether Mardi Gras in the Gulf South began in front of a hardware store in Mobile or a few years later in New Orleans. At the Mardi Gras store, one of the popular beaded necklaces has a plastic medallion/pendant describing Mobile as "The Original Mardi Gras." The mythical story of eighteenth-century bachelor men ringing in the New Year with an impromptu parade with rakes and cowbells was a critical part of the Mardi Gras symbolism, and both rakes and cowbells were imagery used on tourist information, history displays, and prominently in the Mobile Carnival Museum. This imagery worked to portray Mobile Mardi Gras as authentic and traditional. Although the city of Mobile hosts many festivals throughout the year, Mardi Gras is central to how the city is defined not just during the Carnival season but throughout the year. At times, I considered this to be a form of sibling rivalry between two nearby cities, with Mobile positioned as the proverbial neglected stepchild of the Gulf South tradition.

In Mobile, Mardi Gras is a major city festival that resonates through the social, economic, and political structure throughout the year. Mobile Carnival is so large that multiple festival governing bodies interact to regulate the festival: the all-white Mobile Carnival Association (MCA), the Black-run Mobile Area Mardi Gras Association (MAMGA), and an organization of all the parading krewes that coordinates with the Mobile Police Department. Mobile hosts more than twenty-five parades and sixty-five formal balls organized by more than seventy krewes or secret societies—impressive for a city of fewer than 200,000 people.[20]

I selected Mobile as a small city to study for this project, because it holds a more traditionalistic form of Mardi Gras celebration. It is traditionalistic in three important ways: city mythology about the long history of the tradition, the formality of the festivals, and continuing racial segregation. The celebration of Mardi Gras in Mobile is more formal than other cities in the Gulf South. Most krewes are mystic societies with strict confidentiality and masking requirements. The clothing required at most Mobile masque balls is *costume de rigueur*, a strict formal dress code that requires a white tie and tuxedo tails for men and floor-length ball gown for women. Several Mobile informants bragged that the city and Los Angeles were the two major markets for tuxedo tails rentals. But also, Mobile is a formal city. During Mardi Gras this manifests itself as not just attention to clothing, "but highly routinized protocol in the selection of those who will lead the dance at these affairs, close scrutiny of respectability in the selection of the king, queen, and court reigning over the city, and careful all-city supervision of Mardi Gras activities generally, to see that things don't get out of hand."[21]

Mobile Carnival is intimately connected to debutante season in the city, which starts on Thanksgiving week and extends through the

Carnival season. In addition to the young women who debut at krewe balls, two king-queen couples are selected each year to reign over the entire Carnival season. The white couple is selected from MCA, and the Black couple is selected from the active Black krewes organized through MAMGA.[22]

Part of this traditionalism around festivals is racial segregation. Mobile has strongly segregated krewes and a long rich history of Black Carnival events, krewes, royalty, and parading. A few of the white krewes date their membership back to the late nineteenth century. The most elite krewes of white, upper-class men in Mobile join the Strikers Independent Society, Order of Myths, Infant Mystics, or Knights of Revelry, all of which were formed before 1880.[23] The Comic Cowboys, a satirical parade of white men criticizing the year's events, began in 1884. White women formed krewes in the early 1900s but did not have parading krewes until after World War II. As part of this project, I attended non-LGBTQ balls, which were often racially segregated not just in membership but in guests who attended the ball. Explanations for why racial segregation persists in Mobile during Mardi Gras were consistently that "birds of a feather flock together," using what sociologist Eduardo Bonilla-Silva describes as naturalization frames to explain away racism as a natural occurrence.[24]

There have been ongoing challenges to the racial segregation of Mardi Gras krewes. Conde Explorers was the subject of a 2008 documentary on racial segregation during Mobile Mardi Gras called *The Order of Myths*. Although all LGBTQ krewes except one in Mobile have been racially all-inclusive since their establishment, Conde Explorers was the first krewe established as an all-inclusive *parading* krewe with the goal of having a night parade. The all-white krewes that parade at night traditionally hire Black marching bands and dance teams to perform in between floats, including the visibly out and gender-transgressive Prancing Elites dance team. Historically, Black krewes have only paraded during the day, a restriction held in place by the organization of parading krewes and the Mobile Police Department. In chapter 5, I analyze the ways Conde Explorers have contested the limitations on parading in Mobile.

The patriarch of Mobile Mardi Gras is the historical figure, Joseph Stillwell Cain, Jr. (1832–1904), often referred to as "Joe Cain" or "old Slac." Cain was a market clerk in Mobile during the post–Civil War

Reconstruction, a period when Carnival was suspended. In February 1866, he disguised himself as a chief of the Chickasaws ("Chief Slackabamorinico" or "Old Slac") and paraded through town in a wagon with other Confederate veterans as part of a broader protest against Reconstruction and an attempt to reinvigorate Carnival festivities.[25] He is credited with initiating the modern way of celebrating Carnival.[26] The mythology of Old Slac was reinvigorated in the civil rights era during the 1960s in Mobile, with the creation of the Joe Cain Procession in 1966 on Shrove Sunday, which quickly became Joe Cain Day, or the "People's Parade," the common man's Mardi Gras.[27] Cain has come to represent white Southern resistance, festival revelry, and city pride. Even now, participants in the Joe Cain Day parade, which is predominately small krewes and walking krewes, are almost exclusively white, although most of the city turns out to watch the parade. His gravesite was moved to the downtown area, and the Joe Cain Day celebrations start there. Several small mystic groups have formed around Joe Cain, including Cain's Merry Widows and the Mistresses of Joe Cain, two secretive groups of white women (and rumored to include at least one cross-dressing man) who parade on Joe Cain Day and have a public rivalry. These two veiled groups of women were joined in 2014 by the irreverent group, the Secret Misters of Joe Cain, a mixed-gender, all-inclusive walking krewe in short shorts and scruffy drawn-on beards. This depiction of the town's patriarch as a man "on the down low" with a secret mister is part of the growing visibility of LGBTQ groups and culture, which I discuss further in chapter 4.

Mobile, along with San Antonio, has the most significant LGBTQ visibility and involvement in the yearly festival. The Mobile LGBTQ community revolves around the Metropolitan Community Church (MCC), Mardi Gras, and well-established bars in a visibly gay area of downtown. The tradition of krewes for gay men dates back to the 1960s, when a group of white gay men who had attended gay Carnival events in New Orleans formed the Krewe of Pan, which held its first ball in a private home in 1968. Krewe of Pan lasted three years and was followed by a few other short-lived krewes in the 1970s and 1980s, including the Apostles of Apollo, Order of Adonis, and Daughters of Gaia.[28]

Mobile is home to two of the only krewes ever formed explicitly for lesbian, bisexual, and queer (LBQ) women in the Gulf South. The

Daughters of Gaia was explicitly run for and by LBQ women. According to a former member, the krewe could not survive due to its economic circumstances, as women could not financially bankroll the new krewe during lean years. Since the early 2010s, the Mystic Womyn of Color, a women's krewe specifically for Black lesbian participants, has operated in Mobile. Mystic Womyn of Color is the only krewe I have found in the Gulf South that is run by Black LBQ women. The krewe often parades in the MLK "people's parade" that is the Black Carnival counterpart to the Joe Cain Day parade, holds events for the Black lesbian community throughout the year, and hosts a ball of about 250 attendees a few weeks after Mardi Gras officially ends. The year I attended, more than a hundred of these ball attendees came from all over the South and Midwest, including Ohio, Georgia, and South Carolina.

In addition to Mystic Womyn of Color, Mobile currently has three all-inclusive krewes that are mainly composed of white gay men and lesbians but are open to individuals of any race, gender, class, or sexual orientation. The largest of these krewes, the Order of Osiris, hosts a yearly masque ball attended by almost two thousand people.[29] The other two all-inclusive krewes are Krewe of Phoenix and Order of Pan, both of which are a result of schisms and break-offs from Osiris. There are also other krewes that are known for being open to LGBTQ participants, including the racially diverse, all-inclusive krewe Conde Explorers, one men's krewe, and one women's krewe. There is some history of cross-dressing and costuming on Joe Cain Day. The zone of gay-owned businesses, bars, and restaurants downtown was also a place where many krewes claimed spaces to watch the parades.

Baton Rouge, "The Spanish Town Flamingo"

My first impression of driving into Baton Rouge (pronounced BAT-on Roozh) is the overwhelming size of the Mississippi River. The Louisiana capital is nestled on the eastern bank of the large muddy river, on the land of the Chahta Yakni or Chocktaw tribe. Like the rest of the Gulf South, the city has a complex history of being colonized by French, Spanish, and British forces. As of 2017, the city had a population of around 227,000 people, although the larger metropolitan area is closer to 800,000. In the 2000s, Baton Rouge was one of the fastest growing cities in the South, partly due to the influx of migrants from New Orleans after Hurricane Katrina. The city is on the edge of French Acadiana and is linked to the distinctly Cajun city of Lafayette across the long causeway of Atchafalaya, an 18-mile bridge that connects the two cities. In my first drive into Baton Rouge, my assistant Analicia and I got stuck on the causeway in rush hour traffic for hours, part of the traffic issue in which Baton Rouge infrastructure has not caught up to the influx of new residents. The city contains numerous historical political buildings, the sprawling buildings of Louisiana State University, while concealed but merely blocks away are impoverished Black neighborhoods. The city is thirteenth in the country in terms of most segregated cities.[30] The typical Black household in the Louisiana capital earns $34,914 a year, nearly half the $65,842 the typical white area household earns.[31]

Although Baton Rouge is close to New Orleans, its Carnival tradition is relatively recent and decentralized. The city did not develop its own krewes and carnival traditions until the late 1940s, when the first Carnival ball was held in 1948.[32] There are eighteen krewes in Baton Rouge proper and another fourteen krewes in the outlying areas.[33] Ball culture is rich in Baton Rouge, but there is not a long history of major Mardi Gras parades. There were some parades between 1949 and 1956, followed by a two-decade hiatus on parades.[34] According to Costello, compared to New Orleans, the Baton Rouge balls "surpass the New Orleans krewes in elaborateness of court costumes as well as tableaux, usually adhering to each year's theme. Another difference is that the capital-city krewes often adopt Hollywood-like musicals, or other easily recognizable and flashy themes."[35] Many Mardi Gras krewes and parades in Baton Rouge are fundraisers for causes like HIV and cancer, including the two events most strongly associated with the LGBTQ community, the Krewe of Apollo ball and the Spanish Town Parade and Ball.

Currently there are only five parading krewes and two "people's parades" in Baton Rouge, and there is no centralized organizing body, major royalty, or strong Black Carnival tradition in the city. Many locals attend Mardi Gras events in New Orleans. All but one Black person I spoke to about Carnival events referenced going to New Orleans to attend events at Zulu Social Aid and Pleasure Club—the most well-known Black Carnival club—rather than going to local Baton Rouge events.

Mid-City Carnival celebrations in Baton Rouge are more diverse and connected to the Black Carnival tradition.[36]

Costello dates the start of the Spanish Town Mardi Gras Parade to 1981, stating that "the parade had humble beginnings as a walking procession on Highland Road, with a king brandishing a meatball impaled on a long fork as a scepter."[37] Not counting Louisiana State University football games, the parade is Baton Rouge's largest event with more than 100,000 people attending.[38] The plastic pink flamingo is the symbol of the parade, and the appearance of wooden cut-out painted versions of the flamingo in the City Park Lake heralds the ball. The ball "is famed for its excesses in costumes and celebrating."[39]

Many interviewees described the Baton Rouge LGBTQ community as fragmented and hard to organize, particularly the transgender and LBQ women communities. The Baton Rouge Pride is also the largest indoor Pride in the South. There are several long-standing LGBTQ bars in Baton Rouge, including a disco bar. The oldest organizations are an MCC church and the Krewe of Apollo.

In Baton Rouge, there are two LGBTQ krewes: one for gay men and one for drag queens. The oldest krewe is the Krewe of Apollo, a men's krewe that began in 1981, and it is one of many Krewe of Apollo chapters in the Gulf South. According to the longest living founding member, Larry Freemin, in the 1970s, there was a group of about eight gay men in Baton Rouge who became members of the Krewe of Apollo in Lafayette, which was a chapter of the original gay men's Krewe of Apollo in New Orleans. Freemin and his seven friends formed the first board of the Krewe of Apollo in Baton Rouge. Freemin was conscientious that the krewe be a sustainable organization, with board turnover and elections to determine the royalty of the ball. The krewe is a group of thirty to forty-five men, almost exclusively white gay and bisexual men, who put on a ball annually for more than one thousand guests, along with other fundraisers and smaller events throughout the year. For about a decade, starting in the late 1990s, there was also a smaller krewe for gay men, the Capital City Royal Order of the Unicorns, which was also inspired by a chapter of the Royal Order of the Unicorns in Lafayette. Former members describe this krewe as smaller, with about ten members, and more oriented toward a working-class gay aesthetic and fundraising.

The Krewe of Divas formed in 2005 and had its first ball in 2006, specifically to promote drag. The Krewe of Divas functions more as a drag troupe that socializes young drag queens throughout Baton Rouge and southern Louisiana. One of the most visible founding members is the older queen, Miss Chica La Rouge, who announced online in 2006 that the goal of the krewe is "to help us raise money, so we can have a few Miss Louisiana America Prelims, to help a few of these girls get somewhere."[40] Krewe of Divas does host a ball sometimes, often during Pride month in June, and performs as a troupe at Pride events.

Like New Orleans, Mobile and Baton Rouge both follow Mardi Gras traditions of having krewes, parades, balls, and revelry during the Carnival season. However, there are distinct differences between the two cities' Carnival festivities—the size of the event, importance to city life, and the cultural traditions within the event. In Mobile, the traditionalistic culture of the festival prioritizes status intensification for social elites and racial segregation at events. Even the type of LGBTQ involvement in the festival varies between cities, as the Krewe of Apollo in Baton Rouge emerged out of New Orleans krewe traditions for gay men whereas the all-inclusive krewes of Mobile push back against the traditional elite culture of Carnival.

Romanticizing Settler Colonialism in Southwestern Fiestas

Due to effective tourist advertising of New Orleans Mardi Gras, Carnival seems far more familiar to Americans than the regional celebration of fiestas. The term "fiesta" more generally means a festivity or celebration. In Spanish-speaking countries, fiesta often refers to a religious festival, such as one honoring a Catholic saint. Some fiestas in the United States are still religious. These festivals are most common as part of the New Mexican tradition, but there is a history of fiestas in Southern California, Arizona, and Texas.[41] Fiestas often take place over the course of one to two weeks, frequently with events that proceed and precede the official festival period. These fiestas tend to include multiple parades, fairs, theatrical events, and the crowning of festival royalty. These events are usually planned by non-profit organizations and coordinated by a fiesta commission or council.

Fiestas are intimately linked to the production and consumption of the mythical Southwest. Several of these fiestas were started by Anglo, or non-Hispanic White, boosters in the early twentieth century to promote tourism in the Southwest, which was being framed as a mythical, magical place rooted in Native and Hispanic culture.[42] These fiestas were part of the late nineteenth-century Spanish revival that began with Helen Hunt Jackson's book *Ramona* in 1884.[43] Fiesta San Antonio and other major fiestas, like Fiesta de Los Angeles, were founded during this time. Carey McWilliams describes this Spanish revival as about narrating a "Spanish fantasy past,"[44] a mythical reenactment of Spanish history that has a questionable connection with history. For example, during this time Los Angeles created a Fiesta with parades and pageantry that exoticized the Spanish heritage of the city, which was quickly transformed into a generic parade called Fiesta de la Flores.[45] Some regional festivals do not have "fiesta" in the title but follow this spirit of historical pageantry. For example, the Washington's Birthday Celebration in Laredo, Texas, includes such historical pageantry as Pocahontas giving the key to the city to George Washington, a woman dressed up as Martha Washington, and a Hispanic debutante tradition of Las Marthas.[46]

The tricultural power dynamics between American Indian, Hispanic, and Anglo communities and the history of settler colonialism in the Southwest are central to understanding fiestas.[47] Fiestas came out of and are a part of ongoing settler colonialism. Settler colonialism is a history of displacement of indigenous populations with an invasive settler society that creates its own identity and claim to the land.[48] Settler colonialism is not a process that happened just in the past, it is ongoing in the present day.[49] The settler colonialism of the Southwest is multilayered. Spanish conquistadores dominated and decimated indigenous populations, Mexican communities were subjugated by Anglo Western pioneers, and Anglo migrants are part of the gentrification of the Southwest and displacement of Hispanic residents.

In New Mexico, these tricultural dynamics are even more complex, as Latinx identities are more fragmented. Some New Mexican residents identify as part of a lineage of Spanish conquistadores and distinguish themselves from other Latinx or Mexican American residents. They are often described in academic writing as Hispano but use a set of complex identities to describe themselves.[50] There are ongoing power dynamics between Hispano and Anglo residents of New Mexico and the American Indian population of the nineteen pueblos and three reservations that are in the state. Ten percent of the population of New Mexico is American Indian and about 14 percent of all American Indians live in the state.[51] In New Mexico, many Fiestas were started by Anglo boosters but have since been reclaimed as part of New Mexican Hispanic heritage and are now controlled by Hispano-majority festival councils.

Many Southwestern festivals rely on religious imagery and historical pageantry about the Western frontier and stories of conquest. Fiesta de Santa Fe and Fiesta San Antonio began as a celebration of the conquering of American Indians by a Spanish general and the Battle of San Jacinto (the response to the Alamo) respectively,[52] and in New Mexico, Fiesta de Taos celebrates Santa Ana and Santiago.[53] Catholicism shapes the celebration of Fiestas in New Mexico. Fiestas de Las Vegas celebrates Our Lady of Sorrows,[54] and Catholic rituals are a central part of the Fiesta de Santa Fe. Most of this religious and historical pageantry is serious, but there are often events within fiesta celebrations that satirize both the historical pageantry and religion.

Santa Fe "Que Viva"

The full name of Santa Fe (SAN-te FAY) is La Villa Real de la Santa Fe de San Francisco de Asís. The city is on the land of the Jicarilla Apache. Santa Fe is the state capital of New Mexico, one of the least populous states in the United States with a state population of around two million. Many people I met across the state during my research described the state as "a city": small, insular, with a lot of organizing on the state level. Almost 150,000 state residents live in Santa Fe County, just an hour down the scenic highway from the more populous Albuquerque.

The first time I went to Santa Fe, I flew into the tiny city airport and caught an airport shuttle to the hotel. In Santa Fe, the altitude of over 7,000 feet took my breath away during fieldwork, gave me an ear infection during our longer summer stay, and contributed to my exhaustion during my time in the city. Throughout my first long weekend, I was charmed by the hotel employees who drove me to and from the downtown area. Fiesta de Santa Fe is timed as a transition from the summer tourist season to the locals reclaiming the city as their own in the fall, although some tourists do attend Fiesta. So frequently I had the shuttle to myself and peppered the drivers with questions about race, gay life, and Fiesta. My first shuttle ride was with a Hispana young woman who worked at the front desk, and she stressed the authentic nature of the American Indian jewelry vendors in front of the city hall. I wrote in my fieldnotes that day that "there is something that tries to be desperately authentic about tourism in Santa Fe." Santa Fe is marketed as an exotic tourist destination, the "City Different."[55] What scholar Chris Wilson calls the "myth of Santa Fe" is a "constellation of arts and architectural revivals, public ceremonies, romantic literature, and historic preservation."[56] The downtown consists of adobe-style buildings in a few mandatory colors, pricey restaurants, and high-end art galleries. The downtown is dead by around 9:00 p.m. on a weekend.

Santa Fe is shaped by a placemaking rhetoric about tricultural harmony between Anglo, Hispano, and American Indian residents and cannot be understood without examining these power dynamics. Although less than 5 percent of the Santa Fe population is American Indian, to the immediate north and west of the city are a dozen of the state's pueblos, a type of reservation. The historical power dynamics between American Indians and other residents of Santa Fe plays out in the geography of the downtown plaza. American Indian vendors line up in a row against city hall, selling their wares by displaying handmade crafts on blankets on the ground. As an opening event of Fiesta de Santa Fe, right across from the vendors' area there was the pageantry of the *entrada*, a quasi-historical reenactment of the Spanish conquistadores, complete with young confused American Indian children on stage pretending to be baptized by the conquerors.

The population of Santa Fe is almost evenly divided between Hispano and Anglo residents. Hispano residents of Santa Fe often trace their ancestry back to Spanish conquistadores, crafting personal identities as European rather than Latin American, as part of a "fantasy heritage" of pure Castilian descent.[57] There is also a long history of land encroachment, industry domination, and other forms of economic power imbalances between Anglo settlers and Hispano residents.[58] More recently, rising property taxes and Anglo settlers have fueled gentrification and the displacement of Hispano residents of Santa Fe.

Historically, Anglo settlers have come to Santa Fe for purposes like consuming American Indian and Hispano culture, creating art colonies in affordable desert towns, or otherwise engaging with the mythical, magical Southwest. One of the most famous groups of Anglo settlers is the members of the Santa Fe art colony, a group of mostly Anglo settlers who were drawn to the Southwest after World War I as part of the outgrowth of the tourism industry in New Mexico.[59] Colonists came to the Southwest for its ruggedness, American Indian and Hispano culture, and landscape features.[60] According to Sylvia Rodríguez, "the art colony was the mechanism by which a harsh environment and inequitable social conditions became symbolically transformed into something mysterious, awesome, and transcendent."[61] One of the most well-known of these artists locally was William Howard Shuster. Will Shuster, or "Shus," was a visual artist who moved to the Santa Fe colonies in order to recover from poison gas he was exposed to during World War I. Shuster was part of a group of Anglo male artists who named themselves Los Cinco Pintores, "The Five Painters."[62]

The power dynamics of the relationships between American Indian and the Hispano and Anglo settlers infuse Fiesta de Santa Fe. Fiesta de Santa Fe has a strong, explicit Catholic influence and is crafted as a family-friendly spectacle by a Fiesta council that is disproportionately controlled by Hispanic heritage elite.[63] Fiesta de Santa Fe is often marketed as one of the longest continuously running festivals in the United States, and the Fiesta website touts that it has been taking place for more than three hundred years. The origins of the festival can be traced back to a 1712 proclamation that the city should celebrate the 1692 reconquest of Santa Fe by General Don Diego de Vargas.[64] After the Pueblo Revolution of 1680 expelled Spanish colonizers from the area for twelve years, de Vargas conquered the Native population for the king of Spain and the Catholic Church. There has been a small procession carrying "La Conquistadora," a Catholic statue, since the 1700s, along with a series of novena masses every summer. The brutal reconquest and colonization of Santa Fe is typically sanitized in Fiesta accounts as a "peaceful" occupation of cultural unity, enacted as part of the *entrada* of Fiesta until the mid-2010s when it was protested by Hispano and indigenous residents. To date, the royalty of Fiesta de Santa Fe are given the titles Don Diego de Vargas and his queen, "La Reina de la Fiesta de Santa Fe."

However, the structure of contemporary Fiesta de Santa Fe was developed in 1919 by Anglo city boosters and tourist fairs promoting New Mexico for Anglo settlement and development.[65] Early Fiesta organizing committees were dominated by Scottish Rite masons and linked to the museum's cultural revival program.[66] The beginning of the de Vargas pageant in 1911 coincided with New Mexican statehood and a national fad of historical pageants inspired by the English Arts and Crafts movement. Across the United States, these early pageants "allowed the local hereditary elite, whose members played the first settlers, to assert their priority atop the local social hierarchy."[67] Hispano enthusiasm for the festival and the de Vargas pageantry was minimal due to the way the pre–World War II Fiesta de Santa Fe was organized within the museum's cultural revival program by Anglo boosters. American Indian participation was typically exploitative. For example, festival organizers pressured American Indians to perform pueblo ritual dances for the tourist public, dances that were heavily regulated and forbidden by the federal government in private pueblo life.[68] Central to these early festivities were portrayals of American Indian traditions as part of the "past" of Santa Fe, an element of settler colonialism.

In the 1920s, the Anglo artists' colony developed the counter Fiesta to resist the more commercial Fiesta, which at the time was focused on military parades and professional American Indian performances. Art colony residents crafted a less commercial festival focused on local Hispano folk culture and spontaneous bohemianism. In 1926, Anglo artists affiliated with the Modern School instituted their own historical pageantry parade, calling it El Pasatiempo, a kind of pageantry that satirized local culture.[69] The 1937 parade lampooned local culture "satirizing dude ranchers, archeologists depicted as 'lugubrious bonediggers,' an old-time western funeral with the corpse's feet protruding from the coffin, and a fake bullfight."[70] In 1924, the artist Shuster created the first effigy of Zozobra, "Old Man of Gloom," for a private Fiesta party, based on his viewing of a Judas figure filled with firecrackers in rituals of the Yaqui Indians in Mexico.[71] This appropriation of indigenous culture is a key component of settler colonialism. The paganistic burning of Zozobra, a fifty-foot-tall man in a sweeping cloak dress, is now organized by the mostly white Kiwanis Club and attended by more than 50,000 people a year. Santa Fe residents stuff Zozobra full of papers on which they write their worries and gloom, and these are ritually burned away. The symbol of Zozobra is used by the City of Santa Fe marketing to promote the festival, and when I visited the tourism office in 2015 there was a small figure of Zozobra in the office.

Hispano residents used this shift in power to gradually claim the parts of the festival focused on Hispano culture, including many Catholic masses, the reenactment of Don Diego de Vargas's reconquest, and the royalty of Fiesta "refashioning it into a celebration of Hispanos' conquistador origins and prior occupancy of the city."[72] Fiesta de Santa Fe is coordinated by the Hispano-majority Fiesta Council, an evolution that happened over time as Hispano residents reclaimed the festival from Anglo artists.[73] The Fiesta Council closely safeguards a Hispano heritage rooted in the Spanish conquistador's conquest of the area. In her 2010 book, *The Santa Fe Fiesta, Reinvented*, scholar Sarah Bronwen Horton describes the Fiesta Council's work as Hispano cultural preservation in the face of gentrification and displacement of Hispanos from Santa Fe.[74] The Fiesta Council requires that two main royalty of the festival—Don Diego de Vargas and La Reina de la Fiesta de Santa Fe—speak Castilian-style Spanish and have a strong Hispano heritage, ideally tracing it back to the first Spanish settlers in New Mexico. American Indian adults are tokenized in the royal court. La Reina has a "Spanish princessa" and "Indian princessa," and one member of Don Diego's royal court (or *cuadrilla*) is typically an American Indian man. Younger members of the Council that I interviewed describe the Council as outdated, full of "old school politics," and out of touch with youth. There has been some change to Council politics, including responses to protests against the entrada in the 2010s.[75]

The LGBTQ community in Santa Fe is both diffuse and complicated. Based on 2010 census data, New Mexico as a state is in the top ten of states with high rates of same-sex couples, and Santa Fe County has almost twice the rate of same-sex couples as the rest of the state.[76] The mayor at the time of this study, Javier Gonzales, came out as gay in the city newspaper, the city's tourist website has a section for LGBTQ visitors, and the city is the site of one of the country's first LGBT retirement communities.[77] A 2011 article in *The Advocate* named Santa Fe the second gayest city in America, "where seasoned gays come to center themselves, but not in a boring way."[78] But the national coverage of gay Santa

Fe focuses it as a site of tourism and retirement for older Anglo gay men, as a place where LGBTQ people move *to* rather than come *from*. Indeed, gay men have been a central part of the gentrification of Santa Fe. In the Hispano community of Santa Fe, interviewees described coming out as more challenging, but also commented that, as one young Hispano man told me, "there's something in the water," as most long-time Santa Fe Hispano families have at least a few visibly gay or lesbian members.

Yet there is little formal organization of the LGBTQ community, both in general and during Fiesta. The last gay bar in Santa Fe closed in 2014 and had struggled to keep its doors open before that. Sociologist Japonica Brown-Saracino refers to these kinds of accepting small cities as having "ambient community," a place where social ties are based on common politics, beliefs, and practices rather than sexuality and thus typically lack autonomous LGBTQ organizations.[79] During Fiesta, participation by LGBTQ people is less organized, as there are no distinctly LGBTQ events. However, lesbians and gay men are visible and involved in the numerous "people's parades" and large community events, including the burning of Zozobra, Old Man of Gloom. The current director of Zozobra, a Hispano gay man who has been involved in the festival since he was a child, described the gay, bisexual, and transgender histories of the event, including known gay or bisexual men who played prominent roles in the festival and a same-sex couple who lit the tall marionette on fire together for decades. LGBTQ people are also involved as writers and actors in the satirical Fiesta Melodrama, including being the topic of the show at times. The Melodrama has a LGBTQ night for audience members as one of their shows.[80] Fiesta de Santa Fe has also been the site of one of the most visible contestations of major festival royalty by the LGBTQ community (see chapter 5).

San Antonio, "The Fiesta City"

San Antonio is the biggest city in this study, a sprawling city of 1.5 million people in South Texas, with boundaries that stretch out in the countryside. It sits on the land of the Tonkawa people. When I moved to San Antonio, everyone told me that the Alamo "is smaller than you think it will be." And indeed I found this to be true. San Antonio is a solidly working-class town, a majority-minority city in which non-Hispanic Anglo people make up around a third of its residents. I was charmed by the city the minute I moved there. One of my favorite early memories is the San Antonio backlash to the hipster state capitol Austin, which had been doing some placemaking around the slogan "Keep Austin Weird." At local coffee shops and on car bumpers in San Antonio, I was pleased to see a satirical bumper sticker "Keep San Antonio Lame" with a brown picture of the Alamo on it. Austin is known for being more sophisticated because of a larger university presence and a dynamic live music scene, but San Antonio maintains a humble spirit despite its larger size, with complete reverence for its NBA basketball team and tourism industry that is fueled in large part by the Alamo and Mission history and Fiesta San Antonio. However, the Alamo itself is part of an entrenched settler colonialist history of the city. Many of the city's historical landmarks—the Alamo, the Missions—stand and represent the decimation and forced assimilation of the American Indian population or the conquest of Mexican residents by Anglo occupiers. Based on Census data, 64 percent of San Antonio residents identify as Hispanic, 25 percent identify as non-Hispanic White, 7 percent identify as Black or African American, and 0.7 percent identify as American Indian. The poverty rate is 18.6 percent and the median income is low.

Yet the Alamo and the subsequent Battle of San Jacinto (where the infamous shout "Remember the Alamo!" was heard) are part of the history of Fiesta San Antonio. Fiesta San Antonio began in 1891 with a parade that honored the heroes of San Jacinto, the concluding battle in the 1836 Texas Revolution.[81] An impending visit by President Harrison and concerns about the waning interest in memorializing the Texas Revolution led a group of upper-class Anglo women to organize a Battle of the Flowers parade, which would become a long-standing event of Fiesta San Antonio and one of the largest parades in the country.[82] Fiesta San Antonio has gone by many names over this time, including the Fiesta de San Jacinto.

Of the four festivals in this study, Mobile Mardi Gras and Fiesta San Antonio are the largest—both in participation and sheer number and variety of events. Fiesta is a sprawling event that lasts two weeks at the end of April but really runs into a whole season that heats up with pre-Fiesta events at the end of March.

There are several festival events run by Anglo social elites, including the Battle of the Flowers parade, the Texas Cavaliers River Parade, Night in Old San Antonio, and the Coronation of the Queen of the Order of the Alamo. The Order of the Alamo and the Cavaliers crown the two long-standing royalty, the King Antonio and the Queen of the Order of the Alamo. Both royalty figures are selected through an exclusive process and have with one exception been an Anglo social elite, a remarkable feat in a majority Hispanic city. Like most festivals, minority royalty have proliferated rather than been integrated into elite organizations. Since the 1960s, racial minority groups have contested the crowning of elite royalty by creating royalty crowned through transparent and accessible pageants, like Miss Fiesta and the Queen of Soul, or contests, such as the scholarship fundraising contest that determines Rey Feo. Rey Feo was developed as a counter to the Anglo-only King Antonio and was the "ugly king" or the "people's king" who represented the Latinx community in San Antonio. Rey Feo was developed by the League of United Latin American Citizens (LULAC) Council Number Two in San Antonio in the 1940s to raise money for education scholarships.[83]

"Fiesta San Antonio" used to be controlled by an Anglo heritage elite, but this control was destabilized in the 1950s and 1960s through a reform of the Fiesta commission board and the creation of more events and royalty controlled by the Latino and African American communities. However, the Fiesta Commission, or the governing body of the festival, did not recognize Rey Feo as part of Fiesta until 1980 due to broader contestation to recognize royalty in the Latinx and Black communities. The Fiesta Commission was initially a coalition of participating member organizations with representatives, but there was pressure from city residents to broaden the participation of the event and the commission in the 1960s. Some Latinx residents of the city still critique cultural appropriation and racism in Fiesta.

San Antonio has a high poverty rate and a thriving LGBTQ community. There is a history of gay and lesbian bar culture, political organizing, and public visibility in the city that dates back to the 1950s. In 2013, San Antonio passed limited municipal protections against discrimination in public accommodations, employment, and housing.

Like Mobile, there is diverse involvement in Fiesta San Antonio by the LGBTQ community. One of the oldest Fiesta events, Cornyation, a mock debutante pageant and political satire that started in 1951 as a satire of the Coronation of the Queen of the Order of the Alamo by members of a theater group, is now one of the "hottest tickets in town" during Fiesta (see chapter 3) and a major fundraiser for HIV/AIDS organizations. The event was kicked out of its performance space in 1964 for being too vulgar and went on hiatus until its revival in the early 1980s. There is a court theme each year and a dozen "houses" that each make a skit that parodies current cultural and political events. Each "house" has a duchess or queen and one or more designers who plan and direct the skit for each house. The Cornyation crowns a King Anchovy, who is typically not a member of the group but a visible business, social, or political figure in the community. Cornyation has never been an exclusively LGBTQ event, as heterosexuals also participate. However, LGBTQ artist talent, drag, and camp humor form a central part of the show, and historically the artistry of the event has been done by Anglo and Latino gay men.[84]

There are also other official events with a strong LGBTQ presence: a major fundraiser for the LGBTQ-serving San Antonio AIDS foundation called the WEBB Party, which was started by a group of Anglo and Latino gay men in the 1990s; a drag queen chili queen cookoff; and a parade in one of the neo-bohemian gayborhoods of San Antonio, the King William Parade and Fair, which includes everyone from drag queens to roller derby skaters. Informal LGBTQ events proliferated, during my fieldwork, including major fundraisers run by Latino gay men and a Fiesta "hat party" thrown by a Latino gay man and his friends in his father's backyard.

Both Fiesta San Antonio and Fiesta de Santa Fe include some of the cultural traditions of fiesta celebrations, like historical pageantry and promotion of settler colonialism. The cultural structures of Fiesta de Santa Fe are far more traditionalistic, religious, and patriotic than those of Fiesta San Antonio. Additionally, the amount of LGBTQ involvement and visibility at Fiesta San Antonio is significantly more than at Fiesta de Santa Fe.

In all four of these cities, regional culture and local traditions meet to create festivals that are meaningful for city residents. In each of these city festivals, regional customs are developed into iterations of the festival that draw on the city's distinct social life. Each city makes the festival distinct and part of urban placemaking practices. These festivals were central to city life, although they prioritized the traditions maintained by social elites. LGBTQ community members were active, visible participants in each of these cities. Indeed, in three of these cities, LGBTQ-run festivals events were the hottest ticket in town.

3

The Hottest Ticket in Town Is a Gay Ball

On Being Wanted

Scoring a last-minute, day-of ticket for the San Antonio Fiesta event Cornyation is almost unheard of, but somehow, I snagged one the first year I attended. Throughout my research, participants, organizers, and fans consistently said the show was one of the hardest tickets to get during Fiesta time. Newspaper articles describe it as a scarce commodity: "It's always a hot ticket; most shows will sell out."[1] So the second year I attended, I went downtown to the box office at 5 a.m. "Cornyation campers" were sleeping in lounge chairs outside the box office, waiting to buy coveted tickets for the Thursday evening late show—it always sells out within an hour. A year later, I was with one of the Cornyation board members a week before the show as he fielded call after call from city officials hoping to get hooked up with tickets. At another point, on a tour in downtown Mobile, Alabama, the white, middle-aged gay man guiding our group told us that he regularly attended local Mardi Gras events and every year, his out-of-town friends inquire about securing tickets to the Order of Osiris ball—always the first Carnival event to sell out. In both Mobile and Baton Rouge, Mardi Gras aficionados repeatedly told me that the balls put on by the larger LGBTQ Mardi Gras organizations or "krewes" were "the hottest ticket in town." That both LGBTQ and heterosexual folks clamored for a way into these events was a source of pride, a sign that the whole metro community valued the LGBTQ groups' contributions to the festival.

In this chapter I analyze how festival events—especially the big, bold LGBTQ parties associated with these civic celebrations—partially remedy the recognition gap for the LGBTQ community. In the last chapter, I mentioned the Santa Fe event the Burning of Zozobra, a huge fundraiser run by a Hispano gay man that is attended by more than 50,000 people each year.[2] This chapter focuses on three explicitly LGBTQ festival events: the Krewe of Apollo ball in Baton Rouge, the Order of Osiris ball in Mobile, and Cornyation in San Antonio. All three of these "hottest ticket in town" events are attended by thousands, too: every year, nearly 5,000 people attend the six shows of Cornyation, and the Carnival krewes host between 1,000 and 2,000 people at their balls. At these proudly queer events, organizers estimate that approximately one-half to two-thirds of attendees are heterosexual—meaning that the events' popularity is not niche, but widespread. Between 2007 and 2017, time and again, I would read newspaper coverage consistently applying descriptive phrases that matched what I heard in interviews: "the one [event] you never want to miss,"[3] "the hottest ball ticket in town,"[4] and "one of the most coveted [tickets] of Carnival season."[5]

In her book, *The Tolerance Trap*, Suzanna Walters suggests that to be celebrated or included is exponentially better than being tolerated.[6] During festivals, LGBTQ groups are publicly and widely recognized as contributing to the community through their skillful, fabulous productions—often lauded for putting on *the most* professional performances, *the most* amusing shows, *the hottest ticket*.

This recognition and being wanted did not rely entirely on being respectable. There was little of the "covering" or erasure of queer cultural differences that one might expect at a "respectable" event. No, these balls and events were replete with drag, same-sex affection, and campy, bawdy jokes. To be sure, some of this recognition makes gay culture a spectacle, but I argue that these festival events cannot be dismissed as *mere* spectacle or the presentation of a respectable face of gay culture: they are a space where gay culture is recognized as distinctly valuable and desirable. Media coverage coos over the size and scale of the balls and shows, clearly embracing the displays of gay humor, drag, and style. The fabulousness of the events demonstrates the way that gay culture can distinctly contribute to local festivals and urban placemaking. This recognition is inevitably partial; these events highlight the most consumable, recognizable part of LGBTQ culture—the culture of gay men—which obscures the contributions of lesbian, bisexual, and queer women. Still, the overall impression is that, for LGBTQ participants, these annual events create a sense of being wanted and valued for what they contribute to the festivals and to their communities.

TABLE 3.1. Major LGBTQ-run Events in Three Cities

Name of Event	City	Event Type	Gender Composition	Racial Demographics	Sexual Demographics
Krewe of Apollo	Baton Rouge, LA	Annual masque ball, held once with around 1,200 guests	All men	Predominately white men with a few Black male members	Exclusively gay and bisexual men
Cornyation	San Antonio, TX	Annual theatrical event, performed six times in three days, around 5,000 guests	Mixed gender in the cast. Men are more likely to be designers, only women can be duchesses	Predominately Latinx and Anglo participants	LGBTQ and heterosexual participants, although the event is mostly run by Latino and Anglo gay men
Order of Osiris	Mobile, AL	Annual masque ball, held once with around 2,000 guests	Mixed gender. Started out as a mostly men's group, is now 50/50.	Predominately white people with a few Black members	Mostly LGBTQ participants with a few heterosexual members

Apollo, Osiris, and Cornyation are long-standing features of their respective cities' annual urban festivals (Mardi Gras in Mobile and Baton Rouge and Fiesta in San Antonio). They have been included since at least the early 1980s, and each event is run by a board and a crew of members or volunteers working and meeting throughout the year. Krewe of Apollo, mostly white gay men, and Order of Osiris, an "all-inclusive" krewe with no gender or sexuality restrictions (that is nonetheless mostly white gay men and lesbians born and raised in the Deep South), are both Mardi Gras krewes that organize formal masque balls. Their ball guests enjoy refreshments and liquor, sit at assigned and lavishly decorated tables, enjoy a multi-hour tableau of krewe members' costuming, and close out the evening with dancing and revelry. At each masque ball, the krewe crowns two royalty figures (e.g., "kings" or "queens"), often those who have contributed over many years, from their ranks.

Cornyation is an event performed during Fiesta San Antonio. It began in 1951 as a satire of an elite debutante event called the Coronation of the Queen of the Order of the Alamo. It has never been an exclusively LGBTQ event, yet, historically, it has been helmed by Anglo and

Latino gay men. In 1964, Cornyation was kicked out of its performance space for being too vulgar, but it was revived in the early 1980s. Today, a dozen "houses" set an annual court theme, which, under the leadership of their duchesses or queens, each create and present a skit on behalf of their house. The Cornyation also brings the crowning of King Anchovy, typically not a member of the group but a visible figure from the local business, social, or political scene.

Between 2012 and 2016, I conducted participant observation at all three of these events, attending each at least twice, but also working within the lunches, parties, fundraisers, and dress rehearsals of the organizations behind the fabulous festivals. Eventually, I even worked as a stagehand and performer for four years with Cornyation. I interviewed members of each event, including the major organizers, for a total of fifty-one interviews, and I analyzed municipal newspaper coverage between 2006 and 2016, gaining data from more than four hundred articles. The newspaper coverage affirmed the cultural contributions made by each event, specifically highlighting the gay cultural elements that made these tickets so desirable. Some of the journalists were identifiable fans of the events, while others were white journalists and social columnists who regularly write about festival events for major city papers and were supportive of their local LGBTQ community. No matter the journalists' positions, though, they collectively presented an image of each of the three events as desirable events within their city's annual festival.

Thinking about Gay Culture

What do I mean by gay culture? All subcultures and communities have cultural forms. The LGBTQ community is no exception. Like other kinds of cultural forms, one does not have to be a gay man to engage in gay culture, nor do all gay men engage in gay culture particularly well. But these cultural forms—like a certain sense of humor, styles of dressing and speaking—signal and stand in for the broader LGBTQ community.[7] The LGBTQ community is culturally diverse, but straight culture—and at times gay male culture—tends to reduce this diversity down to the culture of gay men.

The aspects of gay culture that make it fabulous are rarely the ones that make it erotic, as fabulousness focuses on the glitter and fashion of queer life rather than the erotic connections between people.[8] Thus, the part of LGBTQ culture most consistently recognized and valued in the public accounts of festival events I studied was gay culture, particularly outrageousness and drag. In newspaper accounts, the aesthetics of gay culture was frequently described as a de-eroticized fabulousness in aesthetics and design, particularly around costumes, table decorations, and performance. Scholar Madison Moore, in his book *Fabulous*, describes the fabulous nature of queer aesthetics—the way it rejects normative styles and embraces fierce outrageousness—as a type of performance for marginalized groups to assert themselves in the public, as a way for "marginalized people and social outcasts to regain their humanity and creativity."[9] Scholars like David Halperin study elements of American gay culture, including camp, the appropriation of non-gay items, attention to aesthetics, being "over the top," and "laughing at situations that *to others* are horrifying or tragic."[10] That camp and the fabulousness of events are often attributed to gay aesthetics echoes research on the ways that gay male culture dominates the LGBTQ community.[11] Gay culture is not the exclusive terrain of gay *men*, either. For example, lesbian designers and cross-dressing heterosexual men performed camp during their Cornyation skits. Nonetheless, there is a long history of gay men being protective or territorial over gay culture, particularly elements like camp and drag, a possessiveness that is often validated by the media.[12]

Drag is an enduring symbol of gay life, particularly in the South, where cultural norms of pageantry support the public visibility of cross-dressing and drag.[13] Drag queens and men doing drag was central to the fabulousness embraced by event audiences. Drag was featured prominently in the newspaper coverage of all three events.

But rarely are drag *kings* celebrated, nor is there any broad recognition that LBQ women do camp and can be fabulous.[14] This absence of recognition may be a result of the lower cultural legibility of LBQ culture for heterosexual audiences; there is, for instance, no equivalent to the television series *Queer Eye* for LBQ women. This recognition gap is amplified by the greater visibility of gay men, particularly white Anglo gay men, as symbolizing the broader LGBTQ community.[15] Media depictions, in turn, rarely feature the aesthetics of LBQ women, ignoring lesbian styles like butch embodiments and rendering female bisexualities invisible.[16] These dynamics of amplifying gay male culture and ignoring LBQ women's contributions were evident in all three cities, although the Order of Osiris, an intentionally all-inclusive krewe, had the most acknowledgment of LBQ women's contributions.

Krewe of Apollo Baton Rouge: One of the Most Beautiful Balls in Baton Rouge

Baton Rouge newspapers do not provide much coverage of the city's Mardi Gras festivities, possibly because it's so near New Orleans, with its world-famous celebrations. Still, their reviews of the Krewe of Apollo's annual ball—the Bal Masque—emphasize its grandeur, fabulousness, and fundraising. They also stress the brotherhood within the organization, including how close the men are with one another and their memorialization of recently departed members. One review reads: "One of the reasons this is among my favorite balls is that it benefits a great cause—the krewe's AIDS-Crisis Fund. Another is that the costumes are amazing!"[17] Another, particularly ebullient review notes:

> From the staging of its first Mardi Gras ball 30 years ago, an invitation to the Krewe of Apollo Baton Rouge's Bal Masque has been one of the most coveted of Carnival season. No one can argue that Apollo's New Orleans-style tableau isn't one of the most elaborate in town; people are talking about the costumes for weeks afterward.[18]

Using the word "coveted" stresses the group's popularity, and, like other reviews, this one favorably compares Apollo's ball to others in the area. After the 2011 ball, we read, the krewe has "proved once again why it has the reputation as staging one of the most beautiful balls in the area."[19] The attention to the beautiful costumes again asserts a joyful appreciation for krewe's aesthetic contributions to the city festival.

The elements of gay culture and commentary on gay politics that are interwoven into the ball, including the emphasis on drag, are central to such descriptions. When krewe members perform in drag as part of the ball tableau performance, their drag names are used in the program *and* in the newspaper. In 2016, the reporter described, excitedly, "the finale of the costume portion of the tableau was Apollo's interpretation of the historical moment when the United States Supreme Court voted in favor of marriage equality, with Bonét and a group of friends brilliantly re-enacting the vote."[20] Mobile's krewes are more secretive, but in Baton Rouge, participants' full names also make it into the local paper.

> Ball Captain Lester Mut made his entrance as Jennifer Marlowe, the Disco Queen, a Caucasian cross between Diana Ross and Donna Summers . . . Joe Boniol, Ball Lieutenant Jim Omohundro and Rick Hamilton emerged from a pink bus in costumes reproduced from the musical "Priscilla, Queen of the Desert" and boogied to such disco hits as "I Love the Nightlife," "I Will Survive" and "Shake Your Groove Thing." Ball lieutenants Tim Rapier and Chad Fernandez captured the essence of New York's Studio 54 followed by a tribute to Michael Jackson's songs from the disco era by former Baton Rouge resident Derrian Tolden, now of New York City. Serving as an introduction to the new king and queen was the appearance of krewe members Scott Blanchard and Eddy Vargas as the Village People.[21]

This account of the ball includes clear references to drag, gay cultural icons like the Village People, and drag-related movies like *Priscilla, Queen of the Desert*. The tone is appreciative and descriptive, absent any shaming or voyeurism. Most coverage, in fact, treats the artistry of the men in the show as a laudable accomplishment.

Drag is an important part of the Krewe of Apollo ball. Drag features heavily in the tableaux, in which krewe members parade down a central runway dressed in extravagant costumes and elaborate back pieces—artistic armatures that sometimes extend four or five feet above the performer's head. At one dress rehearsal, I spoke with the boyfriend of Stan, a slender, twenty-something, white man costuming for the first time. Stan's boyfriend explained that he'd been enlisted because the ball captain was concerned that there was not "enough drag" in the show. Another longtime krewe member remarked that the krewe frequently debated whether they have "too much" or "not enough" drag as they plan each year's events. Because another krewe in town, The Krewe of Divas, is strictly composed of professional drag queens, the Krewe of Apollo's members often drew a firm boundary between Apollo and the Divas. Many members stressed that the Krewe of Apollo ball was not a drag show of professional queens, but rather an event that highlighted one Queen in particular.

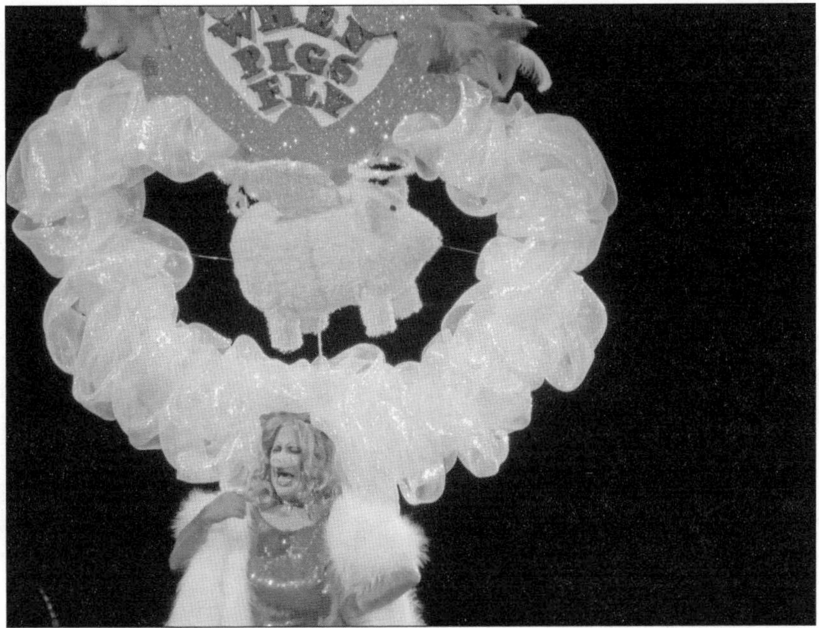

Figure 3.1. Krewe of Apollo member as Miss Piggy during the annual ball

Krewe of Apollo members emphasized the drag performed by their queen, the Apollo member dramatically revealed at the end of each year's ball. She, always a man in drag, will reign over the krewe for the following year. In this men's krewe, the royalty was a king/queen pairing, yet many krewe members said that the ball is "all about the queen." According to one man in his thirties, the queen made the Bal Masque "similar to a wedding," where it's all about the bride. He added that some of the excitement was "probably the aspect of seeing a man look like a woman. And you probably can't tell it's a man," but I noted how queen's drag differentiated the Krewe of Apollo's ball from other festival events in the city. Yes, like a wedding, participants' attention is focused on the production and performance of femininity—in this case, however, it is *male* femininity. Thus, the performance draws from the heteronormativity of rituals like weddings while simultaneously challenging it: Everyone knows the queen is a man, queering the apparent heteronormativity of the ball's king/queen pairing.

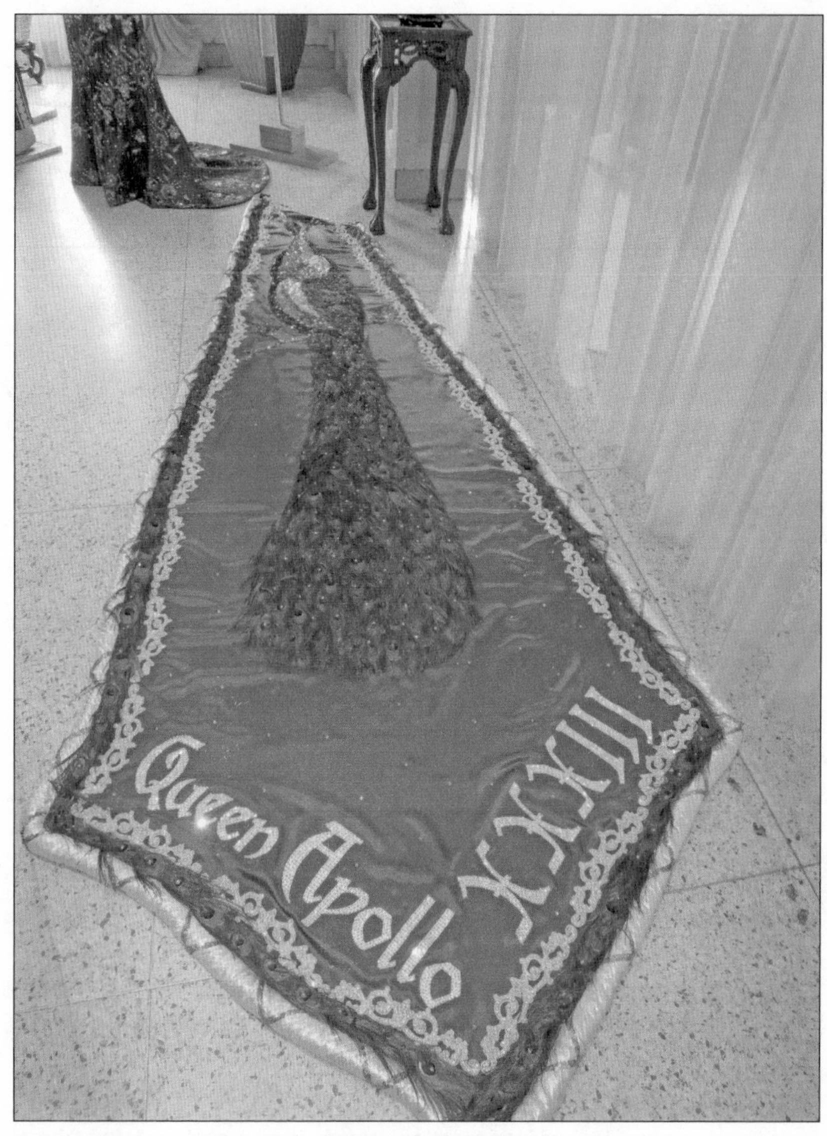

Figure 3.2. Queen of Apollo royal train on display at Krewe of Apollo brunch

To be sure, the gay culture visible in Apollo is predominately white gay culture. Where the smaller krewes in Baton Rouge and Mobile feature more elements of Black gay culture, Apollo balls, especially their music, focus on white Southern gay cultural staples. Ball attendees will hear lots of old-school country like Dolly Parton, songs by diva idols like Cher and Madonna, contemporary pop songs, and Broadway musical numbers, with a few exceptions during performances from the few Black krewe members and Black guest performers. In my first year attending the ball, a Black transgender drag queen (according to a gay bartender, one of the most visible members of the quiet Baton Rouge transgender community) brought down the house with a stunning drag performance to a Motown classic. Another Black krewe member regularly used hip-hop tracks and gestured to Black style in his costuming, while young Black men who performed as part of dance ensembles incorporated the dance style of voguing in sometimes subtle ways.

Women's labor—the work of sisters, female friends, and hired designers—was mostly invisible at the Krewe of Apollo's ball. Cisgender women cannot become members of this krewe, though they are present in the organization and production of the annual ball. At the pre-ball cocktail party, members of this women's auxiliary serve and refill cocktails. During the ball's setup, women work backstage assembling performers' elaborate backpieces or putting the finishing touches on designs they made for the krewe members. And, at the ball, sisters and female friends help decorate the tables throughout the convention center and perform other helpful tasks. Rarely, women performed during the show, but usually only as helpers or members of large ensembles. For example, an older white krewe member costumed in complementary outfits and danced with his sister on the stage. The first year I attended Apollo's ball, I noted that a longtime female friend of the krewe costumed on stage as Mother Goose, and a young white woman using a dildo as a strategic prop was part of the ensemble; the MC of the ball that year, a white gay comic, drew attention to her and joked that she was the "only person with a vagina on stage."

The women's work did not go unnoticed. At the post-ball private awards show one year, a white heterosexual woman who designed many costumes was recognized with an award, as was a white butch lesbian who ran a community gay bar. But apart from the recognition of the

Figure 3.3. Krewe of Apollo member with backpiece at the ball

Black transgender queen, these women's work did not get recognized outside the krewe. Newspaper accounts and public understandings of the Krewe of Apollo were that it was an important part of the city's Mardi Gras celebration—the hottest ticket in town—and that it was primarily a krewe of fabulous gay white men. The coverage of the Order of Osiris in Mobile was relatively similar.

Mobile Order of Osiris: The Gays Do It Up Right

In Mobile, municipal newspapers cover the myriad balls and parades throughout the Carnival season. The lion's share of their attention goes, naturally, to the largest and most well-known of these events. The Masked Observer, a secret reviewer of Carnival activities for the largest city newspaper, regularly writes about the Osiris ball, favorably commenting on the décor and style of the event. Where other journalists use descriptors like "alternative lifestyle," an "over-the-top group,"[22] or "Mobile's most fabulous partying organization,"[23] the Masked Observer typically describes Osiris as "Mobile's most fabulous mystic society."[24] Newspaper accounts describe the Osiris ball as one of the most entertaining Carnival events because of the table décor, the tableau of drag and satire, and the sheer fun: "[D]efinitely the one tableau you never want to miss,"[25] where "the decorations are fabulous" and "carried out to perfection."[26] One year the Masked Observer noted that he "has rarely witnessed tables so exquisitely decorated or guests made to feel more welcome" as at Osiris's ball.[27] In Mobile, where lavish hospitality is part and parcel of Mardi Gras celebrations, these compliments are particularly meaningful.

In newspaper accounts, gay aesthetics get the credit for all this fabulousness. I was struck by one description in which the journalist comments, "the Order of Osiris ball, which is the gay and lesbian society, and my personal favorite—the gays do it up right."[28] This exclamation that "the gays do it up right" relies on understandings of gay culture as oriented toward a certain gendered aesthetic. Again, it reduces LGBTQ culture to its most visible and frequently consumed parts: those created by and for gay men, often assumed to be fashionable, upper middle class, cisgendered, and white. It relies on stereotypes of gay men as campy and over the top. This co-ed group is described by the Masked Observer as

"Mobile's most fabulous mystic society, and the one most qualified to tell you which tie goes with which dress shirt."[29] Or, the "well-manicured hands down, The Order of Osiris has the most entertaining ball of them all. And this year, the organization made up of gay and lesbian members, once again, did not disappoint."[30] These references to "well-manicured hands" and fashion advice build on cultural understandings of gay culture as fashionable in a way that's consumable by but not threatening to heterosexuals, evidenced by cultural visibility of gay fashion designers and the popularity of shows like *Queer Eye for the Straight Guy* and its more recent iteration, *Queer Eye*.[31]

Yet, women's contributions were not absent from newspaper descriptions of the event. In 2017, the reviewer enthused, "Queen Anna and King Heather? Both the queen and king were girls? Yes, that's correct! Confused? I'm a little confused too, but just remember it's the magical Land of Oz where queens can be kings and queens can be queens."[32] The pairing of two women as the royalty pair, as opposed to the male-female pairs common in krewe royalty, disrupted Carnival traditions. This reporter described the gender-bending at the ball as a magical part of the ball, as the "Land of Oz" that allows women to be kings or queens, a description that locates this gender transgressiveness of the women within the narrow context of the ball. When lesbian members of the Order of Osiris were mentioned in the media, it was usually by noting the presence of women wearing tuxedos at the event or lesbian culture in the tableau, such as references to *Star Wars* or *Xena: Warrior Princess*.

In Osiris, women and men are equally involved in the group, including in the royalty and leadership, yet, the labor of women's participation in festival events is often obscured in media representations. In Mobile's Osiris, many gay men and LBQ women I interview mention that lesbians in the group bring organizing power and skills for building to the organizations. One of the oldest members of the group, a senior white man, leaned over to me during one meeting together and said with a wink, "You know, if you want something *done right*, have a dyke do it." He went on to tell me that many of the best ball captains, who conceptualize and organize the annual ball, are women. During the dress rehearsal for the ball, LBQ women in the group bring out their power tools to fix errant floats and to strategize about how to improve the movement of the floats through the convention center. These clear contributions—to organizing, to fixing, and to building—are nevertheless not a prominent part of how the krewe is featured in the media coverage of the event.

This lack of acknowledgment may also come from the devaluation of LBQ women's participation from within the LGBTQ community. LBQ women are more likely to be marginalized in LGBTQ spaces, like gay bars.[33] During the setup for the Order of Osiris ball in 2016, I noticed something as I circulated around the convention center. I investigated a table with a Harry Potter theme designed by a white, older lesbian couple. They showed me the creatively designed props on their table—the various recyclable bottles they saved over the year to turn into potions containers, the pictures they printed from the Internet. They commented that they just do not have as much money as the gay men in the group and thus must be more creative. Across the convention center, one of the most visible tables is decorated with huge, glittery centerpieces that rise above all the others. Someone informed me that the white gay man who had those decorations paid someone to design his outfit, float, and table decorations.

Yet, not all white gay men in the group have surplus income. An older white gay couple showed me how their tables are decorated sparsely, that they used an old, painted Spam can to make the foundation of their centerpieces; they enjoy traveling and do not want to spend their limited income on table decorations. I am hosted by a butch-femme lesbian couple who have spent the last several months constructing elaborate centerpieces to create an Alice in Wonderland–themed area; they made these centerpieces on the weekends with a group of lesbian friends, their chosen family with whom they also regularly vacation. My table is the Mad Hatter's table, which comes with a gift bag full of related paraphernalia, including my own teacup, Mardi Gras beads, and drinking glasses. My seat is labeled with a little card with my name on it. One of the established members of the group, an older white woman, came over to inspect the elaborate tables; she shook her head and exclaimed to the butch lesbian woman who designed the tables, "you out-gayed the gays this time." I was struck by the way the lesbian-decorated tables are described as "out-gaying the gays," pronouncing tables decorated by a group of lesbians to be both a gay aesthetic accomplishment and besting gay aesthetics. In a later interview, a femme lesbian who was known for being one of the best table designers in the krewe described herself as

Figure 3.4. Decorated tables at the Order of Osiris in Mobile

having "a little gay man inside me." In this case, being fabulous is still being gay, even when performed by lesbians.

Newspaper coverage framing events like the Osiris ball is shot through with superlatives—wildest, most outrageous—helps characterize the LGBTQ krewes as something special to the wider (heterosexual) community. This broader respect is notable not only for its recognition of the scale and size of the events relative to the rest of the festival but also for its recognition of the aesthetic talents and detailed attention of the performers. More frequently, disreputable parts of gay culture, such as drag, are publicly portrayed as positive and enjoyable. To the extent that the annual soirees will be recognized as spectacular, and more than just a spectacle, there is added value to throwing an excellent party. According to one white lesbian interviewee, a local native, "Mobile is a party town anyway, so if you put on a good party, everybody respects you for it."

So superlative gay fabulousness is often consciously and pridefully produced. Krewe members spend months creating their outfits and miniature floats for the tableau. In Mobile, the LGBTQ events boasted some of the most elaborate, inventive table designs I saw throughout my research.[34] Huge, decorative, and thematic, the guest tables carve out the ball's space. One middle-aged white butch lesbian told me that Osiris's guests were consistently amazed that a krewe with only a few dozen members could put on such an elaborate event. While showing me around the convention center, another, older lesbian Osiris member recalled a founding member in the 1980s had a catchphrase for the spirit of their club: "never too big, never too much." Indeed, at the annual awards ceremony the krewe leadership presents a special award to the person who did the most elaborate costuming, float, and table decorations for the ball.

The "never too big, never too much" spirit was embodied in all of the events I studied in Mobile, Baton Rouge, and San Antonio. They all had elements that were over the top and outrageous, because these were critical to making these events the "hottest ticket in town." Plus, being outrageous builds on a long history of gay aesthetics of excessiveness and lavish luxury.[35] Being wanted, being a coveted ticket, was about crafting and accomplishing a certain kind of outrageousness that could be positively framed within city narratives.

At Osiris, the size and scale of the event is a point of pride, signifying the effort and attention the krewe members expend on their annual ball. Being grandiose and fabulous is valued by all, including heterosexual attendees. But it is also attributed to gay male aesthetics. Women who contribute will refer, even to themselves, as contributors to that culture—recall the butch woman who "out-gayed the gays" or a femme woman in Mobile who described her artistic ability as having "a little gay man inside me." Sometimes these aesthetics reflect class and economic differences between LBQ women and gay men in the group, although not all gay men are economically well off. Other times, gay men's aesthetic contributions are prioritized even when women show themselves to be compelling and interesting artistic contributors to festival events.

Cornyation San Antonio: Wild, Glittery Drag Queens

In San Antonio, Cornyation is just one of more than a hundred events in the annual Fiesta San Antonio, but it's a hot topic in the news. The show is prominently included in best-of lists and articles full of Fiesta fashion tips for women.[36] Local reporters cover Cornyation, interviewing its royalty, King Anchovy, and even following up on the summertime distribution of its fundraising checks. The newspaper describes the event as "Fiesta's wildest, wackiest event,"[37] "one of the most popular ways to see San Antonio go a little bit wild,"[38] and "an adult-only Fiesta staple loved for its over-the-top spoofs on current events."[39] Consistent themes in the coverage include the way the show satirizes political and cultural events, its vulgar "adult" content, and its fundraising success.

> It's lewd and crude, but the raucous Fiesta variety show that skewers local and national newsmakers, celebrities and politicos is always a must-see. This year's "The Court of the Second Coming" just might have you coming back for seconds with former U.S. Rep Charlie Gonzalez as King Anchovy XLVIII ruling over skits, dancing and drag queens. Shows are always a sellout, but tickets can be had. Just remember that Cornyation doesn't give a hoot, and that's what makes it so good.[40]

What makes it *good* is that it "doesn't give a hoot"—it's celebrated for being "lewd," "crude," and "raucous," and that is why the show is described as "always a must-see" and a "sellout." Within Fiesta's festive, party-oriented program, Cornyation gains recognition and can take pride in its disorder and lack of restraint. There has been some increased restraint in the show, as decades ago audience members wildly threw objects to each other before, during, and after it, including the infamous custom of hurling flour tortillas at one another. Now there is a sign posted on the theater door—"No Tortillas"—and audience members can only throw *cascarones*, or confetti-filled eggs, at one another.

The gay aesthetics of the show are evoked by news coverage in a few ways. Frequently, reporters mention that the show was performed in the 1980s in a "gay dance club" called the Bonham Exchange. Articles also regularly emphasize the presence of glitter-covered, scantily clad men. As one reporter notes, "Cornyation is not a gay event. It's just happy. And there's a lot of glitter and men wearing makeup and spandex."[41] A third theme among these accounts is the near ubiquitous mention of drag queens, although drag is only one component of the show: "A drag queen tartly dressed in an airbrushed wife-beater and plaid miniskirt flirted with the crowd,"[42] one account reads, while another says, "As usual, drag queens were plentiful at the Fiesta event, which skewered headlines from the past year. And, as usual, there were absolutely no sacred cows."[43] The Pointless Sisters, a group of Latino men in drag who have performed at the show for decades, are also covered frequently in reviews and pictures. The year the Pointless Sisters performed in colorful ballet folklórico skirts and blouses, one prominent newspaper photograph featured the lead performer spinning—all you could see was the whirl of his colorful skirt and his mustachioed face. Finally, fiesta coverage of Cornyation emphasizes play and gender non-conformity. Consider the following list of the best parts of Fiesta San Antonio:

1. Can you say "par-TAY?"
2. Eleven nonstop good-time days and nights
3. Cascarones
4. Fiesta queens
5. Drag queens
6. Wannabe queens
7. Order of the Alamo coronation
8. Disorder at Cornyation[44]

In this list, Fiesta queens (the official royalty of the festival, as decided by the Fiesta Commission) outrank drag queens and "wannabe queens," but *barely*.

In San Antonio, the emphasis on gay culture is not always an exclusive emphasis on *white* gay culture. Cornyation drag comes out of a strong Latinx drag community with roots in San Antonio's 1970s bar culture.[45] Thus, the majority of participants in Cornyation have a Spanish surname or are Latinx-identified, and their drag often uses elements of Latinx culture, including Catholic themes, Mexican cartoon characters, songs in Spanish, aesthetic styles like ballet folklórico, and drag techniques associated with drag performers of color, like disidentification (recycling mainstream images and discourses and performing them as subversive).[46] Latinx Cornyation designers and performers often display the fabulousness described by Madison Moore in the book *Fabulous*, a creative eccentricity involving "high levels of creativity, imagination, and originality."[47]

Cornyation's one hundred plus performers are divided into ten to twelve "houses," each led by a female "duchess" (also called their "queen," "vice-empress," or "empress," she is frequently the only woman in each house) and with its own artistic designers. As in the Order of Osiris, LBQ women are integral to the annual celebrations. There are some female designers; in 2017, three of the houses were led by women designers. In the mixed-gender groups, Cornyation and Osiris, lesbians, bisexual, and queer women are an integral part of the show but are often missing from the forms of acknowledgment, including newspaper accounts and even other group members' valuations.

That is, gay male group members frequently devalue LBQ women's contributions to the organization and to its annual Fiesta event. Female designers I interviewed confirmed that it took them a long time to gain the respect of gay designers, who often ignored them unless and until they created an "epic" costume or performance. For example, Martina's contributions to Cornyation were consistently downplayed. She was among the group's youngest designers, but she had been doing the work for more than a decade. I first met this young, bisexual Latina when I was a stage crew member on her team, running on stage to hold up glittery cardboard props of San Antonio landmarks while she and her crew of Latino men danced in crudely made fat suits to parody

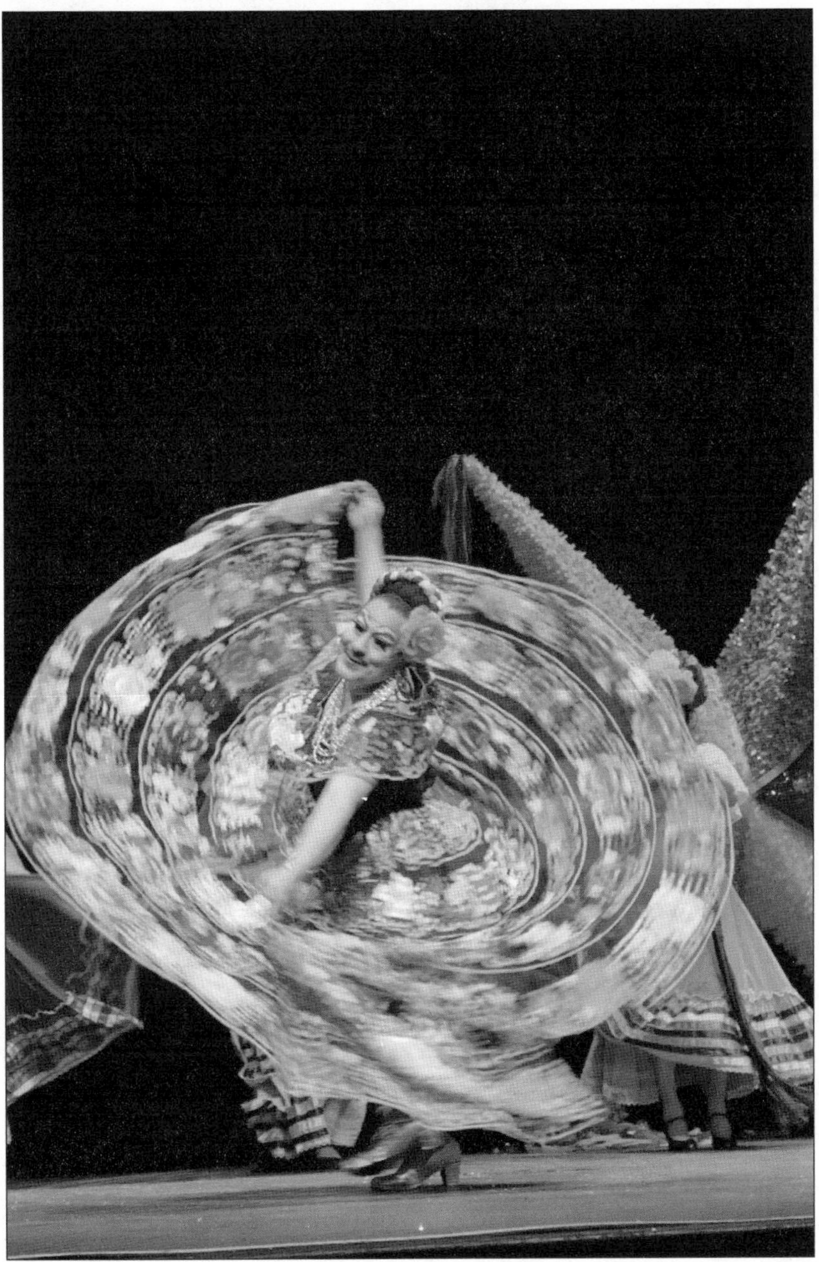

Figure 3.5. Cornyation Pointless Sister dancing. Credit: Lauryn Farris

concerns about the rising rate of childhood obesity in San Antonio. Martina arrived as the "queen" or "duchess" of the sketch, the only role in each sketch required to be filled by a cisgender or trans woman, to rescue the day dressed as a huge pizza. A few months later, we sat at the outside tables of a well-known local gay brunch place. Her partner, Julian, a young Latino who also frequently designed and performed in Cornyation, joined us. I learned that Martina became involved in the show as an older teenager, working with her gay theater mentor from a local children's afterschool program. When her mentor passed away, she stepped into his shoes. At that point, I had no idea that her tenure with the event was more than ten years; when I asked about her experience fitting into the show, she shrugged, "I've felt a little outcast for the most part, but I guess maybe finally just letting it go." She continued, "I've been in Cornyation for so long and even now I feel like 90 percent of the people in the show don't know who I am, but I know who they are. I've always felt like they don't view me as part of the show or something, I'm not part of the clique or something, you know." Martina had seen other female designers come and go over the years, yet she was still not considered a "senior designer." Much like other women participants I interviewed, it seemed Martina had run up against the "old boys club" atmosphere that could pervade even raucous, disordered Cornyation.

Martina was not certain whether she should attribute the lack of recognition to being a woman, being Latina, being perceived as straight, or some combination of all these factors. People do not seem to notice that her crew is entirely Latino gay men except for her, her partner, and one Latina woman who performs with them. Like her, LBQ women described receiving less recognition and respect for their accomplishments, having to work harder and longer to get the same amount of respect men get for their artistic contributions to the event. This echoes the ways that, in artistic fields like fashion design, gay men's contributions are valorized and rewarded above women's and other men's accomplishments.[48] And the lack of acknowledgment of women's contributions within the organization may be shaping how the event is covered in the media and recognized by the public.

I experienced this invisibility firsthand while working on my book on Cornyation, an illustrated romp through the history of the show from the 1950s to 2010s. Board members of the organization read through drafts of my manuscript, and I recall one, an older Latino man, sneering at my description of the show as involving gay men *and* lesbians. "There are no lesbians in this group," he said emphatically, crossing out the parts of the manuscript where I'd mention lesbians. The cognitive dissonance was astounding: What about *me*, a queer woman who had been involved in the show, backstage and onstage, for four years at that point? What about the lesbian and bi-identified women I hung around with backstage between shows, or the female stage manager who mainly dates women and has worked for decades backstage to turn the show from chaos into an organized (if still chaotic) performance? What about the performer, a flirty bisexual woman who groped my comically oversized bra stuffed with socks as she waited to go onstage? That in that moment I felt my own contributions to the organization erased, demonstrated tangibly that gay men's dominance of LGBTQ spaces and events endures. Cornyation leadership describes their event as something "for the entire community," and yet my contributions as a queer woman were being obliterated with the stroke of one man's pen.

More Than Respectability, More Than Spectacle

Proudly, these events put the outrageous (and at times disreputable) parts of gay culture on display. There's drag, cross-dressing, same-sex affection, and bawdy camp. Same-sex couples dance at Mobile's Osiris ball after the tableau is over. Young white and Black men in nothing but short, form-fitting swim trunks dance provocatively on stage at Baton Rouge's Apollo. Both krewes try to avoid being "crude" in their tableaux, but you will see tasteful same-sex kisses on stage, challenging Southern norms about public displays of affection, and campy, naughty gay humor is in abundance at all three events.

Drag and cross-dressing for both men and women are part of all three events. The group of two hundred individuals who put on Cornyation every year include local professional drag queens as well as a dozen or so men pulling together various styles of campy (or not so campy) drag and a few women cross-dressing on stage. Osiris members often cross-dress as royalty—in fact, when the krewe selects two members to be royalty each year, the new royal figures can decide to be *either* a king or queen. Two of the men in the group have been queens, and several butch lesbians have been kings. One year at the Osiris ball, a pair of lesbian couples performed as Han Solo rescuing Princess Leia and as the Mad Hatter with Alice in Wonderland. A few male members of Osiris consistently costume in drag; other male Osiris members do so sporadically. For example, one year two men with hairy legs and beards, dressed in skimpy, lighted neon tutus, sports bras, and wigs came out dancing as Tinkerbell fairies, throwing beads to the ball's attendees.

In the all-gay Krewe of Apollo, drag is an integral part of the ball. Their royalty is always a king and queen pairing (again, both will be men), and many Apollo members described the ball as "all about the queen." To the Krewe, *she* was what made Apollo's ball different from other Mardi Gras balls, and drag was everywhere, even being performed by men who rarely did drag outside the annual event.

Drag and other gender play extended to the attendees, too. At both Mardi Gras balls, cross-dressing and drag is encouraged, as long as guests are dressed formally, in either a ball gown or a tuxedo. That meant that, if for one night only, these events—part of city-wide celebrations—allowed for even heterosexual community members to adopt "disreputable" aspects of gay culture. Not only did these aspects of gay life become visible, they were recognized and celebrated as an integral part of each event by municipal newspapers.

On Being Wanted

LGBTQ festival participation at all three events is valued *because* of gay culture, not in spite of it. LGBTQ labor, creativity, and performance are recognized as important contributions to these cities' festivals, and straight people want to attend these events. The groups seemed both proud and mildly astonished that they were the "hottest ticket in town," in the words of their local newspapers.

Their astonishment stems from the ways their recognition is partial and incomplete. When LGBTQ culture is highlighted and appreciated by mainstream culture, it is disproportionately *gay* culture. At these festival events, there was more appreciation for camp, drag, and other gay aesthetics—along with an ethos of fabulousness—than any other identifiable part of the LGBTQ community. Even the LGBTQ community itself privileges white men at the expense of women, racial minorities, bisexuals, and gender-transgressive individuals.[49] This can be alienating, especially when LBQ women are not publicly recognized for their contributions when the events are celebrated in the media.

Having an LGBTQ festival event be the "hottest ticket in town" is not a revolutionary smashing of the gates of homophobia, a cataclysmic re-ordering of the social order, or a radical transformation of the social system. Being the hottest ticket does not remedy LGBTQ homelessness, poverty, or racial injustice. And yet, being celebrated at all is a profound experience of being wanted and desired for one's unique contributions to city and community.

This desirability, in turn, relies on constant labor. The recognition during festivals comes from the production of an entertaining event. That is, the recognition is conditional and the pressure is constant: You can't get the positive recognition without putting on consistently heightened shows. Ernest, a white, thirty-something member of Apollo, was adamant that "you have to live up to your reputation, year after year after year." This reputation is constantly performed and never fully completed in a way that reminds me of scholar Jon McKenzie's thesis, fleshed out in his book *Perform or Else*, that the freedom to perform can turn into an imperative as powerful as governmental disciplinary forces.[50] Performance can become forced. And what happens if you no longer want to perform?

Rights, however resentfully granted, have more lasting power than being wanted for an entertaining event. During my fieldwork for this project, same-sex marriage became legal throughout the country via Supreme Court ruling. Many of my participants were delighted to have the right to marry, yet they understood that exercising that right would remain a difficult hurdle. State and city authorities begrudgingly and inconsistently performed their duties regarding this newly enshrined rite. In Mobile, some city authorities who resisted same-sex marriage stopped issuing marriage licenses to *any* couples rather than give them to same-sex couples.[51] Festival participants knew what it was to put on a coveted event, to have their performances and spectacles desired by city members and applauded by reporters, an experience that may feel different than being resentfully allowed rights.

The gay balls I studied were potent sites for building value around the LGBTQ community. They did not require respectability, just a good show. And so, festival events help fill the recognition gap for LGBTQ people in the South and Southwest. Because cultural membership is about being collectively defined as valued members of a community, balls can lead to a sense of citizenship and belonging, of meaning and significance. In the next chapter, we will see how attendees, for their part, symbolically recognize LGBTQ progress and work toward reconciliation—through inclusive collective partying.

4

Inclusive Collective Partying

On Making Community

I often bring friends to festival events. For my visit to San Antonio's Fiesta Frenzy in 2012, my fellow professors, Alfred and Habiba, got the nod. By the time I pulled up to the Josephine Theater at 7:30, Alfred was already there—as he put it in a text, he'd arrived "absurdly early." So had a small crowd, milling about outside. Several older Latino and Black men were mingling with curvy white and Latina women. Alfred studies HIV and has frequently attended drag events, but I did not know how much experience Habiba had with drag culture. As I drove to the theater, I caught myself being concerned that Habiba would find the show too vulgar or wild. Just the year before, the politics of vulgarity had been in full force.[1] One of the emcees—a Latinx drag queen—took out her fake breasts and gave them to an audience member in exchange for a grope of the woman's real ones in order to raise money for the cause that night. For Habiba, this might be . . . a lot.

Fiesta Frenzy is an unofficial Fiesta event, a one-night charitable event with local drag performers and guests from around the country. On this night, it's taking place in a 277-person theater. When we enter the bustling lobby, I notice a tall white man dressed in a suit, crown, and a sash bedecked with pins. At first glance, I think, "Is King Antonio here?" No, he's not the major royalty of the entire festival, he's the reigning royalty from the LGBTQ club Alamo Empire. I buy a Fiesta pin that says "Alamo Empire 2012" (bearing names I presume are the organization's royalty), with the proceeds going to Las Mujeres Unidas, a local ASO focused on Latina women. Alfred and I join the long drinks line, buy a sweet cocktail from a young queer-looking man behind the counter, and sit to chat. Watching the crowd flood in, I note that, on the whole, its members are older than I remembered the year before, but still appreciably diverse in terms of age, gender, and racial diversity. A young Black man in a leather vest strolls past a white lesbian couple in their seventies. A large group of Latina women in butch-femme couples who attend every year passes in their fine clothes—colorful vest and tie combinations I've long admired.

The program, I notice as we take our seats near the back of the theater, reads "An Evening of Pride and Patriotism." It is not, as I assumed, ironic: The show starts with a beautiful Black man named Skuddr Jones in a crisp button-down shirt and sleeveless blue hoodie reverently singing the Star-Spangled Banner. Everyone stands. Many put their hands over their hearts. Two people walk slowly down the aisle carrying flags, which they eventually place in stands on the stage. I forget sometimes that San Antonio is, unmistakably, a military town.

The emcees are Eryca Daniels and Amber Nixx, two Latinx drag queens who joke about their weight and their matching dresses. Eryca hypes the crowd, shouting for us to "make some noise," as they toss Carnival beads to the outstretched hands in the eager audience. Amber asks with a winking reference to anal beads, "Do I need to bend over for this?" Eryca throws a huge bunch of beads to people on the side aisle, and everyone goes wild. My friend Habiba arrives and seems to enjoy the show, but, as I'd expected she might, expresses some discomfort with the way the queens disregard any boundary with the audience. The emcees and performers gyrate in audience members' laps, perch on their knees to take photos, and ask probing questions about their sexuality. The emcees encourage us to drink more by making toasts and doing shots on stage, "Here's to all the gays, straight and bisexuals that wish us well . . . All the other sons of bitches can go to hell!" There are several "roll calls" of who is in the audience. "Where are all my lesbians? Where are all my gay men? Where are all my bisexuals? Where are all my transgenders? Where are all my straight people?" Each group cheers, met with the emcees' affirmation: "See! We can all get along!" Based on the cheers when the emcee asks for straights to cheer, there are clearly plenty of people in the audience who identify as heterosexual.

Over the course of four hours, Eryca and Amber give out service awards to community members, highlight the cause for the evening (Pride Center San Antonio), and introduce performers. They swear at each other in Spanish and mock the audience and drag queens alike. When Tencha La Jefa, a local queen known for her campy comedic drag, takes the stage with blacked-out teeth and curlers in her wig, Amber announces, "She was voted most beautiful in her trailer park!" I always enjoy Tencha's performance style, which was developed using Mexican television characters like La India María and Doña Florinda from *El Chavo del Ocho*.[2] Eryca chimes in with Amber, joking that Tencha "is a reason not to do drugs while you're pregnant."

Fiesta Frenzy, like LGBTQ-run festival events, was part of what I call "inclusive collective partying." This high-performance production embraces LGBTQ outrageousness, racially diverse audiences that include many heterosexual and cisgender participants, and public acknowledgment of all this inclusivity. This inclusive collective party was often framed not just as heterosexual cisgender people using the LGBTQ community for entertainment but as creating valuable experiences of being part of a collective celebrating their time together. Classical sociologist Émile Durkheim describes it as collective effervescence, the shared spirit that comes from an experience that is both temporary and meaningful. For many LGBTQ festival events, the pleasure of the event and diversity of attendees was an important part of the collective effervescence, connecting across lines of sexuality, and sometimes class and race as well.

The same inclusive collective partying had different meanings in each setting. At times, it focused on educating the heterosexual public, at others it seemed to be a spectacle of entertainment or a blatant attempt to shape the agenda for cultural change. In the more traditionalistic festivals—Mobile and Santa Fe—the lack of restrictions around attending LGBTQ events was one way of resisting festival segregation practices. In Mobile, inclusivity became a defining characteristic of the way LGBTQ people "did" Carnival (although Black LGBTQ involvement in predominately white krewes was limited). In the city with the least traditionalistic festival—Baton Rouge—there was more ambivalence about heterosexual consumption of gay culture as a spectacle. LGBTQ celebrants tried to harness this spectacle for education. In the large urban festivals in San Antonio and Mobile, participants in smaller LGBTQ events fretted that their events had become too popular with heterosexual attendees and tried to retain control over them. I also saw pushback as participants expressed nostalgia for the days when the events were more specifically and solely run and attended by LGBTQ community members. That is, sometimes values such as strengthening community took priority above—but did not completely displace—inclusive collective partying.

The research for this chapter includes my fieldnotes from attending festival events in all four cities and interviews with organizers of LGBTQ festival events. I also include data on the attendees of events here. My research assistant Analicia conducted interviews with twelve heterosexual Cornyation fans who have attended the show for decades, and I conducted dozens of informal interviews in Mobile and Baton Rouge with Carnival ball attendees. I conducted these informal interviews about individuals' experiences at events at the event itself but also while attending other Carnival events, including public parades. I also asked people about their Carnival event experiences while checking out my rental car, getting fitted for my tuxedo, ordering dinner, touring museums, and checking in with my hotel concierge.

Inclusive Collective Partying and the Spectacle

A lot of heterosexual people attend LGBTQ festival events. It would be easy to dismiss some of these events as mere spectacle, as heterosexual people viewing LGBTQ performers only as entertainment and nothing more. Certainly, in the previous chapter I have demonstrated how many LGBTQ-run festival events are the "hottest ticket in town," coveted for their flamboyant gay culture. A quick read could suggest they are merely a spectacle, a dramatic visual display that may be an object of curiosity or thinly veiled contempt.

I have several reservations about those who are dismissive, believing that these spectacles—and they *are* spectacles—are, for heterosexuals, nothing more than an object of curiosity or contempt. Most theories about spectacle focus on consumption and objectification, and many scholars argue that the spectacle is a commodification of marginalized groups' culture by and for majority groups.[3] For instance, in his book, *Gay New York*, historian George Chauncey describes the way the city's neighborhoods like Harlem could be used as a spectacle for white, middle-class observers who derived pleasure from visiting.[4] In his work, *Boystown*, Jason Orne gives another example, in which straight women's participation in gay spaces is resented as disrupting the sexual energy and culture.[5] In these ways, visitors can engage in "slumming it" or being "tourists" at "gay Disneyland," an act of voyeurism that allows people to enjoy a culture that is not their own while letting their ideas about that culture remain unchanged and by not examining the ways their presence changes the experience.

The tension I observed in three of the cities about the downsides of heterosexual involvement in LGBTQ cultural events—mostly concern that heterosexuals were taking over events—fit well with this idea of spectacle. Yet one of the few sociologists who studies urban festivals, Kevin Gotham, argues that spectacles are multidimensional, complex, and include contested and contradictory meanings.[6] These urban spectacles, Gotham writes, "have a Janus-faced quality. They have the potential for creative encounters and enabling social practices. They can also produce a host of unforeseen and irrational consequences, including period manifestations of social revolt."[7] Even philosopher Guy DeBord, known for developing theories about the spectacle, clarifies, "the spectacle is not a collection of images; it is a social relation between people that is mediated by images."[8] Spectacles should not be dismissed as some form of enacting "false consciousness," researchers in this vein argue, but important creations connected to processes of identity formation and collective consciousness.[9] Sociologist Mary Bernstein argues that groups deploy identity for complex means, sometimes as an "identity for education" to educate others and gain legitimacy and sometimes as an "identity for critique" to confront dominant cultural values.[10] In Baton Rouge, where there was more spectacle around LGBTQ festival events, LGBTQ participants often deployed an identity for education, whereas in cities like Mobile and San Antonio, LGBTQ festival participants were more likely to use their position to critique the status quo.

Attendees to all the LGBTQ festival events are enthusiastic about how much fun they are—and how that fun enhances their appreciation for and knowledge about the LGBTQ community, creating a sense of togetherness across differences. I argue that even if a diverse group of individuals gathers to engage in viewing a spectacle, the experience of celebrating in a diverse collective may be unifying in unexpected ways. Sociologists Josh Gamson, Verta Tayor, and Lila Rupp have found that heterosexual attendees to events like drag shows, or avid watchers of trashy talk shows, actually do learn from watching and come to challenge their preconceived notions.[11] Drag shows, for example, fit into broader LGBTQ social movement goals; through entertainment, they "illuminate gay life for mainstream audiences and provide a space for the construction of collective identities that confront and rework gender and sexual boundaries."[12] These spaces allow heterosexuals some latitude for exploration, particularly cross-dressing for women, though most attendees simply stress the feeling of community and togetherness, especially the fostering of new social connections during festival time. Because the social relations of Mardi Gras are dense, it can be hard to get a ticket to a krewe ball without knowing a krewe member who will host you at their table; with the inclusive collective partying of the LGBTQ groups, diverse groups can have fun creating new connections and a wider sense of community.

Sociologists have long observed that when people come together to enjoy something—whether that be a religious ritual, holiday, or festival—it creates this sense of community.[13] Pleasure and its politics can be trivialized in sociological research,[14] but in her study of Pride parades, Katherine Bruce argues that scholars need to "take fun seriously," especially when this fun induces social change.[15] In their book, *Fabulous*, Madison Moore explains that "the pursuit of fun and pleasure are political gestures too."[16] This fun and pleasure is not just an individual experience but rather a group endeavor. In the words of geographer Kath Browne, "where celebration moves to imagined connections between individuals, there is a sense of collective partying."[17] A "cultural bridging practice" that momentarily brings people together despite their differences,[18] I saw how "collective partying" was integral to attendees' experiences in all four cities.

LGBTQ participants often described their events as the largest inclusive parties during their annual festival. Diversity is an abstract, distinctly American ideal that often signals racial heterogeneity, or, more exclusively, the presence of African Americans.[19] In *Black in Place*, Brandi Thompson Summers argues that Blackness becomes an indicator of diversity and is marketed as a progressive way of being in the city.[20] LGBTQ festival participants rarely described their events as diverse; instead, they stressed their appreciation of how *inclusive* events were, that there were no policies or barriers to participation and the events were open to everyone who wanted to attend (and could snap up one of the hot tickets). Of course, similar to diversity, inclusion is a concept that may hide inequalities within organizations. This kind of inclusivity uses a color-blind logic in which, if everyone is *permitted* at an event, it can be rebranded as inclusive, regardless of actual diversity in turnout.[21] Sociologist Eduardo Bonilla-Silva's theory of color-blind racism includes the use of abstract liberalism frames like "equal opportunity" to explain racial inequalities.[22] That way, the event need not be intentionally modified to be more accessible or interesting to absent participants.

Discussions of diversity (and presumably inclusivity) are also marked by the absence of real inquiries about social inequalities.[23] In festival events, I saw, for instance, social class creating obvious exclusions: Attendees need to be able to buy tickets and, in the case of Carnival balls, rent, borrow, or buy the requisite formal wear. But there are subtler exclusions about what kind of culture is represented at the event, who feels comfortable being a member, and how accessible the event really is. In the city of Mobile, the inclusivity of LGBTQ festival events was an important identity for critique in opposition to the typically racially segregated Mobile Mardi Gras.

Baton Rouge Mardi Gras

Baton Rouge Mardi Gras had a lot of inclusive collective partying, but these events often included more use of gay culture as spectacle. The largest events of Baton Rouge Mardi Gras—the Spanish Town Parade and Ball and the Krewe of Apollo Ball—were described by interviewees in terms that match with inclusive collective partying. These events could be huge and included many heterosexual guests. Some felt they symbolized the apex of diversity and ability of everyone to get along. Compared to other festival events in Baton Rouge and elsewhere, heterosexual attendees at Spanish Town and the Krewe of Apollo Ball seemed to be engaged in more consumption of LGBTQ people as a spectacle and were subject to LGBTQ participants' deployment of identity for education. There was also contention over the Spanish Town Parade, perceived by many gay men as disconnected from its queer origins. In Baton Rouge, events that attracted mostly a LGBTQ audience—Krewe of Divas Ball, and the LBQ women's Spanish Town after-party at a local bar—were small, relatively marginalized, and overwhelmingly without heterosexual attendees.

Something that Brings the City Together

The Krewe of Apollo Ball was initially a near-exclusive LGBTQ event with predominately gay male attendees. Some members did invite parents, co-workers, or neighbors, but for the most part these events were LGBTQ events. Larry, one of Apollo's founding members, remembered running into members of "straight krewes" who wanted to know, "How can I ever get to see an Apollo Ball? I heard about y'all's productions and your costumes." He told me, "We gradually invited those people along, and they were just overtaken. So that's what's opened all the doors up so much for so many people who want to be a part of it, you know?"

Many krewe members understood hetero attendance as a sign of support and community acceptance and felt proud they were part of an inclusive party. When Josh, a twentysomething gay bartender, attended his first Krewe of Apollo Ball, he noticed all the heterosexual attendees of the event: "like, I didn't know there was this much support out there for us, and it's great. Because we're a Southern state, and sometimes people are just not very open and accepting . . . so to go there and see people pay a hundred dollars to hang out with a bunch of gay guys is just *insane* to me." Terrill, a white gay man who had been a member of Apollo for several decades, similarly described the influx of heterosexual attendees as a "symbol of acceptance" for both the krewe and the broader gay community. During our interview outside a coffee shop in Baton Rouge, a young Black member of Apollo marveled, "it's weird, it's crazy, it's the social event of the season. Apollo is the big event that everyone wants to go to. . . . I think it's something that brings together not only the gay community but the city as a whole."

Krewe members were full of stories about heterosexual Baton Rouge residents who learned about gay life by partying with this diverse and inclusive group. Carl, a white gay man in his forties, hosted our interview in his home with his partner, also a krewe member. As my research assistant Elizabeth and I try on his partner's queen outfit from the year before, Carl told us about his co-worker, Sandy, who brought her fiancé to Apollo's announcement party and ball. Sandy's fiancé had "never been around gay people," said Carl, "and I can tell you what made a lasting impression on them . . . when they walked in, the krewe knew who they were. People there remembered their names and greeted them. They were blown away, and it was her fiancé's first time around gay people and people in drag." The krewe "went the extra mile to make them feel welcome . . . but that's what the krewe does, little things to make people feel welcome." Carl proudly framed this hospitality as part of what made the krewe a "very integral part of the city" and noted, "as people open up to more diversity here, then the krewe is still going to lead even more. I believe that, I really do."

Carl's description suggested that it was a combination of hospitality and the krewe's deployment of identity for education that crafted community at the Apollo Ball.[24] This identity for education, Bernstein writes, "challenges the dominant culture's perception of the minority or is used strategically to gain legitimacy by playing on uncontroversial themes."[25] Watching the Krewe of Apollo discuss how it was presenting itself to the public, including discussions of standards of performance and whether there was too much or not enough drag, showed their investment in such education.

Social and romantic relationships between krewe members are visible in Apollo's annual show, both in subtle and obvious ways. Men hold hands, dance sexy, and flirt on stage. During "callouts," when the royalty's family and friends come visit them on stage, partners are described in loving terms ("my best friend and partner"). A Black krewe member noted that the ball helps heterosexual attendees "understand the gay culture a little bit more . . . I liked that at a past ball, everyone did a video that gave you a backstory to each costuming member. It gave the audience the backstory to everything." That year, I had noticed how the videos stressed the connections between men at the ball, whether romantic relationships or friendships. One krewe member costumed with his sister, another described how important his roommate was in his life. Two krewe members who costumed together talked candidly about their twenty-year love story. The ball captain's introduction video was him in a hot tub with another krewe member, alluding cheekily that one was, at the start of the segment, giving the other a blow job underwater. That year's ball theme was "Forever Young," and so each video included a childhood photo. All this had shown gay life as normal, relatable, not-so-different in ways that allowed all attendees to see more similarity than difference across the crowd.

As I kept writing in my fieldnotes, the social relations of Mardi Gras are *rich*. Almost all the tables are assigned to a krewe member, who sells or gives the tickets to family, friends, and acquaintances. The krewe member decorates the tables for their guests according to the theme of the ball and their costume (if they are costuming). As the krewe member parades through the ball, they pause at their tables for a toast with their guests, who sometimes pop confetti "crackers" or wave objects like light-up foam tubes. Throughout the event, it is clear who is connected to who; table mates might not have been acquainted with each other, but they were joined by their relationships to the krewe member. One year, I met my host krewe member's childhood friends, co-workers, and siblings, all seated alongside me.

These social relations shaped the actual diversity of the ball itself. The Krewe of Apollo Ball was one of the less racially diverse LGBTQ balls I attended, with maybe 10–15 percent of the guests Black-passing (varying by year). Tables hosted by Black gay men who were in the krewe and those hosted by white gay men involved in the drag community were typically the most racially diverse. The year their sister krewe, Krewe of Apollo Lafayette, had a Black man as queen, the table of visitors from that Lafayette krewe included mostly young Black men who came with the queen. There were also significantly fewer women in tuxedos at the Apollo ball compared to other LGBTQ Carnival balls. In addition, there was a contingent of white LBQ women who took over a table at every Krewe of Apollo ball. When I interviewed white lesbians and trans men in Baton Rouge, a few were dismissive, calling the Apollo Ball something for "gays and straight people." And, as mentioned previously, the expense of joining the krewe or attending the ball, with its ticket prices and requirement for formal dress wear, may be out of reach for many Black residents of Baton Rouge, who earn significantly less income than white residents.[26]

Apollo's sorting by tables and the lack of mingling between them made it tough for this researcher to meet people beyond my own table. Thus, I made sure that I was extremely chatty (perhaps annoying, in that ethnographer way) in the bathroom and while waiting in line to buy refreshments. Many guest members crowd the edge of the runway, so I sidled up to chat with them about my book and their experience at the ball. Guests expressed excitement and awe over the costumes and gushed that *this* ball was the highlight of the Carnival season. At times, the crowd acted collectively and felt like a vibrant community experiencing something together—this was most tangible in the crowd's emotional reactions to the videos of krewe members and its cheers when krewe members mentioned parents attending for the first time. As the grand finale approached, there was a palpable wave of anticipation. Soon, the new royalty would be crowned. The formality and cohesiveness of this event was a stark contrast to the other major parties of the Baton Rouge Carnival season, the Spanish Town Ball and Parade.

Everybody Having Their Own Party Next to Each Other

Walking through the Spanish Town Ball in 2015, in a convention center packed with hundreds of pink-clad krewe members dancing to live music, drinking, and enjoying the outrageous table decorations (huge light-up penises were an obvious standout), my friend Jason and I both feel oddly . . . uncomfortable. I had been to the Spanish Town Parade before, yet one of my white gay Baton Rouge interviewees had warned me that the Ball was mainly attended by what he called "cool straights" (adding that, of course, "many gays" came to the event). I can't put my finger on this discomfort. Maybe it was the way the décor evoked heterosexual bachelor and bachelorette parties? So many penises, so many people excited to drink body shots off the navels of hot young women and revved up about the party's reputation for being wild and uncontrollable. There are assigned tables, but most are just drop-off points—places where you drop off your own cooler of liquor so that you can dance, unencumbered, to the pulsating live music.

I recognized one of my connections from the Krewe of Apollo, a tall white gay man named Chris, and made my way over. Chris throws shade at my clothing selection—a sports coat with pink stripes and neon green pants he sees as too formal—gesturing to his own pink tutu as more appropriate. "This is like a block party, but inside and for *everyone*," he says, adding that his aunt and several cousins who ride on parade floats are in attendance. When I briefly grouse that this ball feels so much *straighter* than the Krewe of Apollo Ball, Chris nods and pulls me closer in a moment of queer solidary. "*We started all of this*," he says into my ear, sweeping his hand to draw my eyes around the room. Yes, the Spanish Town

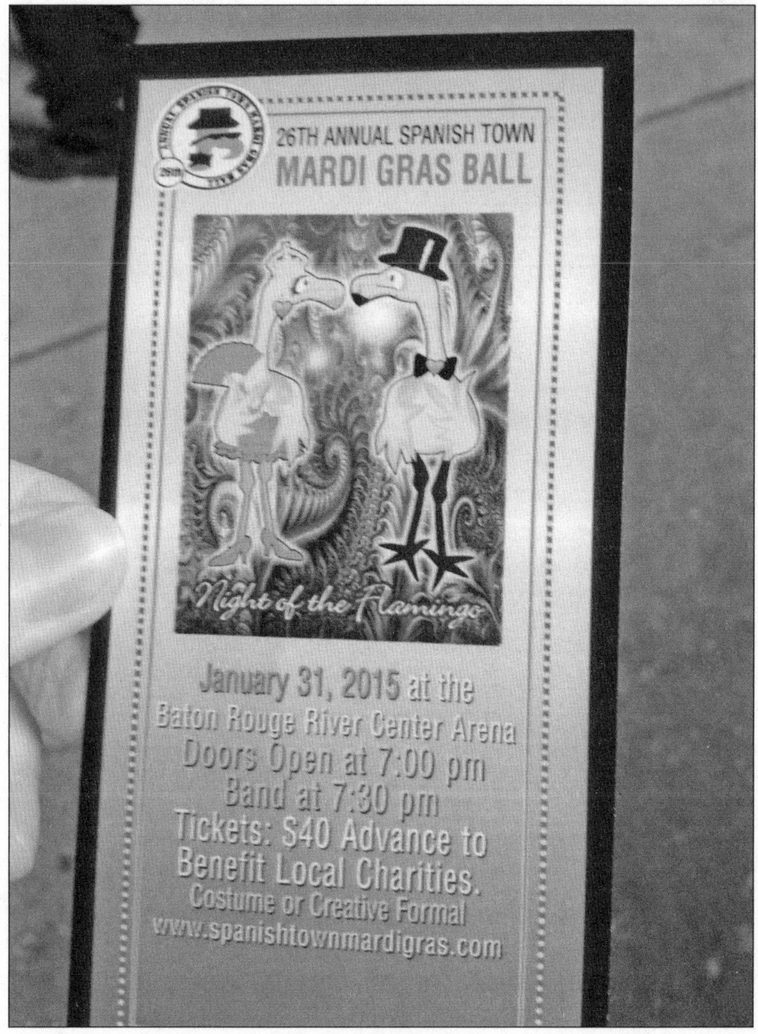

Figure 4.1. Invitation for the Spanish Town Ball

Ball and Parade were now heavily influenced by heterosexual participants and culture, but both had been started by members of the LGBTQ community. By bringing me into his declarative "we," Chris argued that not only gay men but also people like myself—someone he understood to be a lesbian or queer woman—were involved in creating these events, making them hot tickets, and retaining pride in their original ownership.

Chris had never lived in the Spanish Town neighborhood and was a child when the Spanish Town Parade started; still he asserted vicarious citizenship over the neighborhood and parade. Theo Greene has defined vicarious citizenship as "the exercise of rights and entitlements to community participation emanating from extra-neighborhood, symbolic ties to a neighborhood or locality."[27] Chris's symbolic ties via gay identity contributed to his sense that he, too, was an important part of this major Mardi Gras event.

Throughout my interviews and fieldnotes, I often heard LGBTQ people in Baton Rouge describe the Spanish Town Parade as an event with queer origins that came out of an established gayborhood. One of the oldest in the city, Spanish Town was established in 1805 by Canary Islanders coming from Spanish-ruled Galvez Town.[28] It has not, however, ever been an ethnic urban enclave but has a complex history of racial segregation and integration. During the 1980s, as it developed a reputation as a racially integrated bohemian gayborhood, Spanish Town residents staged their own Mardi Gras parade.[29] LGBTQ people—most obviously, white gay men—were visible in both the neighborhood and its parade during this time.

I heard about the Spanish Town Parade during the local Pride festival, on the second day of my research in Baton Rouge. I walked among the tables of organizations, chatting with people about the Baton Rouge LGBTQ community and Mardi Gras. One young Black lesbian community organizer mentioned that, during Mardi Gras, she tended to go to the Spanish Town Parade or the "pink flamingo parade," describing it as "our parade." Similarly, in a phone interview with an older, white lesbian who lived in Spanish Town and who I spotted at almost every Baton Rouge Mardi Gras event I attended, she exclaimed that "make no mistake, that parade was started by drag queens in a pickup truck." Many other interviewees and informants mentioned the presence of drag and drag queens in the parade as an important part of the event's gay cultural history. This claims-making, marking LGBTQ community members as the originators of the parade, allowed informants to emphasize the cultural and social contributions of the LGBTQ community to Baton Rouge history.

Nonetheless, there are multiple competing narratives about the origins of the first Spanish Town Parade, none of which are validated by the local media. Two of these narratives position the origins of the parade within a history of racial integration and contestation within the neighborhood. One white heterosexual male interviewee and Spanish Town resident has loudly claimed that he and a friend started the parade in the early 1980s by paying a few young Black teenage boys to parade around the neighborhood and pound on cardboard boxes the two years before the official start of the Spanish Town parade. When the boys did not reappear after the second year, he got his flatbed trailer and towed it around the neighborhood instead. Other interviewees described that the parade was planned by two "very creative" white men in the neighborhood, one of whom was an anthropologist. Second line parades are walking parades (e.g., without floats) that are part of the Black Carnival tradition. These two men purportedly watched videos of second line parades in New Orleans to get inspiration for the Spanish Town parade. One male interviewee stressed with a positive and respectful tone how "very creative" these men were in a manner that may have been signaling their sexual orientation. These two narratives—that the parade was started by two white men paying Black boys or by two white men culturally appropriating Black Carnival traditions—position white men in the neighborhood as starting the parade by using Black artistry, labor, and culture.

Most LGBTQ people I spoke to emphasized the role of drag queens in the start of the parade. In a journal article about the parade, a Spanish Town resident recalled the 1981 parade, "I looked out my apartment window because I heard some music. A couple of drag queens and maybe two vehicles went by. I remember thinking, 'what the hell was that?'"[30] Many interviewees and informants confirmed that the parades of the '80s prominently featured drag, including the walking krewe "The Sluts of '84." In a magazine interview, a longtime Spanish Town resident waxed nostalgic about it:

> Then there were the drag queens; they would show up in, like, black leather and spiked heels, full beards. And we thought they were great, but they dropped out around '86 or something. *The Advocate* [the Los Angeles-based gay magazine, not the Baton Rouge newspaper] felt that the parade was getting way too heterosexual for them.[31]

Some informants specified that these drag queens had not been residents of the neighborhood—rather they lived "who knows where" and headed over to Spanish Town to join in the parade every year. The description of these queens—with black leather, spiked heels, and full beards—captures an erotic, amateur, gender-fuck style of drag, not the polished, professional, TV-ready drag many mainstream people today may find familiar.

That is, in the 1980s, drag queens were still fairly underground and subversive; they were not familiar sights in the way movies and TV shows like *RuPaul's Drag Race* would make them for heterosexual audiences in subsequent decades. You'd likely have to frequent gay bars or live in a very big city to be acquainted with drag. The visibility of drag queens in this Baton Rouge Mardi Gras parade paralleled other groundbreaking Carnival efforts in New Orleans and Rio de Janeiro. In both cities, throughout the 1970s and '80s, gay men asserted their right to cross-dress and perform drag during Carnival events, often in defiance of municipal or statewide laws against cross-dressing.[32] Drag, in its unmistakable, ostentatious queerness, played a symbolic role in the fight for public space and uncontested existence in and beyond such cities' gay communities. That meant that, as drag performance became a beacon of gay visibility in urban festivals, it didn't much matter whether the queens actually lived in the neighborhood. Like Chris from the Krewe of Apollo, these drag queens from outside the neighborhood could proudly be welcomed into a vicarious citizenship in Baton Rouge's single visible gayborhood just by showing up and showing out each year.

Another reason the "we started this" narratives were emphasized by LGBTQ informants is likely that the queer origins of the Spanish Town parade are not as obvious anymore. In the magazine interview above, the Spanish Town resident decried the end of drag queen participation and said the parade was getting "way too heterosexual." The LGBTQ Baton Rouge residents who attended the Spanish Town parade seemed eager to claim their own vicarious citizenship regarding the origins of the parade and were quick to describe the parade as run by heterosexual, non-resident men and point to moments when the parade had been homophobic and/or transphobic.

In 2014, the first year I went to the Spanish Town Parade, the theme was "Flamingo Dynasty" (a play on the then-popular *Duck Dynasty* reality show set in Northern Louisiana, featuring a camo-clad patriarch with distinctly homophobic views). A few weeks before the parade, I met the organizing committee members as I helped paint large wooden cutouts of flamingos for the annual "flocking," wherein the cutouts would be posted in a Baton Rouge lake. Carnival tradition dictated that people would swim out to steal the cutouts from the posts in the lake and display the flamingos in their houses or yards. I was immediately struck by the homogeneity of the Spanish Town organizers present that day: most were white, straight-presenting men. They answered my questions about the parade as a fundraiser and how to best conduct my research at the event. Chuck, the sixty-something fundraising manager, flirted with me carelessly, slipping me—a genderqueer person here to study LGBTQ involvement in the parade—last year's parade t-shirt as he remarked with a wink that normally he made girls show their boobs to get one, but this time he'd let it slide. According to him, the spirit and intention of the parade were to raise money for charity, have a good time, and enjoy some adult-oriented fun. "Children already have Disneyland," he remarked. "Not everything has to be for children." Indeed, while children do attend the parade, the adult-oriented ethos of the event evoked queer political resistance to heterosexual norms around children, family, and respectability.[33] Thus Chuck confided that one section of the parade route was alcohol-free, while another, in the heart of Spanish Town, permitted the "boobs for beads" ritual disrobement. The Spanish Town Parade is diverse, politically and sexually; there's a little bit of something for everyone—and something to offend everyone, too.

My interactions with the Spanish Town Parade's heterosexual organizers reflected *both* a combination of heteronormativity *and* participation in queer culture. Jones, a white man in his forties with a bushy beard, regaled me with stories about his costuming and cross-dressing for the event. Typically, attendees and parading krewes wear hot pink and flamingo-related accessories and clothing, and so Jones commented that when he laid out all his parade gear, he realized he had more pink clothes than "a ten-year-old girl." He laughed over "bad cross-dressing by straight men" at the parade and ball, using descriptors that reminded me of the kind of cross-dressing used in fraternity hazing rituals and fundraisers. My notes on the aesthetic of parade-goers contained several repetitive descriptions: "white middle-aged women in ponytails with pink tutus," "bad white frat-boy drag," and "white older man in pink shirt that said, 'This is Your Girlfriend's Shirt.'" In her work on Pride parades, Katherine Bruce writes about how these events allow even heterosexual attendees an opportunity to challenge heteronormativity "while at the same time enjoying a rare break from its restrictions."[34] My first and enduring impression was that the Spanish Town Parade today embraces its bohemian roots but is also just an opportunity for everyone to wear pink and be a little wild in public.

Back to that part of the ethos that dictates the parade have something for everyone, including something to offend everyone. Touring the floats before the parade, I noticed prominent political and social commentary. Scathing satire on the year's theme was both supportive and critical of *Duck Dynasty*. There was just as much homophobic commentary as there was LGBTQ-supportive commentary. Among the former, I spotted floats decorated for duck hunting, covered in camouflage, netting, and palm fronds, and carrying slogans like "It's just my opinion!" They clearly supported *Duck Dynasty* patriarch Phil Robertson's anti-gay sentiments, which led to the discontinuation of the show, or at least his right to spout anti-gay messages. Other floats were more blatantly homophobic, with one bearing a photo of Robertson with one of his company's duck calls in his mouth and the slogan "The Only Thing a Man Should Blow Is a Duck Call." Many more floats—more than a dozen of them—mocked Robertson's homophobia. These positioned Robertson as a gay man, a drag queen, or having sex with a male flamingo. One float titled itself Flamingo(phobic) Dynasty and satirized well-known homophobic politicians' statements by twisting their references to gay men to be about flamingos. I remember interviewing two LGBTQ members of the Baton Rouge community—an older white lesbian and a young white transgender man—who abhorred the parade, suggesting it allowed straight people to consume gay culture, offering it up as an object of mockery.

The queer politics of the parade are paradoxical like that. At times, it seems LGBTQ-celebratory. At others, it seems a project consumed by heterosexual participants. Elements of its queer origins are evident, particularly in the parade's anti-family sentiment, cross-dressing, flexibility, diversity, and the continuing ethos of "bad taste." Other scholars have suggested that longtime parade organizers and participants "argue that the high exposure [of the parade] has sapped the parade of its queer

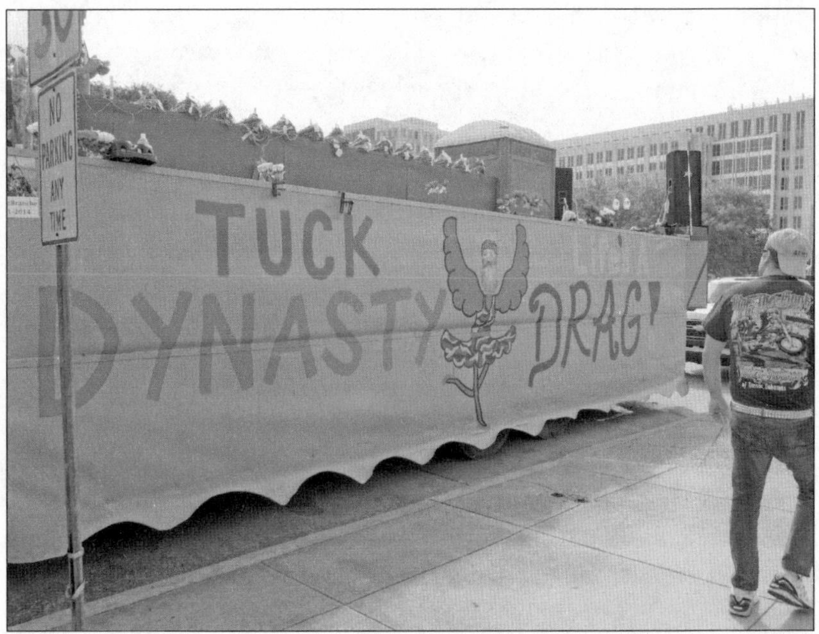

Figure 4.2. Spanish Town float mocking *Duck Dynasty*

politics."[35] Throughout my fieldnotes I did note the consumption of queer culture and fashion by parade attendees, particularly the attention given to white gay men dressed in drag or outrageous costumes. Drag queens I interviewed remarked that they often got frustrated by being constantly stopped by presumed straight attendees to take group pictures with them.

Walking among the parade floats, I was keenly aware of the limitations of inclusivity in Spanish Town. Almost all the floats were occupied by all-white krewes, though I counted about five with Black participants on their floats (these floats were exclusively peopled by Black participants). Racial segregation is startlingly common in Carnival krewes at both my study sites, but I was surprised to see how dramatic the krewe segregation was at an event so frequently described as "bohemian" and "diverse." Indeed, I found that many "people's parades" like Mobile's Joe Cain Day parade and the Spanish Town Parade did not challenge the Carnival norms of racially segregated parades and floats.

Several informants described both the parade and the Spanish Town Ball to me as "everyone having their own party next to each other." The Spanish Town Parade has grown and changed since its start; today it is a large community event rather than the small, alternative celebration of a gayborhood. One year, from my lofty vantage point on the judges' platform, I took a picture of the parade crowd, a sea of tens of thousands of pink outfits crammed into Spanish Town's narrow streets. Coming down to ground level, I wandered through blocks of families barbecuing on the streets with their kids, corners of mostly Black parents with young children, a block of mostly white teenagers making out, and a quiet block that included a large group of white queer senior women. One area in the heart of Spanish Town was blatantly queer, with drag queens, butch lesbians, and other queer partiers celebrating together. I wandered in and out of house parties, unsure whether this collective partying furthered or lessened queer visibility.

It was evident that inclusive collective partying was happening, and that heterosexual participants were learning something about LGBTQ life. But at Spanish Town there were also ways that this LGBTQ cultural visibility was used as more of a spectacle than an educational opportunity. At the Krewe of Apollo, LGBTQ participants had more control over the event and were able to deploy an identity for education during their inclusive collective party.

Mobile Mardi Gras

Mobile Mardi Gras has dramatic racial segregation, and LGBTQ events push back with all-inclusive organizations and events. These events mobilize an identity of critique against local Carnival traditions. In Mobile, three out of the four LGBTQ Carnival krewes defined themselves as all-inclusive, as a resistance to Carnival traditions of racial segregation. The fourth—the Mystic Womyn of Color—used their ball to build Black lesbian community. In an overview article in the local newspaper on the other three—the Order of Osiris, Krewe of Phoenix, and Order of Pan—a trio of traits are listed as differentiators between the LGBTQ-focused krewes and others in town: their "all-inclusive" nature, their "unique tableaus," and "their own twist on the expected dress code."[36]

In other accounts, the *Observer* notes that "based on unscientific but thorough sampling, that Osiris is the most successfully integrated Mardi Gras group in Mobile."[37] In Mobile, being all-inclusive became a queer Carnival tradition; other groups in the city selectively adopted the policy as an act of resistance to Mobile Carnival cultural traditions.

The All-Inclusive Gay Ball

I'm completely overdressed for this pool party; having forgotten to pack my swimsuit, I try to look casual in jeans without betraying the fact that I'm melting in the June heat of Alabama. I am hanging out with the Krewe of Apollo, which splintered off from Osiris in prior years. In between drinking games, playing corn hole, doing the cupid shuffle, swimming, and eating crawfish, I chat with krewe members about their group's history. Rob, a tall, gray-haired gay man who wears a campy pairing of bathing suit and Carnival royalty crown, casually smoked a cigarette while we talked. "It just got too big," he said of Osiris. "We like to keep our ball smaller. When it gets big like that, you lose control over it." The white butch next to him in a tank top and swimming shorts nods enthusiastically. "Last time I went to Osiris there were about 2,000 people there. The line for the ladies' room was almost 30 minutes long." This group's ball, along with Pan, and the Mystic Womyn's, topped out at five hundred guests.

The Order of Osiris, established in the 1980s, was the first all-inclusive krewe in Mobile.[38] Its only membership stipulation is age-related (must be 21 or older), and krewe members told me they had always put inclusivity first. It was a response to their own exclusion from high-status Mobile krewes—and other parts of Mobile society. Typically, the logic was some variation of "We've been excluded, so why would we exclude someone else?" The all-inclusive krewes had a few straight members, often individuals supportive of the LGBTQ community or people recruited for their artistry (especially if the art was queer). One interviewee described some straight members as "six-pack gays"—one six-pack of beer away from being queer—a phrase that reminded me of the term "barsexual," which refers to some cisgender women's proclivity for making out with other women while drunk.

My fieldnotes are full of examples of how inclusive the guests at the ball are and how popular the event is among heterosexuals. "Straight folks love to come to our balls," Louise, a middle-aged white lesbian member of Osiris noted over drinks.

> I would say out of the 2,000 people we had there, 1,100 of them are straight. and because of that, when they see us out in the city, they are like "hey I was at your ball!" instead of "oh my god there's the gay people." It is really, helped the barriers [between gays and straights] go down, and they have a lot of respect for what we do.

Another white lesbian krewe member tells me that friends from her private Catholic high school often arrange their Carnival schedule around the Osiris ball, texting eagerly to try to learn the event's date as soon as possible. It seems that most heterosexual attendees are enthusiastic about the ball, and, as Louise noted, there's a shared belief that the inclusivity breaks down the barriers between heterosexual and LGBTQ people.

Osiris krewe members stressed that the event was still a "gay ball" that heterosexual guests were permitted to attend. A few described tensions about having "so many straight people there because this is supposed to be the gay ball," but that "other people say well, it is a gay ball, not even all our members are gay, but that's who we're putting it on for. If other people want to come and see it, there's no reason not to." And indeed no one in the krewe reported pressure to clean up their acts or perform in a particular way to appease a heterosexual audience. Mostly, krewe members described the thrill of costuming and performing outrageous personae in front of the huge crowd. Jay, a young white gay man in Osiris, was adamant that heterosexual guests attended but did not shape the content of the event.

> I was awed and amazed by the decadence and just the outright ease of *being you* with no judgment, no whatever. Actual heterosexual people of our community and important political people are there and they're not judging. You know what I mean. And now to see they fight for our tickets. And then so if you don't have a positive look at that you could look at it

> in a negative form as well, that we look like monkeys in a cage dancing for them and they just use us for their entertainment. And I've seen it. I've seen their faces sometimes, because sometimes they don't approve of everything that we do. And even I don't approve of everything that we do. Like our 30th anniversary ball was when [two members] did [a performance about] Dirty Catholics. And I'm like, "That's a little bad, you don't need to do that." But do y'all know how many letters we got from the archdiocese? It was bad. Oh, yeah. [The Catholics] rebelled. They were not happy with us. But in that, a positive thing that you find is you find how large your voice is when you get such a negative response, because you've impacted so many people.

Notice the tensions in his comments. Jay was the only Osiris krewe member to suggest their event might be used as a spectacle by at least some heterosexuals, some of the time (that the krewe might be "monkeys in a cage dancing for them"). He also mentions how more controversial pieces, including a sacrilegious mockery of the Catholic Church that was featured by the Mobile newspapers, were met with some opposition from the broader community. But Jay also describes an ease with being himself, unconcerned about scrutiny and sure that even the negative responses to the Dirty Catholics could be framed as Osiris having an impact on the community.

At their essence, Carnival balls are parties. There's alcohol, food, entertainment, and good company. Across Mobile's three all-inclusive LGBTQ-sponsored festival events, there are delighted heterosexual guests, stoked to score tickets, see their first ball, and join in on the fun. Docents at Mobile's Carnival Museum, older middle- or upper-class white women and men who attended Carnival balls, commented to me about Osiris's elaborate and entertaining costuming, high-quality liquor, and excellent dance party. At one Osiris ball, I sat next to two white heterosexual men whose lesbian childhood friend invited them. They were wide-eyed all evening, telling me it was the most fun they'd had that Carnival season and that it bested several other balls. One pointed out that, at other balls, guests are not allowed to eat or drink anything until after hours of krewe member "call-outs." Not here: The booze flows from the first guest's arrival (if not before).

These events also open up the social worlds of attendees, especially those who are relatively unfamiliar with LGBTQ culture. They can explore gender non-conformity in a safe environment. A heterosexual white man seated next to me at the Osiris Ball mentions it was his first LGBTQ event, and when the post-tableau dance party started, he was astonished at the sea of tuxedo-wearing women dancing with each other. Excitedly, he said he had no idea there were these many lesbians in Mobile, Alabama. For their part, heterosexual women report enjoying the freedom to wear a tuxedo to the ball, a pleasant break from most Carnival balls' gendered dress-code requirements (for women, floor-length ball gowns). But at Mobile's LGBTQ-krewe events, there are even heterosexual couples in which each partner striding hand-in-hand wears a tux. A lesbian in attendance described her joy at renting a tuxedo for her mother, a regular Carnival ball attendee who pragmatically enjoys the freedom of warm clothing during the winter ball. Even better, there was no need to pick out accessories—she just put on whatever was in the rental bag and headed to the ball. At Carnival balls, participants let parents and co-workers mingle with their childhood friends and nieces—and everyone *else's* extended networks, forging a sense that the community of LGBTQ supporters can and does expand each year.

Inclusive collective partying creates a sense of community or coming together—a pleasure that can get lost when we do not consider its politics. Members of all three all-inclusive krewes indirectly positioned their event in opposition to racially segregated Carnival events. They stressed the inclusivity, such as an elite white man who was effusive about the Osiris ball, because "everybody comes out of the woodwork . . . it's the only time you see everybody all together . . . it's festive . . . *It is Mardi Gras*." Max, a white straight member of Osiris, regularly sells two tables of Osiris tickets to the men in his other, high-status white men's krewe in Mobile. He told me that one guy, attending for the first time, was profusely thankful for the tickets and told Max, "This is the way Mardi Gras should have been, because it is just so much fun. There's no stress, no problems and everybody, no matter who you are, has fun." This inclusive collective partying is beneficial for some LGBTQ attendees, as well; participants in all three events told me stories about closeted LGBTQ friends cautiously attending, afraid of being outed, and instead running into supportive co-workers, friends, and neighbors at the events. For attendees like these, the ball could offer assurance that, should they decide to come out, they will not be shunned.

Limits to Inclusivity

This approach to being all-inclusive was not necessarily a commitment to racial justice but to lack of restrictions to accessing the event, particularly lack of racial segregation. Several people pulled me aside to confide that, although it was not official policy, Black guests who attempted to attend Carnival balls put on by white krewes were turned away at the doors. Indeed, I attended a Carnival ball in Mobile put on by a white women's krewe, and among the thousands of participants, the only visibly Black attendees were hired bartenders and waiters. By outright stating that they would not turn others away at the door, LGBTQ krewe members practiced what Mary Bernstein refers to as an "identity for critique" of the status quo and insisted they represented the "true nature" of Carnival.[39] Members of Osiris, the oldest of these groups, described how their ball has often been a refuge for interracial couples, even heterosexual ones, as Black-white couples cannot attend many of the other balls in Mobile. Here, at the Osiris Ball, I see interracial couples dancing together late into the night.

While inclusivity was a central part of how krewe members talked about their events, I should stress that the three all-inclusive krewes in Mobile were predominately white organizations. The Order of Pan was the only krewe with more than one or two Black members. Black members described themselves to me as having had experience navigating predominately white organizations and aware that all-inclusive krewes in Mobile had problems retaining Black members. Across krewes, only senior members of the krewe become royalty, making this retention problem visible: At the time of this research, a Black person had never been crowned royalty by any of Mobile's all-inclusive krewes (since that time, in 2016, two Black people have held royalty positions in two different krewes). In the 2000s, a Black drag queen, Miss Venus, was crowned Queen of the now-defunct People's Ball, an open Carnival event that raised money for the Mobile Pride Center during its existence. Miss

Venus commented to me, "I'm the very first one. And it makes me happy. It really never dawns on me until I say it, and then, first of all, I mean being Black. There are no Black kings. There are no Black queens. And I am the first Black transgender male or female—however you—half-and-half, whatever, that has ever made it that far." Remarkably, Miss Venus was voted into the position by a citywide vote and was crowned again two years later.

Because Carnival ball attendees are invited through the social networks of krewe members, the racial composition reflects those individuals' ties; some ball tables are racially homogenous, others are racially diverse. Despite being racially integrated, the music and aesthetics are seen, by Black participants, as boring white culture. A prominent member of the Mystic Womyn once brought a dozen Black lesbian friends to the Osiris ball, where they were unmoved by the program's use of Broadway tunes, disco hits, and references to white culture like *Star Wars*, *Pee Wee's Playhouse*, *Xanadu*, *Alice in Wonderland*, and *The Rocky Horror Picture Show*.

Blackness and Black culture are more prominent at the Order of Pan's New Year's Eve Carnival Ball. A krewe of predominately gay men (with the occasional straight woman), Pan has, proportionally, more Black gay members than all the other, larger all-inclusive krewes combined. When I attended the Order of Pan Ball with my friend Compton, I noticed several ways this event was more connected to Black culture in Mobile than others. Walking in, for instance, I realized the Excelsior Band was playing. The Excelsior Band is a walking band of older Black men that has been part of Mobile Carnival tradition since 1883 and is featured in many Mobile Carnival events. As the ball got underway, some participants engaged in second line parading around the dance floor with colorful umbrellas, introducing another critical part of Mobile's Black Carnival traditions.[40] A local Black drag queen headed up the second line with gusto. And only at the Mystic Womyn of Color and the Order of Pan balls did I hear hip-hop music. At Order of Pan, several songs featured during the tableau came from the music-focused TV show, *Empire*, a kind of hip-hop that was popularized and perhaps "whitened" for a mainstream audience, but it was hip-hop nonetheless. Pan's membership seemed porous, as some of the young Black men parading in the ball were merely friends of krewe members, checking out the event before deciding whether to join the krewe. One costumed during the

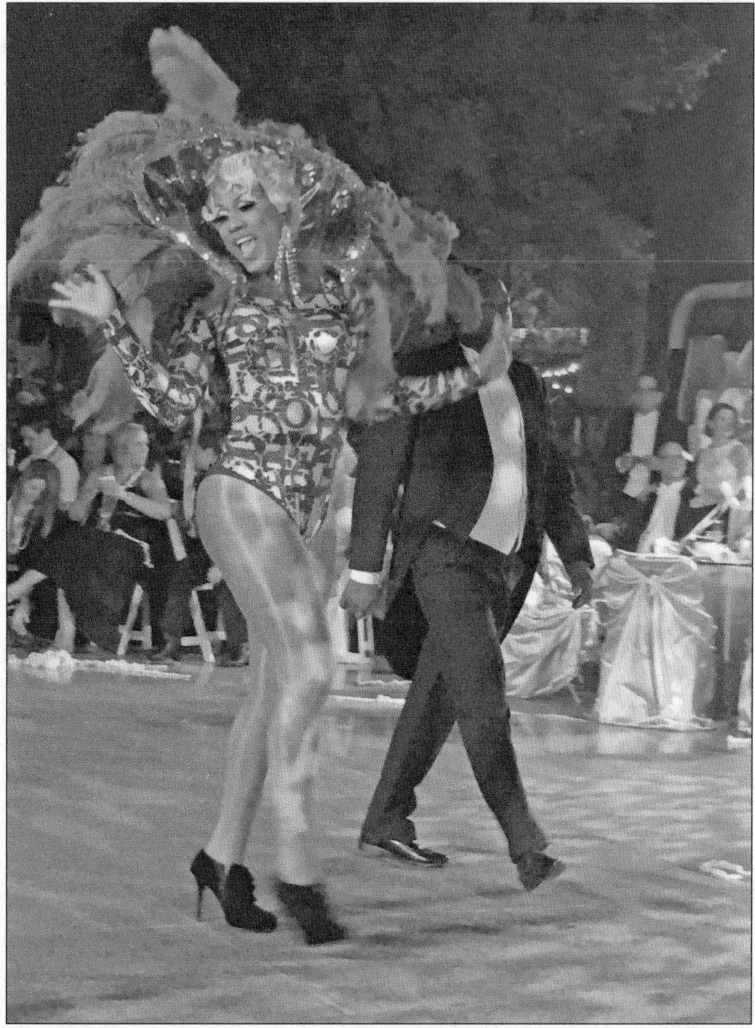

Figure 4.3. Jawakatema Davenport at the Order of Pan in Mobile

show with a glittery loin cloth and huge, sparkling epaulettes. He responded to my outfit compliments by shyly touching his shoulder pads and disclosed that they were repurposed football equipment from his high school football days. He was a friend of one of the white krewe members, a working-class gay man who had a strong social network of Black friends and lovers.

Secret Misters of Joe Cain

This ethos of being an all-inclusive festival group became a queer Carnival tradition that was recognizable outside of the LGBTQ ball scene. In February 2016, I was in downtown Mobile for the annual Joe Cain Day celebrations, surrounded by parade floats, scattered beads, and candies, and thousands of families camped out and barbecuing. Joe Cain is a patriarch of Mobile credited with the initiation of modern-day Mardi Gras festivities at the end of the Civil War.[41] Since 1967, Joe Cain Day has been celebrated on the Sunday before Mardi Gras with festivities that include a "people's parade," an open-entry parade that features floats organized by groups of friends and co-workers, people walking in costumes, and a wagon that pulls a Mobile native dressed as Joe Cain himself. I began the day at a nearby cemetery, where Joe Cain's remains are buried, as the site is ceremoniously visited by a secretive group of white women wearing all black (including veils). Cain's Merry Widows formed in 1974 as a mystic society that mainly appears on Joe Cain Day, on which they mourn their "husband" at the cemetery, toss coveted black beads and garters at onlookers, bicker over which widow Joe Cain loved best, and join the parade procession. Later in the day, the Merry Widows are joined by the Mistresses of Joe Cain, another secret group of women who dress in red, claim that "he loved us best," and squabble theatrically with the widows.[42]

In 2015, the Widows and Mistresses were joined by a new group, "The Secret Misters of Joe Cain who got the party started in 'Daisy Duke' shorts and hairy chests at Church Street Cemetery with the Merry Widows and tossed rainbow beads to the masses while sipping the finest beers Pabst has to offer."[43] (The same year, rumors circulated in the local news coverage that one of the Merry Widows was a cross-dressing man—a rumor confirmed for me by multiple gay and lesbian informants I interviewed.) In 2016, the Secret Misters paraded by me in the marching group section of the parade, a group of white men and women with hairy chests or cleavage on display, beards (if need be, drawn with thick black makeup), and short shorts. They pushed big shopping carts with poster board that read "The Secret Misters of Joe Cain" and tossed rainbow beads at onlookers.

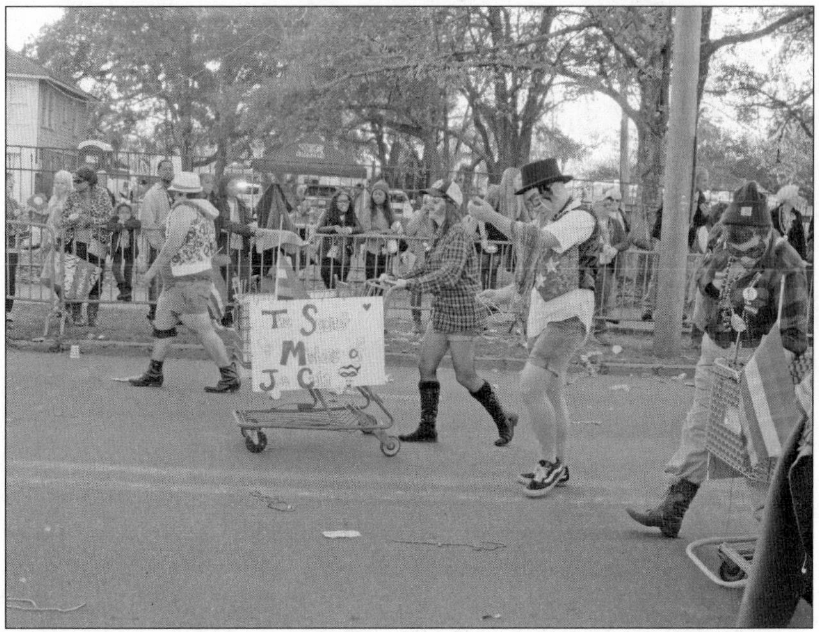

Figure 4.4. Secret Misters of Joe Cain parading in the Joe Cain Day Parade

When I returned to my bed and breakfast, which was run by an older white gay man who is heavily involved in Mardi Gras, he confided that the Secret Misters group were initially scandalous. However, the man who plays Joe Cain every year posed for a picture with the group in the paper, thus giving the Secret Misters his immediate stamp of approval. Members of the group reported that, during their first few years, "parents would turn their children's heads away" as the Secret Misters passed. "And one marching group protested against us because they didn't like the thought of men being flamboyant on the parade route."[44] All this was fascinating for me: at the Joe Cain Day parade, I see firsthand the queering of the city patriarch during a major civic event. Although Joe Cain is already portrayed as hyper heterosexual through his bevy of Widows and Mistresses, the highly visible Secret Misters of Joe Cain imply that Cain was, well, on the "down low." Put differently, their display not only calls for recognition of queer culture, including camp and cross-dressing, but also queers existing festival traditions.

Media coverage of the Secret Misters included them alongside a history of the other all-inclusive krewes in Mobile. In a magazine article, the young white man who created the Secret Misters stated, "One of our aims back in 2012 was to help bring more acceptance to the less traditional and mainstream groups like ourselves. We started off as six heterosexual white guys but now we have grown to include every race, gender, and sexual orientation. Everyone is welcome."[45] The group's leader affirmed for me that it was a mostly heterosexual organization that took an all-inclusive approach to membership. Their queer presentation suggests that the "less traditional groups" they were supporting were the LGBTQ krewes. An ostentatiously queer performance by a predominately white heterosexual men's organization affirms that all-inclusive queer Carnival forms are recognizable outside of the LGBTQ ball scene and can be mobilized by other festival participants.

The Mystic Womyn of Color: It's Our Prom

I spent more than a year researching LGBTQ festival involvement in Mobile before I figured out that the Mystic Womyn of Color (MWOC) existed. They were not listed on the webpage devoted to LGBTQ Mardi Gras associations. They never appeared in lists of the "all-inclusive" Carnival groups known for being led by gay and lesbian people. They were relatively unknown among the white LGBTQ festival participants I spoke with, excepting one white lesbian woman who had attended their ball in the past. I first assumed that few people knew about Mystic Womyn of Color because Black Carnival events often run parallel with but do not intersect with white Carnival traditions in Mobile. When I attended the MLK Parade, a "people's parade" like Joe Cain Day run by the Black Carnival association MAMGA, I was the only white person I could see in three blocks of parade participants.

The mystery of the silence of the Mystic Womyn of Color became less mysterious to me when I finally connected with the group's leader. Shantel, a middle-aged Black woman, is a blur of energy, even in her own living room. Her home is set up for entertaining, with a bar running through the hallway between the dining and living rooms. After an afternoon of hanging out and interviewing Shantel, she invited me to the ball as one of her table guests. For the next seven months, I received regular texts from her about various Mystic Womyn of Color events, including their August All White Party. It became clear that some of these events are attended by women from out of town, and that most of the information about them goes out by word of mouth—texting and person-to-person communication. Below are a couple of texted invites I received in those months:

> Consider MWOC nightlife the ultimate melting pot of fun, allowing you to choose between the laid-back vibes of a traditional southern mansion the chic style of a Magnificent Courtyard draped in White or a trendy scene in Downtown Mobile, No matter what style of nightlife you're craving, you're sure to find it at the MWOC All White Affair August 22, 2015. MWOC-Mobile's Elite Society We Dare to be Different.

> Good Morning i pray that all is well with you and yours. Mystic Womyn of Color will be hosting a Shabby/Chic Christmas party on December 19th from 9:00pm until midnight at Flipside Bar located at 54 Conception Street in downtown Mobile. The cost will be $10.00 per person and food will be provided until it last. We will be raffling off a few 2016 MWOC Ball tickets @$2.00 per raffle, along with a basket of cheer raffle for $2.00 tickets. Before you spend the holiday with your family come spend a few hours with your extended family and friends. Shabby/Chic attired is sequins or Dressy top with jeans or a dress or Formal shirt with Bowtie or Necktie with jeans, its your choice. We hope to see you there and if not we wish you the very best holidays.

My first impression, formed from these communications, was that the group was dedicated to building a Black lesbian community through events. I was even more sure after spending the weekend with MWOC krewe members and guests during their annual Carnival ball. The group was not looking to have an all-inclusive organization or ball but to make a strong Black lesbian community across the South grow stronger. This krewe was specifically by and for LBQ women of color. Krewe members did not invite coworkers, parents, and non-queer friends, so the ball of almost three hundred attendees had fewer than ten guests who were not Black LBQ women, including myself and my friend Rose. It's not that the MWOC Ball is entirely invisible during Carnival, but that, as one participant noted, it's "our prom" (in fact, there was someone there taking prom-style couples' pictures). Cultivating inclusive partying was the job of the other three LGBTQ krewes; the MWOC might have a float in the MLK parade on Mardi Gras weekend, but otherwise, they kept their focus on strengthening Black lesbian community. This focus was part of Black urban placemaking, one of the playful and pleasurable aspects of being Black and in community with other Black people in the city.[46]

I was anxious and intentional about attending. I understood that I was entering what was presumably a safe place for Black women to cultivate their community outside the gaze of white and heterosexual participants. To compensate, I worked to fit into existing group norms and standards. I obsessed over my clothes for the weekend. MWOC does not require *costume de rigeur*, so I searched photos of past years' balls on Facebook and made note of the studs in dapper combinations of shirts, ties, and vests. People tended to attend as couples (specifically stud-femme couples). I was in the middle of a divorce with my Black partner, so I invited my friend Rose.[47] I could pass as a soft butch and frequently wore ties and button-down shirts, so it would not be a huge stretch to fit "the look," while Rose was a white femme with experience spending time at Black queer community events. By this point in my research, I had also figured out that other LBQ women in the South were more receptive to me when I appeared partnered—I assumed it made me seem less predatory—and sure enough, the Mystic Womyn teased me all weekend about Rose. We grinded at the Ball, and I helped her stand up when she had over-imbibed. When I attended the post-ball brunch without Rose (she had already flown home), I had to insist repeatedly, "She's just a *really good friend*, I'm going through a divorce!" Toni, a curvy femme Black woman, winked and teased, "Oh, I used to have lots of *good friends*, and then I had just one *really good friend*." I felt cautious interacting with other women at the event, not entirely knowing the local rules of stud-femme couples and monogamous dating practices in general. I never reached out to shake hands or hug a femme, only followed their lead if they initiated, and I felt restrained when dancing with a few young Black femme women during the Ball.

The Mystic Womyn of Color Carnival Ball comes a few weeks after the end of Mardi Gras ("because space is cheaper," one member explained to me). It's held in a nice ballroom space downtown. The night before the ball I attended, there was a party at Shantel's house, so Rose and I got to meet many of the other guests in advance. I felt awkward sitting at Shantel's living room bar, but that evaporated when our host walked into the room. She lit up at the sight of me and embraced me, saying, "You came, baby girl, you came!" Mart and Celie, seated next to me at the bar, are a Black stud-femme couple in their early seventies. Celie wears a hearing aid and walks with a cane, but her dapper suits are impeccable all weekend long. Both women were in the military, and they had known Shantel for more than twenty years. Celie, in fact, had been a member of the brief all-lesbian krewe, the Daughters of Gaia, alongside Shantel in the 1980s; the pair had performed once at a ball as the Backstreet Boys.

I spent the rest of the night eating gumbo, being plied with shots and drinks by the young bartender, and hanging out with Black women from all over the South. Most of Shantel's table guests were in attendance, hailing from Georgia, South Carolina, and across the South. I met at least six truck drivers who run routes through Mobile. Rose and I were challenged to shots so often that I selected Rose as my "designated drinker" for the evening. Tee, a Black stud from Atlanta with long braids, traveled with twenty of her friends to attend the ball, and seemed determined to teach me how to dance. She led me by the arm to a relatively clear spot on the crowded deck, bouncing to the music with her hand on her hat. I tried to imitate Tee's moves, but I was, apparently, shaking my hips too much. "Just bounce," she directed me, calling her "girl" to come over and bring Rose into the tutorial. They had us dance together, practicing for the ball.

The rest of the weekend proceeded in much the same celebratory, welcoming way. The ball, an affair of three hundred people, focused entirely on attendees connecting with one another. The tableau is short but includes a powerful performance of spoken word poetry and some quick performances by about a dozen krewe members, often dancing in their ball attire with an additional hat or accessory. One of the most dramatic moments of the tableau came when the emcee announced that the "baby" of the krewe, Jada, had suffered an aneurysm and multiple strokes, but was well enough to attend. Jada paraded on stage with a pair of arm braces and walking canes. Clearly, it wasn't all talk: the Mystic Womyn's Ball was about making community. At the center of the party was a packed dance floor, where happily sweating attendees respond to the emcee or Shantel calling out different dances—a swing dance for couples, a big line dance in which the whole crowd snakes and stomps across the dance floor. Women from all over danced and flirted and connected, sometimes pausing for keepsake prom photos to remember the weekend, the community.

At the post-Ball brunch at Shantel's house the next day, I nursed my hangover with macaroni and cheese. I met Shantel's son, a young Black man who told me about other Black Carnival events, including the Great Gatsby Ball, which he learned about on Facebook. In the pictures he scrolled through on his phone, I noticed a Black woman in a tuxedo and wondered more about spaces for Black LBQ women. Although the MWOC event was not an inclusive collective party, the event fit within Mobile's strong Black Carnival tradition. The krewe parades in the Black Carnival "people's parade" and uses Carnival spaces to foster community that extends beyond the city limits. Like other Black Carnival groups, the Mystic Womyn make space for themselves in Carnival traditions that have not always been inclusive.[48] This community making, too, is an explicit resistance to the mainstream, segregated practices of Mobile Carnival.

In Mobile, LGBTQ participants have positioned themselves as the city residents most committed to inclusive festival life, as creating the most inclusive collective party that represents the true spirit of Mardi Gras. This inclusive collective party rarely had ambivalence about the participation of heterosexual guests.

Fiesta San Antonio

Many of the same tensions that existed in Baton Rouge about spectacle and events being taken over by heterosexuals were on display in inclusive collective parties during Fiesta San Antonio. Some small LGBTQ events, including the Hat Party and Fiesta Frenzy (both under the creative control of Latino gay men), resisted official Fiesta designation, trying to keep their events limited, more exclusive. Other once-gay,

DIY events, such as the WEBB Party, had become institutionalized and were run by non-profit organizations. Still, when I attended the WEBB Party, I was impressed by how queer it felt, particularly how many more Black LBQ women volunteered at this expensive event than at the other Fiesta San Antonio events I attended. The event that generated the most discussion about inclusive collective parties was definitely Cornyation, where there was both excitement about inclusivity and the concern that was becoming a common theme in my observations—that the show might not be gay enough anymore.

Everybody's Having Fun and Everybody's in the Same Room

Cornyation and, a close second, the WEBB Party are the most inclusive collective parties during Fiesta San Antonio. In our interviews with Cornyation fans, everyone stressed the *fun*. Anastasia, a white heterosexual woman who had been a fan for decades, clarified: "I don't go because it is a gay event, I don't go because I'm supporting the gays, I go because it's a good show, lots of fun." Similarly, Anna, a white heterosexual Republican, was a frequent Cornyation attendee and told me, "Cornyation is about fun, it's about not taking yourselves too seriously, you can't do that at Cornyation. You just have to enjoy it." Anna was delighted when, one year, Cornyation designer Chris Sauter did a sketch about "gun nuts" in which Lady Liberty got shot, the performers turned into bloody zombies, and one person in a shirt reading "Gun Nut" had two large testicles dangling below,. "When the guy came out with gun nuts, I mean, I was roaring! Cause I'm one of those gun nuts, I hate to say!" Even when Cornyation stretched attendees' boundaries, it was a damn good time. Indeed, the pleasure of the events may make attendees more open and malleable to differences that they would otherwise find challenging. This pleasure of humor, entertainment, and performance is central to the experience.

This pleasure often extends to "unexpected" guests; I hear many stories of family members, co-workers, and members of your mothers' bridge club who unexpectedly love attending these events. All the Cornyation fans I interviewed brought along friends and acquaintances, often in large groups of ten or more people, including business

Figure 4.5. Cornyation skit mocking gun control. Credit: Lauryn Farris

associates, friends of their high school children, debutantes, family members, and co-workers. Most of these "unlikely fans" ended up enjoying the show immensely and returned in future years. Not everyone becomes a fan, of course: A few people report bringing friends who never returned, including a business associate who was so offended he walked out of the show. George, a heterosexual white man who has attended the show for decades, seemed to think this was uncommon. "I have gotten some people who you wouldn't expect to be Cornyation fans to go and they end up going every year. They're the kind of the people that would never be caught dead there." Whether they were labeled "unexpected" because of their political orientation or their lack of exposure to LGBTQ culture and spaces, many immediately felt the inclusivity Cornyation cultivated. George's unexpected fans were "middle-aged, conservative people who don't know anybody that's gay . . . once they went, they saw what it's all about." His guests returned every year, having learned the show was "a place where just everybody gets together and gets along no matter what your culture or your background and that appealed to them."

Many Cornyation-attending groups of friends, acquaintances, and associates only meet up during festival time. Sometimes, this was because the groups included people my interviewees referred to as dramatically different than themselves. One white heterosexual Cornyation fan described the business associates she attended the event with, including a politically conservative business owner, saying "we just have nothing in common other than we happen to go to Cornyation together."

Maria, a Latina heterosexual woman who regularly attends the show with a group of Latina middle-aged women, describes some of her fellow attendees as conservative,

> yet there they are having such a wonderful time and I would just never even imagine them going to a gay bar or anything. But they're here enjoying themselves with a crowd that obviously there's homosexuals, there's transgender people, there's drag queens, and yet they're having a good time. I love that, that everybody just gets along. There's nothing, there's no lines. It's just great.

Inclusive collective partying in which "everybody just gets along" is easily reframed by Maria as blurring the typical social divisions or "lines" between diverse social groups.

Other Cornyation fans said the event broke down barriers, particularly between LGBTQ and heterosexual attendees. For Jack, an older white heterosexual man, "I think that Cornyation is good for the community because it has us come together and we're not afraid of each other." Martha, a straight Latina Cornyation fan, suggested that "because everyone's having fun and everybody's in the same room," including people who are not typically in gay spaces, that it "helps to maybe break the ice" and "show we are all human." She argued, "Whether I'm gay and you're straight, or you're bi and you're not—I think it's saying that everybody's there just to have a good time. I'm a person, I have feelings, I'm human just like you are." Martha and Jack associated inclusive collective partying with recognizing the humanity in LGBTQ people. Importantly, that humanity was not associated with LGBTQ people performing respectability, demonstrating outstanding moral worth, or showing only the most favorable aspects of gay culture. According to Martha, the common purpose of inclusive collective partying was that enjoyment unified participants. Here, pleasure is politics.

Of the Cornyation fans who commented that the show was their first experience with openly out and proud LGBTQ culture, many noted how Cornyation performers were "shameless" and that attendees "love what the gays do and they're not ashamed, they're not embarrassed, and they get up there and they show whatever and they do an outstanding job." For Sebastian, an older heterosexual man with almost no experience in the LGBTQ community, it seemed the main point of the show was to say, "Hey, we're gay, we're open, we're standing up here in front of you doing our thing, and we're proud of it. And *you're* paying *us* to come watch us do it." Before attending Cornyation, Sebastian assumed LGBTQ people were mostly closeted and ashamed, so seeing brazen, fearless queerness on stage altered his understanding of LGBTQ culture and community. Jack, a fifty-something heterosexual man who had been attending Cornyation for three decades, liked how engaging in this proudly queer, inclusive event meant "you leave Cornyation doing a little self-evaluation about 'where am I at on gay lesbian transgender type issues?'" Unlike Rupp and Taylor's study of drag show attendees, I noted that festival event attendees were far less likely to report experimenting with their own sexuality. Jack thought, in general, that Cornyation might help make people more open to coming out, because "if you see, you're watching these people that are totally different than you are and so it's gotta make you think about yourself you know your life, what your lifestyle is like. You see that there is an alternative."

However, like work by Gamson, Rupp, and Taylor, participating in an inclusive collective party that unabashedly featured LGBTQ culture and people was meaningful for audience members. They recognized and valued the inclusive collective nature of the party they attended and seemed to get a lot out of it.

It's So Mainstream

The tensions about this inclusive collective party tended to revolve around the idea that Cornyation was not as *gay* as it once was. One of the directors of the show, a senior Latino gay man, was known for insisting that he does not see Cornyation as a gay event, because heterosexuals had *always* participated. Yet many other gay fans and participants described the show as the Fiesta event with the mostly explicitly gay origins and representations. Gay artists and designers complained the loudest about this perception that the queerness had been watered down, attributing it to the popularity of the show as well as an influx of heterosexual participants and designers.

I felt this tension working as a Cornyation stagehand for two years. Some of my fellow stagehands were former designers. One commonly whispered to me backstage about how he used to be more involved in the show when it was gayer. "It's just not as gay anymore," he exclaimed as we swept the stage between shows. Board members and cast members chatted me up between acts, too, allowing me to learn that the predominantly heterosexual Cornyation "houses" were critiqued in substantially different ways than other acts. Performers in the show often critiqued acts for not being well choreographed, for addressing obscure current events, or not having good music. "They really could have done more with that topic," the lesbian stage manager and former designer would tut. However, every year there was at least one act designed by a straight designer that was critiqued for a different reason. "It's just not . . . funny," a white lesbian stagehand remarked about an act that took on sexual violence in the military. This show has satirized the deadly invasion of the Branch Davidians in Waco, so I am certain her reservations were not about the topic being too dark. The act in question had a vague reference to *The Wizard of Oz*, and a man with a beard dressed as Dorothy was assaulted by cast members in uniforms. Throughout the six shows of that year's Fiesta season, designers kept tweaking the way the act was performed, adding in more exaggerated aspects, but they never quite achieved *humor*.

I think the act failed not because it was put on by a mostly hetero house, but because it was insufficiently campy. Camp is a type of gay cultural humor that has always been central to this show. A lively, audacious artistic style associated with gay male culture, camp can be performed by anyone willing to invert and reverse and twist "normal" aesthetics like beauty and good taste.[49] Camp is not the same thing as wearing drag, although many drag shows are campy. Nor is it apolitical: camp pokes fun at serious things and it is known for revealing that which is typically hidden. In shows like Cornyation, performers use camp to parody the status quo with more glitter, sequins, flamboyance, bad humor, double entendre, and vulgarity than your typical satire. Not only gay men can be campy, camp can be performed by anyone. For example, there is a lesbian style of camp, exemplified in media like *But I'm a Cheerleader* and *Xena: Warrior Princess*.[50]

A second way that the contested gay versus mainstream nature of the contemporary show came up was in longtime participants' frequent assertions that the show was best when it was performed in a gay bar in the 1980s. Because I wrote an entire book about Cornyation, I have interviewed heterosexual and LGBTQ participants who were involved in the event going back to the 1950s. But the participants who had attended or been involved in the event since the 1980s tended to wax nostalgic over the years that Cornyation was in the upstairs ballroom of the Bonham Exchange, revived by veteran Cornyation designers from the 1960s. A disco bar in downtown San Antonio, across the street from the Alamo, the Bonham Exchange was, at the time, a newly opened bar that had a diverse clientele, but catered predominately to gay patrons. When I mentioned once to my senior Latino gay neighbor that it had been known as a "bar for everyone," he rolled his eyes. "Oh please, I got a blow job in the basement of that bar in the 1980s."

Some of the nostalgia for Bonham-era Cornyation was about the intimacy of that setting—a ballroom on the highest floor with a limited occupancy. More often, though, it was about the artistic spirit of the event in the 1980s. According to one Anglo gay designer, "it's mainstream now, and I don't like the energy that it brings. But I miss the intimacy that was there 'cause it was. Now everyone knows about it, and that's what they want to go to and see." Others thought the art was edgier back then. A former designer explained, "It was pushy and edgy because everybody was artists, so their instincts were to be edgy and push a lot."

Certainly, that combination of genuine artistry and cheap, spontaneously created, campy outfits was critical in making Cornyation what it is today. In the early years of the revived Cornyation, designers might only learn the theme for their duchess's costume twenty-four hours before dress rehearsal. The designs embodied the "creative strangeness" that Madison Moore describes, the "style that surprises because it makes fashion out of things that are not made for fashion, or it merges things together in unexpected ways."[51] They would craft the costumes out of everyday nontraditional materials like trash bags, crepe paper, plastic fish, Mylar, shredded paper, aluminum foil, and cellophane. "Part of the challenge back then was to see how cheaply you could do it," I'm told. The designs quickly became intricate, maximizing the proximity of the audience with attention to detail in design.

The audience experience was also dramatically different at the Bonham. There was no real backstage area, and the runway went right down the middle of the ballroom. As the audience crammed into the room, there was an intimate connection between the performers and the crowd. When one Anglo gay male designer attended his first Cornyation at the Bonham Exchange, he instantly wanted to be involved: "my mind just went berserk because actually it was so intimate. They had round tables and the bar with the little lava lamp and they centered the table. It was just like a little romantic restaurant and then everybody else had to stand. There was no A/C, the windows were all open. It was hot in there. But it was just wow, crazy, and it was just such an earth-shattering thing for me. " Many designers remarked on the rowdy, participatory audience pressed together in those days.

Today's Cornyation involves a huge audience over six nights at the Arneson River Theatre each year. But back at the Bonham, for a few years, the show was wild. The audience was an insider audience, and, according to one guest, the night had "more of an underground sort of feel." A designer described the typical audience as "sort of the inner circle of people, arts community, the gay community, political people . . . it wasn't particularly a gay crowd, it was just sort of an insider crowd." A newspaper review of the first show described that "the 246-plus audience read like an Alamo City's Who's Who. Former debutantes, members of the San Antonio Conservation Society and businessmen were among those creating a standing-room only crowd in one of the city's newest gay bars for the 45-minute spoof which has become a Fiesta tradition."[52] In 1983, a journalist noted that Cornyation was fast becoming "the place to be during Fiesta."[53] Some social elites refused to attend—to be seen in a gay bar—but many more were willing to play tourist just to see the show and be part of its diverse crowd. Thus, the nostalgia described to me was not the denial of an inclusive collective party but a longing for one that was more devoted to the gay nature of the show, insiders who appreciated the intimacy of the space, who were willing to come to a gay bar to be part of it all.

Fiesta de Santa Fe

Fiesta de Santa Fe is not an inclusive collective party, nor does it try to be. The core events run by the Fiesta Council promote and maintain

Hispano culture as part of a resistance to Anglo gentrification. Like the MWOC in Mobile, these Fiesta events attempt to shore up an ethnic community threatened by demographic change. The traditionalistic Hispano Fiesta de Santa Fe is also Catholic, meaning I spent more time in Catholic churches during my fieldwork in Santa Fe than I have in my whole life. One of my fondest memories is standing bleary-eyed at 6 a.m. at the back of chapel with my research assistants, Georgina and María, for a novena mass for Our Lady. The entire service was in Spanish, so María quietly whispered to me, clueing me in on what was happening and what the prayers were about. Georgina mostly just tried to fall back asleep standing up. Again, paralleling the Mystic Women's events, this novena was a ritual meant to maintain and support a strong Hispano tradition.

The strictly Catholic religiosity of the event, however, alienates many participants. Though several Hispano gay men I interviewed were devoutly religious and appreciated that it was rooted in faith, many of my Santa Fe LGBTQ interviewees were put off by it. A number mentioned the requirement that all Fiesta de Santa Fe royalty, including the Indian *princessa* in the women's royalty and the American Indian man included in the King's *cuadrilla*, attend Catholic services and be blessed in the Catholic Church. Protest organizers told me there was a history of Indian *princessas* backing out of their royalty roles when they realized how religious it was going to be and pointed out how the practices could be seen as justifying settler colonialism and the way Christian religion was forced upon American Indians.

"You'll never guess what I'm watching," I texted to my friend and colleague Angela Tarango, who studies American Indian religion. I was standing, in awe and horror, watching Hispano men dressed as *caballeros* pretending to baptize a dozen American Indian children on stage. This is the *entrada*, an opening ceremony reenacting the "peaceful" re-conquest of the city by Don Diego de Vargas and his conquistadores. The children roped into this celebration of settler colonialism seem unaware of what is going on; later, an informant tells me that every year the *caballeros* struggle to recruit American Indian participants to enact their show. I am painfully aware that the entrada takes place directly across from a line of American Indian vendors set up outside the Palace of the Governors. One Chicana woman and protest organizer I interviewed in Santa Fe

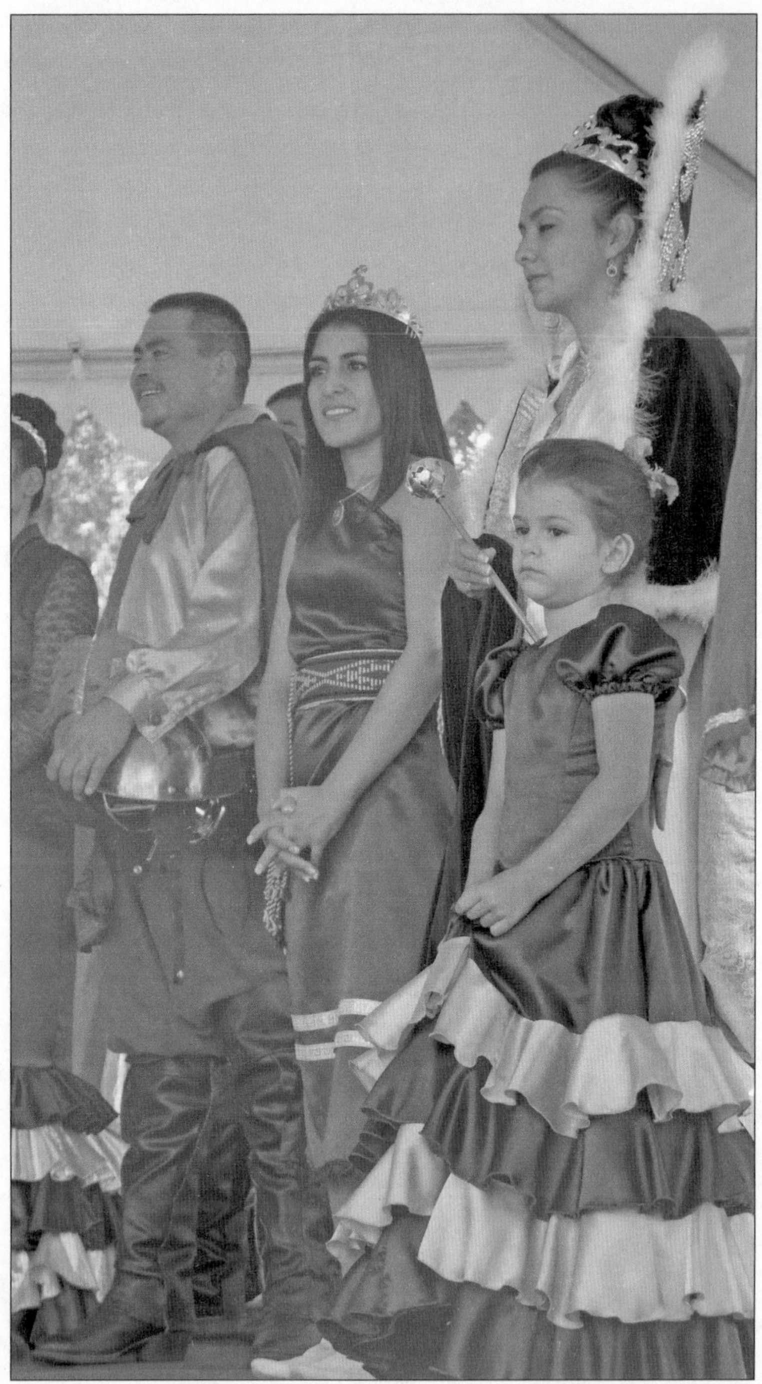

Figure 4.6. La Reina with her page and Indian *princessa* at Fiesta de Santa Fe

described this as "the most fucked up part of the *entrada*," when "Native American vendors have to sit under the *portada* and then there's a whole crowd of people who stand in front of them and they're all faced towards the stage." She told me that, as the performers on stage yell commands like "'Que viva la fiesta,' 'Que viva el Rey y Nuestro Señor,' 'viva Carlos Segundo'—and we're talking about a king of Spain from the 1600s and so it blows my mind—[there is] this real fucked up tension in the plaza at that time."

The rhetoric of Fiesta de Santa Fe is of tricultural harmony between Anglo, Hispano, and American Indian communities in the city. But the entrada makes conquest central. I interviewed two of the people who organized the first protest of the *entrada* in 2015. It was a silent protest in which protesters wore t-shirts reading "1680," the year of the Pueblo uprising, and held signs spelling out an alternative *entrada* narrative. These short revisions were tailored so they could easily be tweeted and circulated through social media, for example: "In 1693, Don Diego executed 70 warriors and enslaved hundreds of women and children," and "Don Diego came in the dark of night."[54] For three years, the protests became more vocal and assertive. The *entrada* was canceled in 2018.[55] In 2020, as I was writing this chapter, the statue of Don Diego was removed from the plaza of Santa Fe.[56]

In contrast, Zozobra is the quintessential inclusive collective party, a festival event with only nominal LGBTQ visibility that aims to be a placemaker for Santa Fe's unity and diversity. Its ostensible purpose is to be an event where the community could celebrate the end of tourist season. The first time I saw Zozobra was in the Santa Fe Visitor Information Center, where a small reproduction of the Zozobra sat, permanently, in the corner of the room. As I described in chapter 2, Zozobra was the brainchild of the predominately white members of the Santa Fe Art Colony, conceived as a resistance to Fiesta de Santa Fe. According to newspaper coverage, "the earliest Zozobra took the form of a conquistador replete with a goatee, his first appearance a parody of Fiestas and the Entrada."[57] Sylvia Rodríguez observed that Zozobra is part of the "unmarked yet core Anglo tradition of Santa Fe Fiesta."[58] Fiesta de Santa Fe scholar Sarah Bronwen Horton describes Zozobra as a "visible public symbol of Santa Fe's unique character as a place of cultural difference and a space where mainstream culture is kept at bay."[59]

Figure 4.7. The burning of Zozobra

The first time I attended the burning of Zozobra, I was joined by my friend Jason. As we entered the huge gates of Fort Marcy Park, we walked into a sea of tens of thousands of guests. The immediate impression was that it was a family affair: Kids tossed balls with their parents, toddlers scampered on the grass, couples laid together on blankets. Everyone seemed inordinately well-behaved. As I commented, Jason reminded me that there was no liquor sold at the festival; when we came in, our bags were searched and I was asked to dump out my water bottle in the grass (the same was not true the next night, at the mariachi extravaganza). The Hispano gay leader of the event would later explain that a few years back, there had been violence after Zozobra; now, they ban alcohol as part of an effort to make it an event "for everyone," especially families with children. Zozobra is one of the few events discussed in this book aimed squarely at an audience of children and families. To that end, the Latino director told me, it was important to keep the ticket price low and hold the event on a weeknight.

I wrote in my fieldnotes, "It felt like a communitarian festival. One where anyone could come and have a good time. One where people knew one another." I noticed Hispano, Native, and Anglo same-sex male couples sitting on blankets or standing to watch the show, shoulders and knees touching, leaning against one another. Zozobra emphasizes local Santa Fe traditions. Close to the entry of the park that first year, I saw a huge chalkboard emblazoned "I Like SF Because. . . ." Attendees had scrawled their responses, ranging from "Zozobra" to "It has great people!" The entertainment ranged from an all-female mariachi performance to children running around as ghosts, in sheets with holes for eyes. Jason and I enjoyed the evening, watching the entertainment, visiting concession stands, and eating. The evening would culminate with the burning of the huge 50-foot marionette, stuffed with gloomy notes (and, that year, the head of the Fiesta Council's divorce papers).

Yet, Zozobra is run by the Kiwanis, a predominately white organization. Zozobra organizers *have* worked to involve Native people in the celebration. In my Fiesta de Santa Fe fieldnotes, Zozobra is the only event where I saw some visibly Native participants who were not being used in performative or exploitative ways. In a piece written by Jason Asenap, a Comanche and Muscogee Creek writer,

> There was a time when Native people participated in the burning of Zozobra, but that ended in 1958. This hasn't stopped Ray Sandoval from reaching out to Pueblo and Native communities, asking people to return to the celebration. But his overtures have been largely ignored. "For many years, Pueblo dancers danced with fire in front of Zozobra and helped light Zozobra on fire," Sandoval said. He spoke to me as if addressing the Native community directly: "We want you to come back home to Zozobra. You were there at the inception and you were there from the beginning and we miss you and we need you back."[60]

In sum, Zozobra is a more inclusive collective party than the Fiesta Council events, though it still struggles with meaningful and involved Native participation. Of all the events in this study, Fiesta de Santa Fe struggled the most with having lively inclusive collective partying. Although Santa Fe is, on paper, the most LGBTQ-friendly city in this study, the cultural traditions of Fiesta de Santa Fe were not focused on inclusivity but rather on maintaining Hispano cultural heritage.

On Community

Different kinds of community are being made at festivals. For some groups—MWOC, the smaller LGBTQ krewes, Hispanos in Santa Fe—bolstering group solidarity is an important part of festival organizing.[61] For others, the goal is creating an inclusive collective party in the style made so prominent by many LGBTQ festival organizations. The benefits of these inclusive collective parties are many. Heterosexual attendees to LGBTQ events, for instance, go beyond experiencing LGBTQ culture as a spectacle; these events provide opportunities for heterosexual people to experiment with cross-dressing, experience the LGBTQ community, enjoy gay culture, and get to know the LGBTQ people in their lives better. Although part of these events being the "hottest ticket in town" is this proud display of gay culture, attendees tended to tell me they were drawn by their inclusivity.

Festival events may be ephemeral, yet the community created through these events can be long-lasting. The Black lesbians across the South, brought together at the Mystic Womyn's Ball, were maintained throughout the year with ongoing events and through social networks extended in its spaces. Whether or not the connections made between attendees persist, scholars point out that even short-term rituals and events are meaningful for making community. That LGBTQ festival participants are recognized and identifiable as urban residents adept at making inclusive communities during festival time is important. Valuing the inclusive collective party creates a community norm that can be mobilized by alternative festival organizations for years to come.

The recognition that LGBTQ people get from these festival events is enhanced by their appeal to a heterosexual audience. Yet in the three cities with distinctly LGBTQ events, there were consistent tensions about the disadvantages of large numbers of heterosexual attendees and event participants. These concerns included expressions of homophobia and transphobia at the event, performing as a spectacle, and losing control over the content of the event.

In the most traditionalistic festivals in this study—Mobile and Santa Fe—inclusive collective parties were a resistance to racially segregated festival practices. These inclusive diverse parties, particularly those that started as predominately white organizations, rarely fully overcame the racial segregation of festival events. At times, white LGBTQ festival participants lapsed into understandings of inclusivity that mirrored the way diversity talk operates, as about creating equal opportunities rather than altering organizational practices to include more diversity. However, the aspirational nature of inclusive collective parties—that an event *could* be open to everyone who wants to attend—is itself an important resistance within the generally segregated practices of urban festivals.

These inclusive collective parties resist the way city residents maintain symbolic boundaries to enforce social inequalities in the city. In the next chapter, I analyze how LGBTQ city residents push for access and acknowledgment from social elites during citywide festivals.

5

Social Elites, Glass Closets, and Contested Spaces

On Being Treated the Same

When I began spending time in Santa Fe to study Fiesta, multiple people told me I should talk to Paul. A slender Hispano gay man, he had achieved notoriety for the dressmaking skills that he developed at his grandmother's knee, and together the two were commissioned to dress Santa Fe's social elites, including debutantes and Fiesta royalty. When his grandmother died, Paul's "bravery" was documented in the *Los Angeles Times*, as he wore a black, homemade Victorian-style mourning gown to the funeral in the Cathedral Basilica of Santa Fe.[1] The people who suggested I seek him out called Paul "the seamstress of Our Lady."

La Conquistadora or "Our Lady" is a 28-inch-high icon of the Virgin Mary that plays a central role in Fiesta de Santa Fe rituals and processions. The dressing of La Conquistadora in these gowns was an important part of Fiesta de Santa Fe events, and many of Santa Fe's prominent Hispano families have contributed dresses to Our Lady's extensive wardrobe. Paul had made more than thirty, explaining, "it's a very time-intensive thing because I treat it as if it were commissioned by somebody that were drawing breath and living." As he participated in the rituals of Fiesta de Santa Fe and clothed La Conquistadora, Paul was also enacting his specific experience: Catholic, Hispanic, gay, male. "I doubt over every little detail about the dress and make sure that everything is perfect when I go to give it to her because she's so important to me. Because she's a living part of New Mexico history." Making dresses for Our Lady was, he told me, deeply satisfying:

> I'm very lucky to have a relationship with Our Lady, because she doesn't see me as queer or as a drag queen or a lot of different things. It's just me as me, and she accepts me as me. And I think because my grandmother had so much love for me, I experience that love and acceptance through

> the Holy Virgin the same way. There is no delineation of who I am. I'm not man nor woman, I'm just a child to her. And that is something that's very special to me, something that's very lovely.

Other kinds of Catholic ceremonies could be alienating for men like Paul, but with Our Lady, he experienced the same unconditional love that his grandmother gave him. To be clear, his was not a *satirical* engagement with Catholicism, of the kind that has made the network of queer "nuns," the Sisters of Perpetual Indulgence, increasingly visible activists. Paul's work as one of La Conquistadora's dressmakers was a tender, meaningful way to embrace his Hispano Catholic heritage and feel loved by Our Lady.[2]

Like Paul, dressing and designing costumes for social elites was a way that Anglo, Black, Latino, and Hispano gay men across the cities I studied participated in cultural festivals and, indeed, in the cultural life of their cities. They designed mannequins and stage props for exclusive events, sometimes even for organizations that would deny them membership. LGBTQ participants in festivals operate in many of these contradictory relationships, and they were careful to include the paradoxes as they brought me into their traditions. One Hispano gay man noted:

> It's strange because [social elites] want our opinions on how they dress and [to help] make sure that everything is historically correct, but the moment that you try to become visible, they become almost enraged that we would "take away their history, their culture." But *it's as much my culture as it is their culture.*

In other words, participating in festivals' cultural traditions was about rejecting exclusion, claiming this culture as his *own* culture. But social elites only allowed participation in festival traditions if LGBTQ people remained invisible. In this study, the meaningfulness of festival life is often about being able to access these traditional rituals and experiences, about being included in their own culture and traditions in an equitable way. Being included was about having a sense of belonging in the place you lived and the traditions that were important there.

In chapter 3, I considered the ways that three major LGBTQ events were valued and wanted as culturally distinct—*as queer events*—amid

Figure 5.1. The Caballeros carrying La Conquistadora during Fiesta de Santa Fea

their city's festival celebrations. In this chapter, I turn to questions of access and acknowledgment within the most exclusive, high-status festival events in this chapter, and I analyze LGBTQ people's simultaneous desires to be treated the same. Having the same access and enjoying the same acknowledgment as others—in this case, as heterosexual festival organizations, organizers, and events—is an important component of cultural citizenship, which sociologists define as the paired right to recognition "as a moral equal treated by the same standards and values and due the same level of respect and dignity as all other members" and the "right to be different."[3] For LGBTQ festival participants, gaining access and acknowledgment was a way of recognizing their moral equality. To follow the same standards, to be treated the same, to have access and acknowledgment, was part of this moral equality.

In this work, I borrow from disability studies to construct access as a perception of one's location and *belonging* in the social world.[4] According to Tanya Titchkosky, access is "an interpretive relation between bodies . . . a way people have of relating to the ways they are embodied as beings in the particular places where they find themselves."[5] Place and feeling a sense of belonging to a particular place is an important component of access. In many ways, the opposite of belonging is being "out of place." I draw on concepts of being "out of place" as spatial power relations that are articulated in both Black geographies and disabilities literatures.[6] To "know your place" is to fully understand the relational elements of place and the ways it combines the spatial with the social.[7] According to geographer Tim Cresswell, "territoriality is an intrinsic part of the organization of power and the control of resources and people."[8] In many elite-run festival events, to know your place as a LGBTQ person was to be quiet about one's gender or sexuality, to be discrete, or to be absent. The expectation of absence was exerted most forcefully on Black LGBTQ people in the Gulf South, where racial segregation practices during Mardi Gras excluded many Black LGBTQ people or policed their presence. According to Radhika Mohanram, "racial difference is also spatial difference, the inequitable power relationships between various spaces and places are rearticulated as the inequitable power relations between races."[9] And to violate expectations about social space is to be looking for "trouble."[10] Within city festival traditions, LGBTQ participants were often looking for "trouble," at times consciously troubling the assumptions of heteronormativity and at other times trying to fit themselves within social elite traditions.

Further, access differs from acknowledgment. Commemorations like street naming or representations of history or social life in museums are rich moments for the reproduction or remediation of social inequality.[11] These processes are part of the "politics of citizenship, conferring a greater degree of belonging to certain groups over others, while also serving as sites for battles to widen the 'distribution of citizenship' and the use of space."[12] Museum displays, for example, can be "involved in defining the identities of communities—or in denying them identity."[13] These processes can be acute moments of exclusion but also moments of intervention in which marginalized groups assert their citizenship.[14]

Social elites are often the gatekeepers mediating LGBTQ access to the cultural traditions of these festivals. Typically wealthy members of the dominant racial group in the city, they control some of the most prestigious festival events and their children are featured among the major festival royalty. Historically, with control over festival organizing bodies, event access, and the processes of acknowledgment (including commemorations and awards), they have also enforced racial segregation and status intensification during festivals. That's not a big surprise, given that a robust stream of research has documented the ways social elites reinforce cultural inequality by drawing symbolic boundaries and distinctions of taste, along with reinforcing systems of cultural imperialism, in multiple domains.[15]

Social elites played a critical role in the access and acknowledgment of LGBTQ people during city festivals. In comparing these four cities, where urban festivals are elite-controlled to varying degrees, I show that not only highly traditionalistic but also less traditional festivals run by social elites restrict the access and acknowledgment of LGBTQ participants, organizers, and celebrants. Within my case studies, I learned that access and acknowledgment were uneven, attenuated by the degree to which each city's festival was traditionalistic, especially regarding racism and racial boundaries. Broadly, the more the social elites control the traditions and organization of a given festival, the less access and acknowledgment LGBTQ participants will have. In religious festivals like Santa Fe's, social elites heavily regulated LGBTQ Hispano participants who wanted to be involved in the elite-run high-status organizations and major royalty. Like the Black, Native, and Latinx minority festival participants described in chapter 2, LGBTQ celebrants in urban festivals were constantly pushing for recognition of minority royalty, access to similar spaces and opportunities, and public recognition of their contributions. Most festivals work to neutralize issues around access for racial minorities by reluctantly recognizing alternative organizations and royalty made by minority communities, rather than allowing them access to elite white organizations. With regard to LGBTQ participants, elites enacted similar boundaries, though more often by regulating heteronormativity within the elite organizations.

Access and Acknowledgment

In this study, access and acknowledgment was often contingent on heteronormativity. The enforcement of heteronormativity involves the requirement that LGBTQ participants either be closeted or treat their sexuality as an "open secret," with but a tacit visibility. Eve Sedgwick calls this state of others knowing but not openly acknowledging a person's non-heterosexual orientation the "glass closet,"[16] and sociologist Katie Acosta refers to the open secret as living in the "in-between spaces," neither wholly in nor out of the closet.[17] Operating tacitly can be a complex form of visibility and liberation, particularly for LGBTQ people of color.[18] Carlos Decena, in a translation from the Spanish *sujeto tácito*, writes about the tacit subject, "neither silent nor secret."[19] The Dominican immigrant gay men he interviews both assert their homosexuality through contextual references and avoid allowing it to be an explicit discussion or confrontation with family. Different from being closeted, the tacit subject keeps "the closet door ajar," allowing others, in the right contexts, to peer inside.[20] Yet both practices are promoted by heteronormativity. In one of the most blatant indicators of the strict bounds of heteronormativity enforced through social elites in festival cities, I learned a new acronym in my research for this project: MGM. It stands for married gay man—a shorthand for the white male social elites "known" to be gay but married to women. The existence of the acronym suggested a phenomenon that was at least believed to be widespread and symptomatic of the requirement that lesbian, gay, or bisexual people hoping to be in elite organizations or be major festival royalty must, at the very least, stay in the glass closet.

Heteronormativity operated in a complex social system, repeatedly and relentlessly intersecting with racism and settler colonialism.[21] Sexual regulation and discipline is a central component of US colonization.[22] There is a long history of indigenous practices being figured by policy-makers as other than heteronormative, and settler assimilation forcing heteronormativity on native populations through spatial relocation and force.[23] Geographer Carolyn Knowles argues that race is made through the arrangement of spaces, which function as "active archive[s] of social processes and social relationships composing social orders."[24] Both race and sexuality are actively shaped and formed through power relations in spaces.[25] Indeed, elite events—the "spaces" of focus in this chapter—are part of the local geographies of race in all four cities.[26] Racism and heteronormativity work together through anti-black heterotopias, spaces that combine the anti-black racism and heteronormativity to create an exclusive space.[27] For example, many elite festival organizations have maintained strict racist boundaries, often limiting both minority membership and guest attendance at events. These boundaries, like heteronormativity's, are policed informally, through pressure, harassment, and exclusion, rather than formally, through organizational operating rules. Either way, racism and sexual discrimination deny full access to social elite organizations.

In interviews and fieldwork, access came up in four ways. Where access means having permission, being at liberty, or having the ability to join or enter a place or organization, it was curtailed around the governing of festival organizations, inclusion among major royalty figures and elite organizations' membership, and event spaces and venues. Access to organizations, spaces, and roles dominated by elites has long been a goal of civil rights activism, though access does not in any way guarantee equity in domains including education,[28] health care,[29] public spaces,[30] and information technology.[31] For example, rarely are prohibitions against access for LGBTQ people written into formal policy, and yet my respondents repeatedly raise access issues attributed to informal policy—cultural traditions, social norms, and an understanding of places that one belongs (and does not belong).

This access was intimately linked to feeling welcome in spaces and not "out of place." In the Gulf South, gay men and lesbians I interviewed frequently emphasized that they did not want to "go anywhere I'm not welcome." One white gay man shrugged, "if they don't want me, why would I want to be there?" For these participants, a sense of belonging may be linked to Southern norms about manners and a history of post–civil rights backlash against insistence on access to space.[32] For Black LGBTQ people, attending often all-white elite events means interacting with a space long since organized to keep people "in their place" by ensuring that out-group members feel "out of place."[33] The racism embedded in festival geographies is an enormous component of these moments of dislocation. But LGBTQ festival participants sometimes push back against these exclusions, resisting the attempts to put them "in their place" and fighting for their own access and belonging.

Processes of acknowledgment from multiple arenas—elites, the mayor, the festival organization—help constitute LGBTQ festivals' participants as urban citizens, integrated into the fold of city life.[34] As I conducted my research, whether during a formal interview, sitting around decorating ball tables, or having brunch after events, people brought up the elite processes of recognition and acknowledgment—the neglect of LGBTQ events by social and political elites was a consistent theme. LGBTQ festival aficionados in all four cities were attentive and vocal about whether they were getting treated fairly among festival events, particularly those run by social elites. To be sure, some LGBTQ people wanted their events and involvement to fly under the radar of these official processes, while participants in the largest events often deeply desired widespread recognition.

Elite Royalty and Organizations

In December 2018, Louise Deser Siskel wrote an op-ed for the *Los Angeles Times*. She declared: "I am Jewish. I wear glasses. I am bisexual—and I'm the Rose Queen."[35] Media reported how Siskel was the first openly bisexual woman to serve in this role, as the royalty presiding over the famous annual Tournament of Roses Parade in Pasadena, California. To some, this may not seem newsworthy, but festival royalty are prominent within urban festivals—these queens, kings, and royal figures preside over festival events and are expected to maintain a certain (hetero) respectability. This strict surveillance of sexuality is generally regulated more heavily for women than men. We can trace that back to the tradition in which many festivals in cities like Mobile and San Antonio have been entangled with debutante season. That is, being major festival royalty was historically part of young, elite women's debuts into the upper-class marriage market. Pageantry like debuts and beauty pageants are deeply rooted in social, political, and economic ideals of society.[36] For example, beauty pageants are a site where "structures of power are engaged: the power to control and contain the meanings mapped on the bodies of competitors, the mechanisms of this power, and the spaces where this power is resisted."[37] Debutantes and royalty within festivals clearly reify femininity, respectable (hetero)sexuality, and heteronormativity.[38] Heterosexuality and gender conformity are, even today, prerequisites for occupying these hyper-feminine roles.

The heavy regulation of race, class, gender, and sexuality messily winnows those eligible to serve in major royalty roles. Social class was a sort of first-order requirement: Anyone hoping to be major festival royalty needs enough status to be considered for the position and enough money to pay for the extravagant outfits and travel expenses. Then race, gender, and sexuality further constrained access to the court. There are far fewer constraints for becoming minor festival royalty, the royalty for krewes, and events like Cornyation.

In Baton Rouge there are no major royalty, but in the other three cities, LGBTQ people's limited access was blatant. In both San Antonio's and Santa Fe's traditions, the queen or *la reina* is a young unmarried woman, whereas the king is an older man, typically an established businessman in the community. In Mobile, two pairs of royalty are crowned—one by the all-white and one by the all-Black festival associations—all of them unmarried young adults. The white royalty pair historically reign over Mobile's Mardi Gras, symbolically receiving the key to the city from the mayor at the start the festival, whereas the Black king and queen serve as the royalty of their festival organization with some citywide recognition of their roles. In all three cities, the royal pair have a court of princesses, duchesses, pages, and dukes. The most restrictive royal courts are in San Antonio and within the white-run Mobile Carnival Association, where kings and queens are selected without a visible public contest. These royal courts are also the most racially exclusive, dominated for decades by white and Anglo participants from the richest families.[39]

In Santa Fe and within the Black Carnival association MAMGA, the process of selecting royalty is a more transparent one involving application and selection. Inclusion in Mobile's Black major royalty was less likely to hinge on debutante marriageability than on community service. This emphasis on community service evokes the differences between white and Black sorority life on college campuses, where Black sororities encourage members to strive for professional and community achievements more than "getting a man."[40] Indeed, as I toured the Mobile Carnival Museum, I saw that the trains on the elaborate costumes of Mobile's Black royalty display insignias from their college sororities and fraternities, whereas the trains of Mobile's white major royalty employ iconography related to family members who were past festival royalty.

It is common for gay, lesbian, and bisexual royalty to come out after their reigns, but never to reign openly. I could write a whole chapter on the hushed, conspiratorial whispers among LGBTQ locals, the gossip about which major royalty were suspected to be gay, who came out later as gay, who hooked up with whom, and who "everyone knew they were but no one said anything." Apart from one rumor about two Coronation duchesses who dated each other in San Antonio and a former Santa Fe La Reina who came out as a lesbian after her reign, almost all of these rumors were about men. Older gay men lowered their voices to tell me,

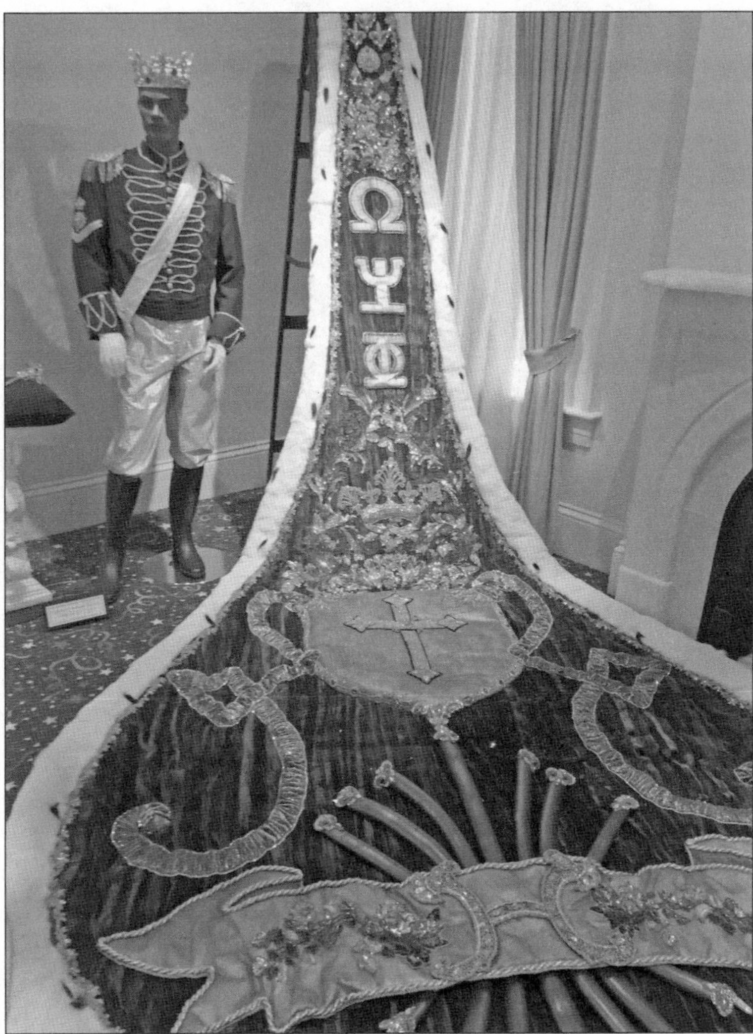

Figure 5.2. Black Carnival train in Mobile Carnival Museum with fraternity symbols on it

in Mobile's Carnival Museum, about one of the white kings in the 1950s, known for throwing exclusive parties for gay men in hotel rooms, and a Black king who had both a wife and a male lover. People seemed to relish telling me these stories of closeted royalty, like there was something amazing about having "the dirt" or having hooked up with one of the royalty figures. Knowledge is, of course, one sort of access, a small signifier of being on the inside. I do not have any stories of transgender people either running for major royalty or coming out after the fact, and in the gender-segregated world of major royalty the participation of transgender people may be significantly more restricted than LGB participation due to the regulation of transgender participation in same-sex activities like sports.[41]

LGB people faced fewer barriers accessing elite organizations and events than inclusion in major royal courts, although this access was often restricted by race and gender. At this level, I found two layers of access: membership in elite organizations and attendance at their events. Elite events include private events related to festival royalty, those hosted by exclusively upper-class organizations, and events that required vetting or social network ties—knowing the right people—to receive tickets. They also included some ticketed, public events, including the major coronations in Mobile, Santa Fe, and San Antonio. Thus, attendance was far less regulated by sexuality than membership. A surprising number of white LGBTQ people I interviewed spoke of attending elite events at some point, even though they tended to describe these parties as "boring" compared to those where queerness was centered and celebrated.

LGBTQ festival participants pointed my attention toward the festival associations and coordinating bodies that decide about which events are officially promoted by the association, which event anniversaries are commemorated, and which royalty are "official" and supported by the association. In Mobile and Santa Fe, festival associations select the major festival royalty; in San Antonio, the festival association confers legitimacy on some events' and groups' royalty and not others. Being recognized by festival associations can come with resources; official, promoted events often receive tangible benefits like being covered by the festival association's insurance policy, receiving free or reduced-price event security, securing funds to support the event, and getting free promotion in programs and websites.

Access to major spaces was also symbolic of seniority, power, and visibility. Many scholars analyze the way space is contested and symbolic of power relations, as a place where race, class, and gender conflicts, frequently obscured, can be observed.[42] Festival venues, typically large, privatized spaces serving as festival staging grounds, were coveted by all the organizations. There were many events crammed into a short period of time, so space was at a premium. Being in major spaces in the center of the city was an important kind of access for some group members. The LGBTQ festival events used venues that ranged from the largest convention center in town to gay bars and even an organizer's father's backyard.

Access to space was shaped first by money and resources, and smaller LGBTQ events often ran on meager budgets. To secure cheaper venues and catering costs, two of the four LGBTQ krewes in Mobile, for instance, hold their balls before or after the Carnival season. Baton Rouge's Krewe of Divas moved their drag ball from festival to Pride month—June—to keep costs down. Like the Mystic Womyn of Color in Mobile, the Krewe of Divas was financially strapped and economically precarious, both in finances and membership.

My case studies can be organized from the most traditionalistic and elite-controlled festival, Fiesta de Santa Fe, to the least, Baton Rouge Mardi Gras. Santa Fe's and Mobile's festivals were marked by expectations about glass closets and more blatant policing around gender nonconformity. Some LGBTQ interviewees in these cities also expressed more longing to be a part of festival traditions. In San Antonio and Baton Rouge, there was less concern about accessing elite traditions than competing with social elites for spaces and acknowledgment.

Fiesta de Santa Fe: Glass Closets

Santa Fe is the city in my sample with the highest rights for LGBTQ people, even a reputation for LGBTQ tourism and migration. Many interviewees described long-standing Santa Fe Hispano families as full of gay and lesbian members (one Hispano gay man described it as "like every family is one-fourth gay . . . it's in the water here"). When, however, LGBTQ people participated in Hispano Catholic events, heteronormativity was strictly regulated and my interviewees spoke of the great pressure to retreat to glass closets, at least for the duration of festival.

Fiesta de Santa Fe was the most traditionalistic in the sense that it elevated Hispano Catholic practices, especially when it came to the major festival royalty. During Fiesta de Santa Fe, I attended Catholic masses in which the royalty were blessed in the Cathedral Basilica of Santa Fe, as well as standing-room only 6 a.m. Spanish-language novena masses to view La Conquistadora, religious processions, and inaugural event prayers. Even at the wildly paganistic Burning of Zozobra, the head of the Fiesta Council prayed, saying plainly that "Fiesta begins and ends in prayer."

The Fiesta Council

In Santa Fe, the Fiesta Council governs, simultaneously resisting Anglo gentrification of the city, enacting settler colonialism against American Indians, and maintaining the heteronormativity of the organization and festival. The Fiesta Council is Hispano-majority, the result of an evolution as Hispano residents reclaimed the festival from Anglo artists.[43] Today, it closely safeguards a Hispano heritage rooted in the Spanish conquistadors' conquest of the area. In her book *The Santa Fe Fiesta, Reinvented*, scholar Sarah Bronwen Horton describes this as Hispano cultural preservation in the face of gentrification and displacement of Hispanos from Santa Fe.[44] Younger members of the Council told me the group was outdated, full of "old school politics" and out of touch with Santa Fe's youth. Recently, Council politics have undergone some change, spurred by the younger contingent and protests about the entrada I cover in chapter 4.[45]

The Fiesta Council seems supportive of its individual gay and lesbian Council members if they remain tacit subjects. The three gay and lesbian Hispano former and current Council members I interviewed described, for example, an older, openly gay Hispano Council member who never became president, because a scandal would "arise" whenever it was his turn. They all referenced closeted or secretive Council members (including one of their fellow councilors described as "an older man that is *confused*"). Interviewees revealed that Fiesta Council politics renders LGBTQ people invisible—just one result of the intersections of settler colonialism and heteronormativity in this southwest city.[46]

The first time I met Pilar, he was in drag. A slender Hispano gay man dressed as Santa Fe Pride royalty, Pilar explained that the year he was Queen of Pride, he was offered tickets to the Gran Baile, a historical procession of royalty from Santa Fe and surrounding cities' festivals. But Fiesta Council politics includes denying "out" royalty. Pilar reported that he went to Fiesta Council, insisting, "I'm a crowned queen of Santa Fe,

I'd like to be formally announced on the bandstand just like the rest of them" because "they have Taos queens and everybody from everywhere and they all get introduced and invited to do the *marcha*." Pilar's request was voted down by the Council: Pilar could have tickets to but could not be announced at the ball. As we spoke, Pilar noted that he had "earned my crown just like the Fiesta queen, just like everybody else," but the Council did not "wanna draw too much attention" to his gender and sexuality. He thought, for optics, the Council "couldn't possibly have somebody that was gay on stage, they had to get all butt hurt." Amid his history of involvement with the Council, the denial of Pilar's own royalty status was a revelation. He upheld the Council, but they offered him only halfhearted support—he could attend the event, but not be visible.

The Fiesta Council requires that two major royalty—Don Diego de Vargas and La Reina de la Fiesta de Santa Fe—speak Castilian-style Spanish and have a strong Hispano heritage, ideally tracing their heritage back to New Mexico's first Spanish settlers. American Indian roles in the royal court are tokenized: La Reina has a "Spanish princessa" and an "Indian princessa," and one member of the Don Diego's royal court (*cuadrilla*) is historically an American Indian man. The racialized purity of the Fiesta de Santa Fe royalty extends to the requirements for sexuality, always framed in heteronormativity. Note, for instance, that the requirements for La Reina include being over the age of twenty-one, never married, with no children—very much in line with the determinants of eligibility for debutantes. Some Council members chafe at the gender rigidity of the rules, yet they persist.

At the same time, the Fiesta Council selects its major royalty through an open contest, which allows for more agitation around who can be the major royalty. Fiesta de Santa Fe was the only site where I observed open dispute about visibly "out" major royalty. I spoke with three members of the Fiesta court who were openly gay or lesbian; all three had been court members within the last decade, and two ran for either Don Diego or La Reina. I knew that there had been at least one closeted Don Diego and some royal court (*cuadrilla*) participants. One former La Reina came out as a lesbian after her reign, and Santa Fe's openly gay Mayor Javier Gonzalez opened the first Fiesta de Santa Fe event I attended by talking about how he, his father, and his uncle had all reigned as Don Diego. But the experiences of out and open royalty figures were often negative.

Pilar, who was an openly gay cuadrilla member in his youth, said he was constantly picked on for his feminine appearance. Hispano men, he argued, "tell you one thing to your face and then they shame you behind your back," revealing that four men had "pestered and poked and bugged until I left, I never came back." Pilar may have been picked on and ultimately excluded because of his sexuality or his femininity—most likely, both.[47]

A Gay Don Diego

No openly LGBTQ person has ever reigned as Santa Fe festival royalty. The first to try was Doug. I met Doug in 2016 in the living room of his grandmother's house, with family members going in and out of the room as we spoke. A muscular young Hispano man, Doug was particularly masculine. He had a penchant for telling long stories, eagerly devoured by my research team (myself, along with research assistants, María and Georgina). He told us of his experience as an openly gay man, serving in the cuadrilla royal court several times and running for Don Diego.

My first impression of Doug was that he had a strong devotion to Catholicism and Fiesta traditions. This may trace to the fact that, in our first conversation, Doug, my students, and I were all bleary-eyed and tired from attending the 6 a.m. Fiesta Catholic novena mass (these masses are held for a week each summer). At different points in the interview, he showed us his religiously themed artwork, including the tattoo of La Conquistadora on his arm and a drawing of himself carrying La Conquistadora as part of the cuadrilla. Doug explained that "Our Lady" watched over him, stating this in language that echoed the devotion of other gay and lesbian Hispanos, including Paul at the beginning of this chapter.

Doug was just as well known for this devotion to Our Lady and the Fiesta de Santa Fe as he was for being a gay activist. A business owner, he ran Santa Fe Pride for several years. Equality New Mexico, a statewide LGBTQ rights organization, financially sponsored his run for Don Diego, during which he and other interviewees describe harassment from Council members. Hispano male councilors made wisecracks about Doug running for La Reina instead of Don Diego. Other members circulated social media photos of Doug performing drag for a HIV/AIDS fundraiser, stating that the Council needed a "real man," not a "drag queen," as its Don Diego. This harassment and gatekeeping reinforced heteronormativity as well as gender norms surrounding the Fiesta's major royalty figures. To Doug, who only performed "charity drag" and was otherwise masculine presenting, Fiesta Council members' concerns about being a "real man" revealed their inability to disentangle sexuality from gender and gender presentation. To them, Doug couldn't possibly be both openly gay and a "real man." They sought a very narrow conformity and dismissed anything else as unthinkable.

Doug intentionally and transgressively challenged Fiesta de Santa Fe traditions. He refused to be a tacit subject. During the contest for Don Diego, Doug's male partner escorted him to the stage and bestowed him with a chaste kiss. When Doug lost, a few Council members attributed it to mistakes in his Spanish speech, yet his open gayness was certainly a point of contention. Doug mused, "If my mama just walked me, would it have been different? But I didn't. I ran gay. I got up there, I was who I was, you know . . . To me, it's anybody can get up at Pride and wave a flag, but when you go before your culture and your traditions. . . ." He trailed off. For Doug, this cultural challenge was more significant than attending Pride, a specifically queer space. It suggested that the discrimination inherent in the Fiesta was a deeply meaningful exclusion; he had aspired to be Don Diego since childhood, and to be denied this position based on his sexuality was devastating for Doug.

Just as lesbianism or bisexuality challenges the heteronormativity and femininity of female debutantes and royalty, the conflation of effeminacy and gay identity challenges the masculinity of male figures like Don Diego, who is supposed to be the figure of a masculine conqueror. The conflation of Doug's openly gay sexuality with effeminacy excluded him from full participation with his own culture and traditions, including his Don Diego aspirations. Even men who were closeted as royalty recall onlookers chanting "La Reina" at them during events. Latin American machismo may have its roots in the masculinity of the Spanish conquerors and their reactions to indigenous two-spirit gender non-conformity, but these boundaries are clearly upheld even today.[48]

Doug was proud and out during his competition—and there is a clear distinction between being openly gay and being tacitly understood to be gay. Festival associations safeguard and serve as gatekeepers for some of the strongest festival traditions, simultaneously protecting the racial homogeneity and heteronormativity of these traditions. In Santa Fe, the festival royalty operate at the intersection of settler colonialism and heteronormativity, attenuating the access of LGB community members to traditions they love as much as anyone else. Their choice effectively is to limit their royal and elite membership aspirations, live in a glass closet, or walk away. Doug gave up his dream of being Don Diego.

Mobile Mardi Gras: Contested Glass Closets

Mobile's festival is also heavily influenced by white social elites—what those throughout the Gulf South consider a more traditionalistic approach to Mardi Gras than the weeks-long debauchery in New Orleans. Mobile Carnival is so large that multiple festival governing bodies interact to regulate the festival: an all-white Carnival association (Mobile Carnival Association), an all-Black Carnival association (Mobile Area Mardi Gras Association), and an organization of all the parading krewes that coordinates with the Mobile Police. Among the cities I studied, Mobile was the site of the most contestation around elite organization membership.

Regulation of Racial Segregation, Gender and Sexual Conformity

Carnival krewes across the Gulf South, except for LGBTQ krewes and a few others, are racially segregated (see chapter 2), but this racial segregation is more strictly enforced in Mobile. In Mobile, just three LGBTQ krewes and one "all-inclusive" krewe, Conde Explorers, were fully integrated, and the latter had a long history of being policed by the social elites of Mobile Mardi Gras.

Conde Explorers, featured in a 2008 documentary on racial segregation during Mardi Gras (*The Order of Myths*), has no restrictions on gender, race, or sexuality. Several members told me that, along with Order of Pan, it was one of the most comfortable krewes for Black gay and bisexual men (although these men mostly operate as tacit subjects within the predominately Black Conde Explorers). All but one of Mobile's LGBTQ krewes has been racially all-inclusive since their establishment, but Conde Explorers was the first krewe established as an all-inclusive *night parading* krewe. The city's all-white krewes have historically paraded at night and hired Black marching bands and dance teams to perform in between floats, including the visibly out and gender-transgressive Prancing Elites dance team. Meanwhile, Black krewes had only paraded during the day, a restriction held in place by the organization of parading krewes and Mobile Police. To secure their right to parade after sundown, one of the leaders of the Conde Explorers, a broad-shouldered Black heterosexual man named Tom, described jumping through bureaucratic hoops. There were arguments about tradition, the group's viability, seniority rights in the parading schedule, and whether the Mobile Police could "secure our safety" in a night parade. Even after securing the right to parade, Tom detailed years of ongoing issues with police and paper-pushers: "it's a constant, there's always a hurdle," every year. Conde Explorers is not treated as a LGBTQ group in its interactions with the parading krewes or the Mobile Police—part of a long historical conflation of Blackness with heterosexuality[49]—instead, it is treated, within a racist legacy, as a Black krewe that is policed and regulated.[50]

Race and gender conformity are enforced within Mobile's elite festival events, often run by white men's mystic societies. A young Black woman who was a member of a LGBTQ krewe recounted being invited to be the first Black *guest* at a local Carnival ball put on by a white women's krewe. Many LGBTQ people tell me that, at exclusive white Mardi Gras events, white gay men still attend with a female guest rather than bring a male partner. And it's common for invitations to elite balls to explicitly forbid cross-dressing. A white gay man from the Order of Pan explained that "the straight organizations—this is how it is. White only, Black only, men only, they've even got mad at us and said no cross-dressing allowed. They didn't say that before, but now they don't allow drag queens to come to their balls." This stands in contrast with some of the major Black events of Mobile's Carnival, where Black drag queens regularly attend in ball gowns.

Membership in elite organizations and non-LGBTQ festival organizations hinged on "discretion"—the willingness to join as tacit subjects. Lesbian, gay, and bisexual adults in this study were most likely to report being or having been members of same-gender organizations which, in Mobile, were sometimes more open to gay men or lesbians (assuming their presence did not necessarily alter the heteronormativity of the krewe's events). For example, I was told several times about one white women's krewe that had an all-lesbian board of directors that year, but when I attended their ball, there was no visibility for this queerness. Indeed, members of the krewe were expected to have a male escort when they were announced on stage. A lesbian LGBTQ krewe member explained that she had left her all-women's krewe when she realized there were other options—"I can't ever dance with who I want to dance with" at the ball in women's krewes, she said forthrightly. Another respondent, Martin, a white heterosexual man, was a longtime member of a popular, long-standing men's krewe with a growing reputation for being gay-friendly. He described gay and bisexual white men who had joined the krewe in recent years, using language that suggested an uneasy arrangement of semi-silence: "they bring their partners to functions but to actually talk about it, you'll never hear them saying 'this is my partner.' It's really not open . . . but they're not treated any differently."

Nonetheless, there were out gay and lesbian members in even the most secretive and elite Carnival organizations in Mobile. They were legacies, folks with a family heritage of elite organization involvement. Among the most highly pedigreed elite and out white gay men I interviewed was a member of one of the two elite white krewes his father had joined—the other would not vote him in because of his sexuality. I also heard many rumors, including speculation in the newspaper, that an elite gay man cross-dressed and paraded as a member of the most secretive society in Mobile, the Widows of Joe Cain, a mystic society that wears both masks and veils over their faces. He winked at me when I mentioned this rumor to him.

I had the unexpected pleasure of interviewing Joe, a closeted white gay octogenarian who had founded one of Mobile's major men's krewes after World War II. Another interviewee brought Joe to a lunch interview, and Joe walked in wearing his krewe t-shirt and carrying a stack of memorabilia and trinkets for my research team to take home. Joe flipped through old pictures of himself as a young man, a member of Mobile's business elite, founding the new krewe with some friends. His sons help lead the group now, part of the reproduction of white elite social networks in the city. He talked both about his wife, who has passed away, and his male "friend" who used to go with him to Osiris balls, where they would dance together. Joe's face glowed as he recalled the year he wore a dress to the ball, but he adds that he stopped attending the balls when his friend passed away over a decade ago. It was likely Joe operated as a tacit subject in his krewe, his sexuality an open secret that everyone knew but, discreetly, did not mention. Sometimes elite white gay men were not tacit subjects in their krewes and instead were visible within the group and to the public.

The Pink Float on Parade

One of my Osiris interviewees warned me: There was a "gay float" in the Comic Cowboys parade, a pink painted wagon. The Comic Cowboys are one of the most secretive mystic societies in Mobile. They rarely throw public balls. Since 1884, their most visible endeavor has been their satirical Fat Tuesday parade on the day before Lent begins and the Carnival festivities end. In it, some four hundred white men parade in simple wagons adorned with white posters bearing inflammatory, ostensibly funny commentary on social and political events. I stayed to watch the parade because I had heard it often featured homophobic and transphobic content. And sure enough, a pink wagon trundled by.

It took some sleuthing to find the gay Comic Cowboy member, Karl, who turned out to a white man in his late sixties. With his slender, younger partner, Saul, we got together at a loud and rowdy tapas restaurant in downtown Mobile. Saul joined Karl on his pink float in the parade every Mardi Gras weekend.

The interview started with the obvious: What was up with the pink float? Initially, it was the only painted wagon in the parade, and the Comic Cowboys gave it to Karl every year for almost a decade straight. Saul leaned across the table to emphasize, "I was disappointed, because I know they did it to be ugly. But I kind of embraced the pink monster." Like Doug being called "La Reina," the Comic Cowboys' assignment of the pink float was meant to bully and mock the purported femininity of gay men—or, as Karl acknowledged, to taunt him.[51] Instead, Karl, tapping into a long history of LGBTQ people appropriating slurs as badges of pride (think, for instance, of the evolution of the term "queer"), embraced and transformed the "pink monster" into his signature.[52]

Family heritage had been Karl's pathway into the Cosmic Cowboys. Most of the members were pleasant to him, but a few krewe members still refused to acknowledge him during meetings and events. Karl was assertive, even threatening to "out" other men as members of the secretive krewe as he warned, "if they ever mess with me . . . they won't be closeted anymore." He felt he was just as entitled to be a Comic Cowboy as any other member and was willing to exert his own personal power to maintain that position. For Karl, he would not allow homophobes to restrict his access to this organization that was part of his family festival heritage.

Saul, on the other hand, expressed a lot of ambivalence about the Comic Cowboys and hesitated when it came to the line between irony and offensiveness. He did not attend the parade for many years after the Comic Cowboys, at the height of the AIDS epidemic, parodied the Centers for Disease Control as the "Sick Fags Over Georgia." Karl interjected that he has, on occasion, objected to the floats' posters. As a group member, he gets to preview the posters and says he intervenes with overtly homophobic and otherwise offensive slogans. "I don't like a lot of it, I object to it, and I do it privately. But I just call the captain of the float and let him know what I think. Sometimes it works, sometimes it doesn't. Nevertheless, I let them know. There are some things that you just can't do." Though his membership in the group was entirely predicated upon his elite family connections, Karl used his position to subtly influence the krewe's brand of satire behind the scenes. He made his own access to the group by making space for himself in the organization. But just these contrasting anecdotes made it clear: Elite organizations can be a hostile place for LGBTQ participants, especially if femininity was made into an issue (or conflated with homosexuality, as it was for Doug) or when racial exclusivity was defended with territorial zeal.

Museums and Commemorations

The Mobile Carnival Museum is the epitome of a racialized space. I sat in the hallway of the museum for a long afternoon, listening to tour guides narrate the history of the festival. The Carnival Museum was founded by the all-white Mobile Carnival Association, which crowns the white royalty of the festival. Most of its rooms are full of memorabilia and regalia celebrating white krewes' costumes, royalty dresses and trains, and decorations, though one is dedicated to the MAMGA and Black Carnival royalty, featuring the colorfully decorated umbrellas used during parading at Black Mobile Carnival events, and another room, which focuses on music as part of the Mobile Carnival tradition, featuring the Black men's Excelsior Band, a brass band with a 100-year Carnival tenure.

The hallway is dominated by a large mural, a timeline detailing important events in the history of Mobile Mardi Gras. It is a study in racialized histories, listing, for instance, the Civil War as the "War of Northern Aggression."[53] Sandwiched between "1974: Alexis Herman (future U.S. Secretary of Labor) named Queen of MAMGA" and "1990: MAMGA celebrates its 50th anniversary" is the entry "1980: Order of Osiris, the first gay Society in Mobile, holds its first dance." Though several krewe members had donated materials, this was the sole mention of LGBTQ Carnival participation in the museum. None of their ephemera was on display, no other history was listed.

The tour guides who passed me that day narrated the history presented on the timeline. Most emphasized that there were krewes "for everyone" in Mobile, listing not only the racially segregated krewes, but also krewes for "couples, singles, young people, and even alternative lifestyle groups." I assumed that last one was a reference to Osiris, which generally only made it into the diversity-of-krewes narrative at the very end—as an add-on. There seemed to be more wavering and uncertainty about discussing gay krewes than the blatant racial segregation of Mobile's Mardi Gras events. Tour guides used neutral, almost positive tones to describe racial segregation as they told visitors that "birds of a feather flock together" during Mardi Gras.

Certainly, it is *generally* unusual to see LGBTQ life and contributions represented in mainstream museums. Indeed, the museum displays about festivals were often the only places I saw LGBTQ contributions in Baton Rouge, San Antonio, and Mobile on display. I was also struck that day that the representation of Osiris, Mobile's first openly gay krewe, was so deeply embedded in the racist histories of Mardi Gras and the racialized spaces of Mobile's museum.

Commemorations and representations can be simultaneously exciting and unsatisfying for LGBTQ participants. I thought of this ambiguity as my research assistant, Danielle, and I interviewed a trio of Osiris members over a long, decadent meal at Ruth's Chris Steakhouse. What was supposed to be a solo interview turned into an hours-long group storytelling session. In the middle of the dinner, I asked Buck, Jimmy, and Todd (all middle-aged white gay men) whether it seemed Osiris was treated the same as other krewes in Mobile.

> BUCK: We are now. For years we were not included in any of the line-ups, you know the cups that have all the ball dates and stuff like that.
>
> JIMMY: We're in the museum.
>
> BUCK: The museum and the parade society. We are now . . .
>
> JIMMY: But for a number of years we weren't.
>
> BUCK: And in our twenty-fifth year, MCA gave us a plate commemorating it.
>
> TODD: And in the museum we're on their timeline since the 1980s.
>
> BUCK: We are actually listed on the list of balls in Mobile.

Buck remembered he squealed in delight when he found the Osiris ball listed alongside other ball dates on the little Carnival calendars, cups, and handouts found at local businesses. But other discussions about commemoration and acknowledgment were more emotionally mixed. Like many other Mobile LGBTQ participants, the men remarked on their limited representation in the Carnival Museum and their omission from documentaries on Mardi Gras. On another occasion, at the Krewe of Phoenix pool party, people told me that the Carnival Museum only included Osiris in its timeline five years before, at the insistence of a gay historian, and still refused to accept their royalty trains as donations for display. Josie, an older white lesbian and longtime member of Osiris, felt sure the twenty-fifth anniversary commemorative plaque was only presented because "someone in there thought it was important." Still she added, "it was really nice just to be recognized by a group that should be important to us." Her comment fit with the many LGBTQ people who felt ambivalent or tokenized by the scant recognition that came to their krewes. Jeremy, one younger white gay man, noted that "we are good enough for your entertainment to watch, but we're not quite good enough to be accepted into a Carnival Association really. But you can give us a [commemoration] plate saying 'ta-da.' So it's bittersweet. I can get bitter, but I'm not." Jeremy sensed elite boundary-making and seemed resigned to it.

One gay member of Osiris told me that space and access to venues was the only way that Osiris was treated the same as straight elite organizations, and that was because access to venues was organized by seniority. Osiris members expressed delight at this access, at their use of space in such a prominent place in the city. Unlike Pride events in all four cities, which were protested regularly by anti-LGBTQ protesters, the festival events I observed were never visibly targeted. However, krewes in both Mobile and Baton Rouge reported having had bomb threats at some of their balls in the 1980s and 1990s. Jimmy, a longtime Osiris member, recounted one year, in the early 1990s, when they had to make the difficult decision to move forward with their Mardi Gras ball, in spite of a bomb threat called in thirty minutes before guests were set to arrive. These bomb threats were part of violence and direct discrimination against any group seen as undermining the heterosexual and racial norms of Mobile's Mardi Gras.

In Mobile, festival traditions of racial segregation and expectations of heteronormativity stymied LGBTQ participants and organization members from being involved. Yet LGBTQ participants were not cowed into their "place" by these informal regulations. LGBTQ people pushed back on attempts by elites to police or taunt them into removing themselves from these spaces. LGBTQ groups like Osiris have worked their way onto ball calendars, major venues, and commemoration plaques.

Fiesta San Antonio

Unlike the more traditionalistic festivals of Mobile and Santa Fe, LGBTQ participants in Fiesta San Antonio had a long history of contestation with social elites over festival culture, including ongoing conflicts over space and recognition. These frictions rarely involved the gender policing at stake in the more traditionalistic festivals.

Recognizing Royalty and Official Events

The opening of the Fiesta San Antonio event, Cornyation, begins with the two masters of ceremony coming onto the stage. For several years in a row, these emcees have been Rick, a white gay man with a penchant for dramatic theatrical performances, and Elaine, a red-headed female journalist who has been King Anchovy (Cornyation royalty) in the past. They joke at the start of each performance that it is "yet another year that we are an official Fiesta event," often feigning surprise that the Fiesta Commission has not kicked them out yet or that Cornyation is *still* an official event.

Being "official" is important in San Antonio. Events sanctioned by the Fiesta Commission are often supported by the commission's insurance, promotion, and authorization, setting them apart from the dozens of unofficial festival events in a way that becomes a badge of honor. During Cornyation cast parties, backstage between shows, and in my interviews, event participants often mentioned their official event status. Older participants, for instance, emphasized that, when Cornyation was re-started in the 1980s, it took *forever* to become an official event. The first advertisement for 1982 Cornyation ran in the local gay newspaper, *The Calendar*, and stated firmly (perhaps inaccurately) that it was an "official event of Fiesta 1982." Whether or not that was true, Cornyation participants spoke a lot about when they became an official event, how long or laborious that process had been, and whether they were going to remain an official event. These discussions were symbolic of their incorporation or marginalization in the festival and city more broadly: When participants engaged with "being official," they were discussing whether the Fiesta Commission was treating Cornyation the same as other festival events, unfairly penalizing it for being too bawdy and campy, or trying to push it out—to assert the event did not actually belong in the festival.

This treatment of the show by the Fiesta Commission fit into a long history of race, access, and recognition during the festival. At the start of each Cornyation show, the emcees announce which Fiesta royalty are visiting the show that evening. Typically, they point out one of the two major male Fiesta royalty, King Antonio or Rey Feo. Both kings come with their own entourage of followers, black SUVs, and police escorts, and each has an official schedule by which they attend major, official Fiesta events. The two kings, however, have different histories. King Antonio is elected by the predominately white Cavaliers, a festival organization that also hosts a river parade. Rey Feo was developed as a counter to the racially exclusive King Antonio and was considered the "ugly king" or the "people's king" representing the Latinx community in San Antonio. Rey Feo was created by the League of United Latin American Citizens (LULAC) Council Number Two in San Antonio in the 1940s to raise money for education scholarships,[54] but did not gain recognition from the Fiesta Commission until 1980, amid broader demands to recognize royalty in the Latinx and Black communities. So, at Cornyation, when the emcees introduce the male royalty, there are multiple symbols at play: They are emphasizing the importance of Cornyation by pointing out that it is being visited by the royalty, but they are simultaneously pointing to the festival's history of racist hierarchies.

Official organizations often uphold heteronormativity and racism in their community during festival time, yet Fiesta San Antonio's Commission was the least restrictive about race and sexuality among the contemporary festivals I studied. Some of the gay and lesbian commission members reported having positive experiences serving on the Commission. And Cornyation was not the only official event serving the LGBTQ community. There was also the WEBB Party, a fundraiser run by the San Antonio AIDS Foundation, and the Chili Queens Chili Cookoff, a food competition hosted mostly by drag queens at the Bonham Exchange, a historic gay bar. As the website for Fiesta San Antonio put it in 2019: "Each chili must be represented by a queen. Being glamorous won't win you this competition! We are looking for a queen who redefines the 'tacky'! The man or woman who can get the crowd to say 'wow that's tacky!' will be given the one-and-only Whoochie award."[55] The Fiesta Commission has even approached the LGBTQ organizers of some unofficial events to encourage them to apply. Organizers explained they declined due to concerns about size of the event, autonomy, and, according to one LGBTQ organizer, morality regulation by the commission, although the commission does not seem to regulate Cornyation's bawdiness.

In the few instances that I saw overt challenges by the Fiesta Commission to LGBTQ events, it involved things such as LGBTQ-event ephemera like medals not being sold in the festival commission's store due to being too explicit, including my illustrated book on Cornyation. Much like Osiris in Mobile, Cornyation was recognized on a major anniversary (its fiftieth). However, one of the board members complained to me that it took some wrangling and initiative on the part of Cornyation to get Fiesta Commission members to attend.

More Queens Than Expected

Just as in Mobile, San Antonio's major royalty are regulated by race, class, and gender, and, along with elite organizations, have strong expectations of adherence to the glass closet. This city's major royalty are the previously mentioned King Antonio, along with the Queen of the Order; Rey Feo has, however, nearly eclipsed King Antonio in popularity. Even in majority Hispanic San Antonio, Queen of the Order of the Alamo has been an Anglo young woman for the past century, and only in 2016 did the Cavaliers organization elect their first Mexican American King Antonio.[56] In several interviews, gay and heterosexual members of elite organizations in San Antonio described the operation of privilege around the MGMs, older white closeted elites. Perhaps the best example was the Order of the Alamo, which hosts the major Coronation in San Antonio under the Lord High Chamberlain. During the coronation of the duchesses and queen, the Lord High Chamberlain takes the stage theatrically in white gloves, a cape, and a top hat, while a small group of men colloquially called "the duchess pushers" prepare the court to promenade down the runway. A few interviewees suggested to me that these positions were frequently outlets for MGMs who wished to express their artistry during Fiesta.

Cornyation, on the other hand, began as a satire of the Coronation of the Queen of the Order of the Alamo in 1951. Its first script was written by a gay white member of the social elite who, in later years, performed as the Lord High Chamberlain. The first fourteen years of show were performed at a major outdoor theater venue as entertainment during a food-related festival. At the height of the show's popularity in the mid-1960s, more than eight thousand people attended the show in one week.[57] In the early years, the script was enthusiastically focused on satirizing social elite rituals, debutantes, corrupt local politics, and the cultural conservation society using campy, coded language. When the show was revived in the 1980s, this sense of poking fun at social elites remained vibrant.

There are still ongoing contestations about space. The first year I worked backstage at Cornyation was also the year that the Coronation of the Queen of the Order of the Alamo, the all-white debutante pageant run by the social elites of the city, moved to the stage next door. At the Cornyation party the weekend before the event, Cornyation performers watched videos of the Coronation debutante pageantry on a living room television, remarking on both how boring and how fancy it seemed. One of the stagehands had participated in the Coronation as a teenager and narrated as we watched: "She's wearing her Daddy's wealth, that one," the stagehand commented when a small young woman on the screen could barely pull her heavy, rhinestoned train down the runway.

In downtown San Antonio, the adjoining Majestic and Empire Theatres share a backstage area, divided by a door that was kept shut during the show days. So, at the Cornyation pre-party and later, backstage during the show, rumors flew fast. Some said the Order of the Alamo was having the backstage doors guarded so that drag queens would not mix with their young debutante queens ("they had everything but the army reserve out there with their M-16s," insisted one stagehand), others that the event had stolen Cornyation's parking and dressing rooms. Coronation, they whispered, had even tried to have Cornyation moved to a different venue, but the venue owners refused.

Separation was, sometimes, blatant. The smoking area outside the backstage doors was partitioned into two separate areas: in one, six-foot-tall drag queens in Twinkie costumes and women covered in glitter smoked between shows, and in the other, old white men in tuxedos smoked anxiously. The cast t-shirts and bags for that year had a clever logo with Coronation in the shadow of the Cornyation with the tagline "More Queens Than You Expected," drawing parallels between the Queen of the Order of the Alamo and the drag queens and duchesses of their neighboring event.

On the night before the show, a lesbian stage crew member told me she had been checking out the downstairs backstage area and found a heap of Cornyation props and costumes piled in the hallway outside a dressing room. The mother of one of the Coronation duchesses thought their dressing room was too small and had simply moved over to the Cornyation side. The stage crew member insisted they move back to the Majestic's backstage area, purportedly responding to her protestations by warning, "you don't understand at all, that this is going to happen, and you're going to do it with my help or you're going to do it listening to the [gay] queen whose stuff this belongs to." I giggled as I imagined a drag queen or flaming designer berating a debutante's mother, arms full of her daughter's gaudy Festival accouterments.

Regardless of their veracity, these rumors demonstrate the symbolic significance of space and access to venues in these important civic celebrations. The LGBTQ festival events had used venues ranging from the organizer's father's backyard to a gay bar to the largest convention center in town. Though the rise to prominence and recognition brought Cornyation into more visible venues, designers and fans from the 1980s waxed nostalgic about the intimacy and community created in the overcrowded barroom at the Bonham Exchange. Smaller, private venues can be a source of community-building and mutual protection so often harder to cultivate once social elites have granted conditional acceptance onto larger stages.

Baton Rouge Mardi Gras

Mardi Gras in Baton Rouge is the least traditionalistic festival of the four case studies in this book. It has no coordinating committee or association controlling festival events and promotion, nor are there major royalty in this small and decentralized festival. Even so, I witnessed ongoing contestation over space and venues.

Being in major spaces in the center of the city was an example of being "treated the same" for some group members. The three largest LGBTQ festival events—Osiris, Apollo, and Cornyation—had had multiple venues over the course of their history and now all used some of the prime major venues in the heart of the urban downtown area. This history of venues was narrated by group members as a sign of success and progress following years of struggle. According to a longtime member of the Krewe of Apollo, "our first ball, we couldn't get a venue, because who would rent to a gay person?" They ended up renting a banquet room in a small catering business owned by a business connection of a krewe member. In just a few years, Apollo's event outgrew the cramped banquet hall. For the next ten years, they rented a Black union hall in the town of Plaquemine, a majority Black suburb of Baton Rouge. It was the only venue in town that was large enough and willing to rent to them in the 1980s. A senior member of the krewe explained that "we met a guy who was gay who managed it" and "thought it was great, because we wouldn't want to do a gay ball in Baton Rouge, but we could go out of town and do a gay ball just 30 minutes away."

In retrospect, Krewe members had mixed feelings about Plaquemine. They described driving across a long, icy bridge to get to the winter event, but also how getting away from the city of Baton Rouge meant more freedom, more privacy and confidentiality. Using a hall in a Black suburb as a refuge fits within a larger American history of white gay men visiting Black spaces in which to enact some sexual freedom, such as bars in Harlem, New York.[58] But after Plaquemine, the krewe used several other venues, including the fairgrounds, where members reported that the staff of "mostly rednecks" liked working with them.

In the 2010s, the Krewe of Apollo moved their ball to a huge civic center, sandwiched downtown between the casino and the World War II museum on the banks of the Mississippi River. Larry, a long-standing krewe member of Apollo, recalled:

> [W]e worked our way up into this expensive 20-something-thousand-dollar civic center that we had to get into, you know? So it took a great effort to do it, but—and we're locked in here now, and this is the best thing for us. We're the biggest thing in the city, and we're locked in four years ahead already, the date for the future balls. You work your way into a seniority thing, and we're like third in line to pick our ball date . . . and everybody rents to gays now. We can go anywhere and have parties. Vendors now rent to anybody that has the money to pay for it.

While performing at the major venue is described as an accomplishment, seniority in access to space was tempered by the discrete regulations white social elites placed around certain high-profile spaces.

The Krewe of Apollo in Baton Rouge occupies one of two event spaces at the River Center downtown; the other is occupied by a white wealthy Baton Rouge krewe that hosts a ball on the same night. Some comments vividly reminded me of the placement of Coronation and Cornyation, side-by-side, including commentary that the Krewe of Apollo Ball was more fun and better decorated.

Issues of race, queerness, and belonging in space came up in accounts of the River Center. Lamar, a young Black Apollo member, was briefly disoriented when he accidentally walked into the other krewe's ballroom during the morning setup time before the ball. "I came through the wrong door," he told me. "I went through their side and they were, like, an all-white krewe, and I'm walking in with my feathers and stuff." He laughed nervously as the other krewe's members turned to stare. "I think I'm in the wrong section," he said, backing out. Lamar's nervous laugh reminds me of the complexity of Black entry into predominately white spaces. His emphasis that he went through the wrong side of the ballroom, "their side," the side of the all-white krewe, signaled to me that he felt Black out of place. He used the word "wrong" twice, signaling that he entered a space that was implicitly forbidden to him. He emphasized that not only was he in white space, but he was carrying an armful of feathers for the backpiece he was making for the tableau, marking him as queer as well. In a white-only space, Lamar's Blackness and feather-bedecked queerness created a jarring, if momentary, dislocation—a reminder of what it meant to stay in one's place. A reminder that his festival was, perhaps, not *the* festival.

On Homonormativity and Belonging

One recurring theme throughout these accounts of access and acknowledgment is feeling out of place and/or yearning for belonging. This yearning for belonging was especially poignant in Santa Fe and Mobile, where festival traditions were often restrictive and exclusive. This chapter opened with Paul, who expressed that longing for belonging as the seamstress of Our Lady and attempt to incorporate himself into the traditions of his Santa Fe Hispano Catholic community. The story of Doug is one of a Hispano gay man who as a child longed to be Don Diego.

Queer scholarship often ignores the way that LGBTQ people crave access to long-standing cultural traditions; researchers dismiss these desires as desperation for assimilation, expressions of internalized homophobia, or acquiescence to homonormativity.[59] Geographer Gavin Brown suggests that this attention to homonormativity denigrates the lives of "ordinary" gay men and lesbians, privileging instead metropolitan ideas about queer politics that often emerge from a privileged position.[60] I agree with Brown that we need to take seriously the lives of "ordinary" LGBTQ people. In this case of festival histories, I approach these questions of access and acknowledgment by attending to the ways people living in these cities understood them. Not only a queer scholar, but a qualitative one, I am, after all, interested in people's complex experiences. Instead, I felt in these stories about access the joy and contentment of belonging. I think of how Buck squealed in delight when Osiris was listed alongside the other balls and events in Mobile, how LGBTQ participants described with a smirk on their faces their event as more fun and less "boring" than elite events, and how LGBTQ events that took place in major venues were a source of pride for participants and attendees.

There were also acute feelings of pain and exclusion. Gaining access and acknowledgment *is* often about joining mainstream institutions like the military and marriage, which simultaneously feed systems of race, class, and gender inequality while providing benefits like employment, rights, and recognition to selective members of the community. In this study these desires for belonging run up against elite gatekeeping over festival rituals. The LGBTQ access and recognition I saw within these four cities' urban festivals were highly conditional: inclusion in elite organizations and events nearly always required remaining in the glass closet. Elite lesbian, gay, and bisexual people who were "tacit subjects" and willing to be less vocal about their sexuality could have access to more roles. Even then, gay men operating tacitly were gender policed with references to their supposed gender non-conformity, called "La Reina" and allocated the pink float during parades. Even in the less elite-controlled festivals of Fiesta San Antonio and Baton Rouge Mardi Gras, LGBTQ participants described contestation for space with elites or feeling distinctly out of place in elite spaces. Additionally, for Black LGBTQ people during Mardi Gras, all-white elite organizations intentionally excluded them and reinforced a sense of being Black out of place in the city. Regardless of how tacit Black LGBTQ people were about their sexuality, histories of racial segregation and segregated spaces during festivals persisted in both cities. These experiences of conditional access and acknowledgment dampened LGBTQ participants' sense of belonging and recognition in the city.

On Access and Acknowledgment

Like most festival processes in this book, access and acknowledgment for LGBTQ people during festivals is mostly symbolic and cultural. At times, it involves access to social networks and resources like space. *Access* was a sign that LGBTQ people were welcome in the festival and thus in the broader city. *Acknowledgment* reflected my respondents' deep desire for progress, acceptance, and belonging. Access and acknowledgment are corrections from decades of being "out of place" in some city spaces.

Being included in these respects is inherently comparative, requiring a referent "other" in the form, most typically here, of each city's most elite organizations, but also festivals' broader base of heterosexual participants. LGBTQ interviewees did compare their treatment to other festival groups, particularly elite ones. And when those books seem balanced, the processes of access and acknowledgment can fill some of the "recognition gap" described by Lamont, even within a geography of festival space that is organized by race, gender, and class.[61]

Access and acknowledgment may remedy questions about the moral worth of LGBTQ citizens of the city. However, requirements for heteronormativity in social elite organizations reinforce the notion that LGBTQ people are not morally worthy citizens. During festival time, LGBTQ residents had other ways of proving their moral worth as citizens even when denied access and acknowledgment by social elites. In the next chapter, I analyze how LGBTQ participants in festivals engaged in fundraising as a kind of benevolent aid that often bested similar fundraising work of elites.

6

Fundraising and Benevolent Aid

On Taking Care of Our Own

My flesh is sticking painfully to the seats at The Friendly Spot—it's June. In Texas. The Friendly Spot is an outdoor icehouse in San Antonio's Southtown. It's owned by couple Jody Bailey Newman and Steve Newman, who were crowned royalty of Cornyation the year before (the honor is usually bestowed upon local figures outside the Cornyation community, like the Newmans). Staffers from BEAT AIDS and a trio of college students sit nearby, all of us waiting in the muggy afternoon for the ceremony to begin. On behalf of her organization, BEAT AIDS director Michelle Durham stands to receive an $80,000 check from Cornyation—an influx of funds that will keep this smaller ASO afloat for another year. The director of San Antonio AIDS Foundation (SAAF), arriving late after being stuck in traffic, also remarks at the importance of the $80,000 check his organization receives: It is more money than SAAF raised at their own Fiesta event, the WEBB Party, and will be instrumental in keeping SAAF going. The three college students rise to accept individual checks, the Robert Rehm Theatre Arts Scholarship for the performing arts, from the eponymous Robert Rehm, a paraplegic local, and longtime Cornyation designer.

Fundraising was a part of Fiesta San Antonio. Fiesta San Antonio is branded as "a party with a purpose,"[1] and every official Fiesta event raises money for a local organization or charitable cause. It did not surprise me that most of this Cornyation fundraising was for ASOs, particularly for ones that explicitly serve the LGBTQ community. Many LGBTQ community fundraisers focus on HIV and ASOs, in part due to the long history of government neglect and underfunding.[2] Fundraising for ASOs is one way that LGBTQ people engage in mutual or benevolent aid, aid between community members that is largely unmet by existing social systems.[3] In this chapter I demonstrate how this fundraising relied on festival traditions and established respectability for some LGBTQ participants, but mostly I emphasize the ways that this fundraising was focused on mutual or benevolent aid, as a way of taking care of their own community.

Respectability and Benevolent Aid

In two of my four case studies, fundraising was central to LGBTQ participation in the festivals. Charity is a "semi-autonomous field of social relationships and cultural practices"[4] that operates within the larger cultural structures of festivals. Some festivals even make fundraising part of their values or ethos. Each year, Fiesta San Antonio brings in hundreds of thousands of dollars for local scholarships and non-profit organizations. The LGBTQ-run events that seem to proliferate during Fiesta San Antonio—from the drag show Fiesta Frenzy to the drag queen chili cook-off—focus their efforts on donations to LGBTQ causes. This fundraising creates both visibility and a reliable funding stream for LGBTQ-related issues. In Baton Rouge, Mardi Gras events function as fundraisers, too, though it is not part of the city tradition. Thus, both the Spanish Town parade and Krewe of Apollo ball raise funds, but their fundraising tends to be unpublicized and entirely focused on taking care of one's own. My other case sites are less tied to fundraising as a primary (or even secondary) purpose, yet in Mobile, many Carnival organizations engage in donation-gathering events throughout the year and, in Santa Fe, the burning of Zozobra operates as a major fundraiser for youth causes. This festival fundraising operated under multiple recognition logics. Philanthropy can be translated into recognition and status enhancement.[5] Charitable fundraising events can be part of a broader status intensification, differentiating the haves from the have-nots.

And yes, it would be easy to interpret the fundraising I witnessed as *strictly* about respectability politics; instead, I argue, LGBTQ participants' intensive fundraising efforts are also about bringing benevolent aid to their own community. Fundraising does allow marginalized groups to fill the recognition gap with a politics of respectability, or the demonstration of worthiness through respectability and morality such as work ethics, caring ethos, or the performance of "good works."[6] The easiest route to respectability would be to only highlight the most morally upright parts of the LGBTQ community publicly. Erving Goffman described "covering" as this act of stigmatized or discredited individuals downplaying differences in order to be less obtrusive.[7] That is, marginalized groups become more "respectable" if they downplay the ways they are different. More recently, law scholar Kenji Yoshino has equated covering with a "hidden assault on our civil rights," as even individuals who have fought for and won legal rights may be expected to obscure their differences in order to be perceived as deserving of those rights.[8] In the fight for same-sex marriage rights, for example, LGBTQ organizers frequently stressed the ways that same-sex couples were similar to male-female couples, emphasizing commitment, love, monogamy, and child-rearing.[9] When fundraising was a cultural value within the festivals I studied in Baton Rouge and San Antonio, members of fundraising LGBTQ festival organizations gained recognition as industrious and community minded—respectable contributors who use their time and talents on behalf of the community.[10]

Recognition for respectability through fundraising prowess, in this way, becomes part of the creation of moral boundaries that determine social membership and belonging. Distinctions about who is morally worthy of social membership are framed as meaningful differences between groups, creating a morally worthy "us" and an unworthy "them." Cultural membership often involves drawing such moral boundaries between groups as a way of vying for respectability and valuation.[11] In her work on race and culture, for example, Michèle Lamont identifies moral boundaries around being hard-working and responsible and how these operate as a form of racism for white working-class men.[12]

In respectable fundraising, LGBTQ groups become part of the morally worthy "us." For LGBTQ people in the South, being recognized as morally worthy—part of the local "us" and respectable contributors to the community—may counterbalance religious traditionalists who marginalize LGBTQ people as immoral or unworthy.[13] In San Antonio, where LGBTQ group members operated alongside philanthropic and social elites, their fundraising industriousness was sometimes used to draw moral boundaries that make LGBTQ people superior to social elites. Fundraising can operate as a moral good especially when directed at deserving subjects.[14] Some charity efforts express morality of human values by promising to "restore a nostalgic community" or "forge a community among contributors."[15] In Cornyation and the Krewe of Apollo, this manifested in moral boundaries involving the virtues of the organizations and people involved in them. The fundraising prowess was also used to construct moral boundaries that differentiate gay fundraising from other festival organizations.

Again, though, respectability politics, in my research, did not emerge as the primary motivation for fundraising for LGBTQ festival groups. LGBTQ groups did not engage in fundraising to earn respect. Instead, I saw a focus on the ethos of taking care of one's own, caring for their own dispossessed and neglected community members. Such mutual or benevolent aid is typically focused on serving an organization's or community's members and their dependents, often those that have been neglected by the government and other social institutions. At times, this aid expanded outward to other vulnerable members of the community, but most fundraising was centered on taking care of one's own.

One of the most documented types of festival fundraising is the longstanding relationship between second line parades and the social aid and pleasure clubs (SAPCs) that form the foundation of Black Carnival traditions in New Orleans. SAPCs are part of a *gemeinschaft* model of fundraising often adopted by immigrant communities and other marginalized groups. In New Orleans, SAPCs that emerged out of Freedman Societies and fraternal organizations began as dues-paying clubs that assisted Black working-class ward members with emergency, medical, living, and funeral expenses.[16] From these, Black Carnival associations such as The Zulu Social Aid and Pleasure Club, the most well-known Black Carnival organization in New Orleans, grew.[17] These mutual assistance societies focused on fundraising to benefit the immediate community. For example, the K-Doe Baby Dolls, a small group within the long New Orleans Carnival tradition of Black women dressed as baby dolls parading, are a SAPC donating money and time to causes like homelessness and support of local music.[18]

In Baton Rouge and San Antonio, the LGBTQ community focused festival fundraising for ASOs or individuals with HIV—causes that, for the participants, were personal and highly important. In most of the cities, fundraising occurred for individual LGBTQ community members who were economically vulnerable. This chapter will attend, in particular, to the ways LGBTQ groups work throughout festival season fundraisers to "take care of our own."

San Antonio: Besting Elites at Fundraising

On my desk there are three Fiesta medals. They have lingered there since 2018, among the detritus of academic swag from conferences, post-it notes, and snacks. Festival celebrants buy, trade, and collect these small metal pins, wearing them on huge sashes or vests during the festival, and an official contest rewards the wearer of the heaviest sash: the Fiesta Medal Weigh-In. Both fundraising tool and advertisement, these medals highlight city organizations, politicians, and causes. The first pin on my desk is from The Center, the small, mostly volunteer-run Pride Center of San Antonio. For the past three years I have collaborated with the executive director of the Pride Center, Robert Salcido, Jr., on a research project on LGBTQ resilience in San Antonio, and I got this pin from him at a meeting of our project community advisory board. The top of the pin has rainbow cloth folded over with a small metal pendant dangling down. On the pendant, line drawings depict two figures: The larger wears a rainbow sombrero-style hat, the smaller holds a maraca in the pink, blue, and white colors of the transgender pride flag. In 2019, the Pride Center sold around 350 medals; at about $5 profit per medal, these tokens are a boost to the small organization's annual fundraising efforts.[19]

The second medal on my desk is also rainbow-topped with a dangling fob. This one is a metal rectangle that looks like a lotería card, a Mexican bingo card with a picture, name in Spanish, and a number. The picture is of Rosie Gonzalez, a Latina lawyer in chunky glasses, spiky salt-and-pepper hair, and a suit and tie. The name on the medal is "LA JUEZ" (the judge, masculine version). Engraved on the back are the words "Grass Roots Fiesta 2018." During the Pride festival in June 2018, Gonzalez was running her second (ultimately successful) grassroots campaign for a position as a Bexar County Judge—when I received the medal, not at Fiesta but at Pride, I assumed that it was a festival leftover, but it may have been a tangible symbol of Gonzalez's adamancy that her campaign would not involve expensive, slick ad campaigns, but grassroots connections.[20] That is to say, adopting a Fiesta medal to tout her campaign may have both raised funds and signaled that, like festival fundraising efforts, the money was going to a cause that would truly help the people.

The third pin has a pink topper and its fob looks like an intersection of two streets, framed by a rainbow crosswalk. In the center, it says, "My Pride Crosswalk Fiesta 2018 San Antonio." On the back, engraved in small print, is "Councilmember Roberto C. Treviño District 1 thestripsa.com." I purchased this pin from one of Treviño's staff members at our community advisory board meeting at the Pride Center. It was a creative fundraising effort to right a perceived wrong: When the city balked at the cost of installing a Pride Crosswalk in "the Strip," an area of LGBTQ-owned businesses and bars slightly north of downtown, business owners and District 1 Councilmember Treviño responded by raising $10,000—enough to have the crosswalk installed before the 2018 Pride Festival.[21] The medal directly helped achieve a symbol—the rainbow crosswalk—that has become increasingly common as a way of placemaking in gayborhoods (LGBTQ neighborhoods).[22]

Fundraising is a visible and expected part of Fiesta San Antonio, whose tagline is "Party with a Purpose." Fundraising ranges from the medals to reserved bandstand seating that raises funds for scouts and high schools to major fundraisers that fund the ongoing work of non-profit organizations. Many of the Fiesta events are fundraisers run by non-profits (with more than one hundred accepting donations for scholarships and other causes), but almost all Fiesta events have a "giving" component to support a local charitable cause. According to one newspaper report, "it takes a small army of non-profits to bring Fiesta to life,"[23] LGBTQ non-profits among them.

Accordingly, Fiesta events run by LGBTQ individuals were fundraising machines, raising money for children's welfare programs, the local LGBTQ archive, ASOs, LGBTQ youth groups and shelters, and non-profits that serve the LGBTQ community. And it's not just the annual Fiesta ball, Midnight in the Garden of Good and Evil, which brings in money for the Fiesta Youth program. Small, unofficial fundraisers are hosted by LGBTQ people in their backyards. During my research on Fiesta San Antonio, I attended numerous unofficial Fiesta events that operated outside of the purview of the Fiesta Commission. These unofficial LGBTQ events included a major drag show called Fiesta Frenzy performed mostly by Black and Latinx drag queens from across the South to raise money for San Antonio LGBTQ organizations and people. Its beneficiaries included the LGBTQ student group at a local community college and a member of the San Antonio drag community who could not work due to health problems. The emcees, two Latinx queens, actively fundraised during the show, walking through the audience with a huge hat for donations, pressing the audience between acts to reach a dollar amount before the next act, and dumping the dollars on a small table on the side of the stage where volunteers conspicuously counted the money throughout the night. Across the city, in its northern reaches, a large household of gay men on a spacious property regularly sponsored a fundraising event called Project Fiesta, in which participants paid money for t-shirts, grab bags, and silent auction items for local causes. The first year I attended, the event raised money for Any Baby Can, a non-profit family organization unrelated to LGBTQ issues.

The two biggest fundraisers for the LGBTQ community during Fiesta San Antonio are Cornyation and the WEBB Party, an evening event of music, food, and guests in elaborate, themed costumes, to raise funds for the San Antonio AIDS Foundation (SAAF), which grew out of the gay bar community as a response to a void of state support and care. The WEBB party began as a private fundraiser in 1993, hosted mostly by Anglo and Latino gay and bisexual men raising money for AIDS services as the pandemic reached critical impact. According to one of the original organizers, the WEBB event grew out of gay-themed Fiesta parties like Mentenniel and an underwear party held at the gay bar Casino Club in the early 1990s, as well as the Octopus Club, a major men's AIDS fundraising collective in Austin (80 miles north) that benefitted ASOs. The name of the WEBB Party came from an Ethiopian proverb that "When spiders unite, they can tie down a lion." The first printed invitations had a typo—an extra "B"—and it stuck. A group of Latino and Anglo gay men, along with a few women, got together as official hosts, hand-delivering the first year's invitations. The WEBB Party would remain invite-only for a few years, with attendees in Fiesta costumes raising money for SAAF, the first grassroots ASO in San Antonio.[24] As the party grew over the years, ownership passed to SAAF, where it remains a significant part of the organization's annual fundraising. The WEBB Party is one night of dancing, performances, silent auction, food tasting, and costuming according to the year's theme (say, 1990s-style vogue or

Alice in Wonderland). In 2004, the WEBB Party was recognized as an official Fiesta event and it now raises up to $100,000 for SAAF each year.

During that same time period, in the early 1990s, long-standing Fiesta organization Cornyation shifted from fundraising for the San Antonio Little Theater, the theater company that started the event in the 1950s, to raising funds for external causes. They focused particularly on local ASOs and charities serving youth.[25] When I interviewed Latino and Anglo gay men who became involved in the show in the 1990s, many stressed that supporting HIV/AIDS charities was a big part of the reason they joined.

By the 2000s, Cornyation had become a fundraising force. With a volunteer crew selling t-shirts, seats, tables, and advance tickets to the event, Cornyation was raising more than $100,000 each year, almost all of which went directly to charities. By 2016, the show had cumulatively raised more than $2 million for local charities, including the ASOs, a LGBTQ youth shelter, counseling services for middle school students, other health-related organizations, and theater arts scholarships.

The sheer scale of Cornyation fundraising became a critical part of the ethos and values of the organization. It was often used by participants to establish the event's respectability and to create moral boundaries between Cornyation cast members and the non-profit foundations run by social elites. In fact, more than any other LGBTQ fiesta organization I interviewed, Cornyation participants told me they frequently engaged with social elites—and were most likely to articulate moral boundaries distinguishing their group from those other efforts. Cornyation practically shared a backstage with the social elite event The Coronation of the Queen of the Order of the Alamo and was listed as a major Fiesta event alongside other major events mostly run by elite organizations, yet it retained its sense of "outsider" status as an explicitly LGBTQ group participating in Fiesta.

The scale and focus of this fundraising were enormous sources of pride for Cornyation cast members I spoke with in the course of my research. Apart from the union stage crew, who are hired for the show, Cornyation performers repeatedly bragged that "no one gets paid," focusing my attention on the show's efforts to keep expenses low and donate as much money as possible to charity each year. The designers who organized each sketch comedy act were even responsible for coming up with the money and materials they needed on their own often by fundraising on a smaller level to cover those expenses. As a Cornyation board member put it, "They don't get paid, nobody gets paid for this, so you're donating your time, your money. The designers who aren't so good at prolific fundraising come out of pocket for a lot of this stuff. So these are people, great people, who are dedicated to doing something significant for the community." Philanthropy and dedication together establish the participants as "great people" contributing good works for good causes during festivals.

Cornyation participants contrasted their fundraising with other Fiesta events, pointing toward their frugality. They were less indulgent than other groups when it came to extravagances like fancy medals and car entourages, they insisted. One Cornyation board member remarked that "our royalty pays for their own parking," in stark comparison to the multi-car entourage and police escort afforded to major Fiesta royalty. Cornyation participants showed me the elaborate medals made by the major Fiesta royalty. Prime among them were the medals made by the El Rey Feo, a festival royalty "elected" by crowning the person who raised the most funds for a Hispanic college scholarship.[26] When cast and board members critiqued other Fiesta events, they often focused on the most elite ones, including the Coronation of the Queen of the Order of the Alamo, an Anglo debutante pageant performed in a theater next door to and concurrent with the Cornyation. Their event, Cornyation participants enthused, was far more fun, exciting, and dedicated to fundraising.

Cornyation participants have a long history of positioning their show as anti-elite and democratic, an event of the "common people." Simultaneously, they elevate their event as a sophisticated, gay critique of the status quo.[27] In the 2000s and 2010s, these moral boundaries identified Cornyation participants as *better* fundraisers than social elites as the show became a fundraising powerhouse for ASOs and other important causes.

Baton Rouge: Our Own Charity

The first time I went to a Krewe of Apollo ball, I was early. I was among the first people through the open doors, passing by a line of club officers greeting guests. As I moved toward the inner sanctum, the large space in which the ball would be held, a younger, associate krewe member sold me a small red-ribbon plastic pin that blinks. The packaging labeled it "Blink the Night Away," a fundraiser for the group's charitable foundation Apollo AIDS/Crisis Fund. Twenty dollars later, I affixed the pin to my tuxedo lapel and entered the ball. I immediately noted a large runway extending down the center of the large room—flanked by a clear plastic container shaped like a memorial ribbon and scattered with cash and coins. In the krewe president's opening speech, he emphasized that the evening was about fun and fellowship, but also fundraising. It seemed clear that the aim was to make sure the memorial ribbon—as well as the Apollo AIDS/Crisis Fund—was overflowing with funds by the end of the night.

Baton Rouge Mardi Gras traditions do not center fundraising in the way San Antonio's Fiesta does. Still, two of the Baton Rouge Carnival organizations with gay origins are visible and active charitable organizations. Mystic Krewe for the Preservation of Lagniappe in Louisiana (SPLL) is the full name of the 501(c)(3) non-profit organization that puts on fundraisers including the Spanish Town Mardi Gras parade, ball, and golf tournament and raises money through membership and parade dues. SPLL was developed in 1984 through the creation of the Spanish Town parade, and the term "lagniappe" is a French Acadian term that technically refers to a small gift given to a customer at the time of purchase, such as a complementary bowl of soup with an entree. But more broadly, *lagniappe* channels understandings of unexpected gifts or benefits and links the Krewe's event to the Acadiana region of Louisiana and Cajun culture.

In 2018, SPLL donated $120,000 to local causes, on par with other years' giving, mostly to non-LGBTQ causes. David, an older white man who helped run the board, said board members have some discretion in selecting the charities each year; choosing a preferred charity foundation was a celebrated part of board participation. David's son, who I met in passing while painting wooden flamingo cutouts bright pink, has cerebral palsy. In his honor, the Krewe was a gold-level contributor to a developmental learning center that he attended as a child. Wherever I interviewed people who parade in the Spanish Town, they emphasized the visibility and importance of the charity work their group was doing.

For gay men in the Krewe of Apollo, fundraising created a public profile—both for the group and individual members—of giving to and caring for their valuable communities. The Krewe of Apollo AIDS/Crisis

Fund began in 1993 and gives grants to individuals and families facing financial crisis. The fund emerged from the informal support group members had already undertaken: pitching in to help friends who often had few other social supports. At the time of my research, only one original founding member was still alive; many had passed of AIDS-related illnesses or other health issues. I interviewed Larry about the history of the AIDS/Crisis Fund before his death:

> I never thought about [the Krewe] being a legacy or anything. It's like, we did it for fun. We were a little private club that pooled our resources to have a good time. And we didn't think about our organization, in the beginning, as being something that we did for charity and for good for other people. We were raising money to have a party, you know? Then, when the HIV/AIDS thing came along within our first five years, we had our own members that were dying, right there in our faces, and most of them back then, because of the closeted thing and the lack of government help in the beginning and stuff, they just literally were being thrown out of their houses. They had no income. And so we started pooling our money together, like, "Our friend so-and-so needs his rent paid this month." Well, we even talked about, "We can't afford costumes for a ball. Let's help our friends for a couple of years, and when this is over, we go back to costuming." Which never had to happen, but it started in that, and then from there, when we realized how many thousands we were putting together amongst ourselves to help our friends, we said, "Let's make this a thing." So, we started our AIDS/Crisis Fund, and that was mostly to help our own.

Larry explicitly framed the Krewe's support within the context of social stigma and government neglect.[28] In the 1980s, the government neglect of AIDS funding and support led to the growth of mutual aid networks, fundraising and ASOs run by LGBTQ community members.[29] There is a long and colorful history of gay men using performance, theater, and drag to fundraise for AIDS, but the AIDS/Crisis Fund grew out of mutual support networks cobbled together to "help our own."

Today, the AIDS/Crisis Fund has expanded to help the entire community, even those not living with HIV/AIDS. For example, one krewe member had a neighbor who was a single mother fighting cancer, and the Krewe of Apollo came to her aid. My interviews with krewe members were full of stories like this—about people helped by the fund, neighbors or co-workers whose insurance deductible or rent was paid as they endured medical crises and job loss.

The Krewe of Apollo members were not searching for respectability and recognition when they began the AIDS/Crisis Fund. They were not jockeying with elites or positioning themselves as extraordinary fundraisers, but the growth and visibility of the fund soon positioned the krewe as a major player among the city's charitable organizations. According to one of the Black krewe members, "we're trying to evolve the krewe into something different and not just being a gay krewe that puts on a Mardi Gras ball every year, but being a gay krewe that does different things for the community. And we have a presence in the community and different things like that." The Baton Rouge newspapers report on the Krewe's philanthropy throughout the year, right there alongside debutante balls and museum fundraisers, in the social column. In articles about church potlucks and Pride parades, Krewe of Apollo men are described as philanthropists and members of a gay organization. Most notably, newspaper obituaries frequently highlight the decedents' participation as members of the Krewe of Apollo.

The AIDS/Crisis Fund was a stepping-stone toward respectability laid through ongoing, earnest charitable work. One white krewe member described how "The thing about the krewe is we do help out people, but we don't limit it just to gay people. We had a family that we didn't even know—a friend of mine's family—and they lost everything in a fire, everything they had. So the krewe helped them out by going to Walmart and getting basic things." One krewe member Chuck described the outcomes of this charitable work, including allowing the krewe to be seen as an "integral part" of the process "as Baton Rouge progresses." "It made people see us more," he said, adding, "the krewe does give back."

Co-founder Larry recalled that the trajectory of the krewe becoming a charitable organization led to corporate sponsorship and involvement in other city-wide charitable events:

> We were never dreaming it was going to expand into where we actually help—we send money off for research and everything else. We've just been connected to so many HIV things throughout the country. That

> wasn't our intent, to start with, but it rolled that way. And, of course, then, as we came out into the public and our corporate sponsors started asking us to help with different other charitable things, from Children's Miracle Network to Halloween Ball to the different things that we've supported and helped put on, you know? And so that has just been unbelievable. I mean, I have a plaque on the wall there from—that kids made for me at the Children's Hospital here, and they did me a Halloween thing and stuff, you know? It's one of the most treasured things I have, and—oh, yeah, now I'm really proud of our krewe, because I wanted it to continue so that, in the thirties and forties and fifty years of existence, it'd be like other old clubs, and as royalty came along, they'd appreciate those of us that came from the beginning, that made it start and happen. But now I'm so proud of us because of the charity work we do, and the fact that we raise so much money for charity, and we have the support of the city and the corporate sponsors . . . It's like the support of so many people came along, and when Sandra of [local corporation] first approached me, and she said, "Larry, y'all work so hard to raise money. You need corporate sponsors." And I said, "Could we get that many corporate sponsors unless it was gay-affiliated business or something?" And she said, "You bet you can. The charity work that y'all do, I will help you with that." And so her name went a long way by being our first corporate sponsor.

Larry, who had not originally planned that the krewe's legacy would be tied to charitable work, stressed that his plaque from the Children's Hospital was among his most treasured possessions. His account suggests that the charity work of Krewe of Apollo has brought recognition and access to new networks, corporate sponsors, and other opportunities that will extend their charitable work into the future. Neither the Spanish Town Parade nor the Krewe of Apollo's masque ball was originally about charitable fundraising, but today, the charitable focus of both groups is key to their reputations as positive contributors to the city, during and beyond festival time.

Mobile: Taking Care of Our Own

It was not apparent at first glance that fundraising was a common activity for any, let alone LGBTQ, carnival events in Mobile, Alabama.

Fundraising was never mentioned in newspaper accounts or even organizations' own descriptions, and the fundraising that was associated with Mobile Mardi Gras mostly came in the form of groups using festival names and Mardi Gras-themed fundraisers. Thus, for example, the Mystic Mutts of Revelry, a dog parade with its own royalty, is the largest fundraiser for the Haven Animal Shelter in Fairhope, a Mobile suburb. Krewes and mystic societies, including the LGBTQ organizations, sometimes host fundraisers outside of Carnival time, but that is usually just to fund their own ball activities when Mardi Gras comes around.[30]

The four LGBTQ krewes in Mobile, however, absolutely undertake efforts to "take care of their own." I learned about these charitable activities through casual conversations as we put together ball decorations or with krewe members tending bar at work. Several members of the Order of Osiris told me that 10 percent of the ball's profits are donated to charity, although several also confessed that the ball rarely made a profit ("some years we do, some years we don't," according to many krewe members). They mentioned a Mobile AIDS support foundation and animal rescues as the main beneficiaries and noted that the krewe used their broad social media reach to bring attention to these causes. Osiris used to hold an annual fundraiser golf tournament, but like most LGBTQ Carnival krewes in Mobile, their efforts in this vein were mainly intended to cover the costs of the annual ball or parade.

Individual members spoke especially about organizing and participating in small-scale fundraisers for economically vulnerable members of the LGBTQ festival community. Jack, a white gay Osiris member, specifically pointed to the way they take care of each other.

> One year we gave a contribution to a lesbian teacher [in a LGBTQ krewe] who had breast cancer. So, instead of doing a contribution to a charity, we gave a huge contribution to her. And then we've supported [an] animal rescue foundation, we supported Mobile AIDS Support Foundation for a while . . . now another thing about us being a family, is *we take care of our own*. The former king from two years ago had a heart attack, and he was a hairdresser so he wasn't able to work. Anyway, we came together with the other organization, the Krewe of Phoenix, at the time and we

> all came together and had a huge fundraiser. Everyone was so sweet, and how much money did we raise that night, almost $10,000? Every one of those ones. We stayed up till daylight counting all that money. But everybody comes together 'cause *that's what we do*. He was in need, and he wouldn't ask us for it, so we all got together and did it.

At the time of this fundraiser, a sometimes-contentious schism had splintered the Order of Osiris, creating the Krewe of Phoenix. Not always friendly, the organizations came together because taking care of one's own was such an important ethos. It's "what we do." One of the members of the Order of Pan, a krewe of white and Black gay men who hold a Mardi Gras ball on New Year's Eve, chatted in his interview about his plans to put together a multi-krewe fundraiser for his best friend, a krewe member and well-known hairdresser fighting brain cancer. By taking care of their own, Mobile krewes operate as benevolent aid societies. However, unlike the Baton Rouge groups' focus on supporting community organizations, Mobile's LGBTQ krewes primarily fundraised for those near and dear.

Santa Fe: Zozobra as Fundraiser

Fiesta de Santa Fe, like Mobile Mardi Gras, does not include fundraising as part of its cultural tradition. According to one longtime Fiesta participant, most of the events run by the Hispano-led Fiesta Council "raises no money for anything other than the Fiesta Council." At the same time, the burning of Zozobra is both one of the largest Fiesta events and a highly visible fundraiser benefiting the Santa Fe Kiwanis Foundations' scholarships and youth program funds. Since 1952, Zozobra, an event with a history of placing Hispano and Anglo gay men in leadership and creative positions, has raised more than $300,000 for the Kiwanis.

The first time I attended Zozobra, I had seen Zozobra swag at other events, including a table in the Santa Fe Plaza that included Zozobra t-shirts, posters, and programs for sale. There were also little donation cards that participants could fill out for different Kiwanis causes; each came with a Zozobra doubloon that helped the giver signal their monetary support for one cause or another. "I support Zozobra SF Grants!" one card declared. Another card, dedicated to a Kiwanis/UNICEF program for the prevention of maternal/neonatal tetanus, exclaimed, "I support Zozobra saving Lives!" The woman trying to sell me swag reminded me that the proceeds go toward Kiwanis causes, mostly serving youth and women.

Although gay men are a part of the coordination of the event, the burning of Zozobra is understood as a communitarian event. It's for everyone, and accordingly, the fundraising fits with the understanding of Zozobra as a positive good for the broader community. Often, the event is contrasted with other Fiesta Council events, which emphasize religion and Hispano heritage and are often described as more exclusive than Zozobra. It is set apart by its egalitarianism, but its fundraising and leadership are not publicly understood as *LGBTQ*. Instead, LGBTQ leadership and participants fit within the communitarian whole, as one part of a multifaceted diverse community.

More Than Respectability

To be sure, some of the LGBTQ fundraising during festivals—partying with a purpose—is about recognition and respectability, particularly in cities like San Antonio and Baton Rouge where fundraising is part of the city festival. LGBTQ members of festival organizations demonstrate their prowess as fundraisers, locating their groups and the LGBTQ community at large within the city landscape with a positive reputation. For Cornyation, the show's accomplishment as a major fundraiser even allowed Cornyation participants to differentiate themselves *morally* from other events and from social elites who use their positions more for status intensification than charitable giving.

At the same time, the story of LGBTQ fundraising during festivals is truly incomplete without recognition that, at its core, it's not about respectability but about mutual aid for the LGBTQ community. Partying for a purpose is explicitly a means toward an end—taking care of their own. Taking care of one's own was about contributing to one's community. Similar to benevolent aid societies, the festival organizations in Baton Rouge and San Antonio focused their fundraising on community members who all too often were neglected by family, the city, and the state. By prioritizing people so frequently excluded, LGBTQ participants were able to translate the popularity of their festival events into tangible, positive outcomes for the LGBTQ community. This fundraising was a complicated progress, as complete success would be the elimination of the need for this kind of fundraising to begin with. The next chapter focuses on more straightforward symbols of LGBTQ progress, the attendance of parents and political figures at these festival events.

7

Partying with the Mayor and Your Mom

On Progress

In the middle of the Krewe of Apollo Ball, an older white man struts down the runway in drag to a Dolly Parton classic. Next, the evening's emcee introduces the mayor of Baton Rouge— "the best dressed mayor in the United States"—Mayor Kip Holden. Holden, an older Black man in a tailored tuxedo, steps out onto the runway. He starts by thanking the Krewe "for making me blush so many times" this evening, then gives a short speech. "[W]e're one family, and everyone here is making a great contribution to this country of America. I love each and every one of you, and we are one family . . . Don't ever let anyone separate or degrade us . . . We *are* family. God bless you!" With the words about family, love, and God, Holden evokes Christian blessings on attendees while simultaneously employing gay cultural frames about the support of "chosen family." And by calling for resistance to division and marginalization, the mayor's speech is layered with reparative tones.

"This is a whole book chapter right here," says my wide-eyed friend Jason. A white, gay history professor in his early thirties, Jason bought a tuxedo and drove me from San Antonio to Baton Rouge for a long weekend of Carnival research. Now, from our spot leaning against the Krewe of Apollo's runway, I look around at this crowd, dressed in their finery, and take in the race and gender diversity in the room. Jason grew up in Appalachia; watching an incumbent mayor in the South proclaim his support for LGBTQ people is new to him. Yet, later, a krewe member tells me that the mayor attends and says a few words at the Apollo Ball every year. It's a very public display of respect and support and love that, not incidentally, adds to the cachet of the event.[1] At the same time, Ernest, an Apollo member, assures me that it's not all about optics: that the mayor "gets out there and he laughs and he's humorous, but he is so supportive behind the scenes, it's not just about showing his face one night a year . . . he is working with our community to make it a better place to live."

The evening culminates with the grand entrance of the new royalty, the King and Queen Apollo who will reign over the coming Carnival season. Before this spectacle, thousands of attendees turn to watch a short video about the new royalty, projected onto the ballroom screens. The most poignant moment is when the incoming Queen, Ernest, larger-than-life on the screen, tearfully remarks that this is the first year his father will attend the ball. Like others in the room, I know that Ernest's father, a rural Louisiana Catholic in his late eighties, is an unlikely guest at a gay Carnival ball—so this is a big deal. The entire ballroom erupts into applause. There is a dramatic pause as the video ends, then Queen Ernest takes the ballroom runway, pulled in an elaborate metal carriage drawn by strong young men. His impeccable gown trails a long train of peacock feathers and rhinestones, and a tiara sparkles atop his head. The entrance is profoundly emotional. Ernest's sister, seated at one of Ernest's tables with my research assistant, bursts into tears, telling tablemates she's crying because he looks so beautiful. As Ernest walks up the stairs and onto the runway arm-in-arm with his boyfriend, both tables occupied by the new Queen's family members rise. The boyfriend's mother sobs and clutches her neighbor, referring to Ernest as "my son." Ernest later tells me that his parents attending the ball was a deeply meaningful show of support.

Hundreds, sometimes thousands, of people attend these annual festival events, and that broad support is happily received by the LGBTQ people whose events are so often the hottest ticket in town. Still, the participation of *certain* people—the Mayor, Ernest's father—carries more weight. LGBTQ community members notice when political figures like mayors, major royalty, and festival commission leaders attend LGBTQ festival events—and when they do not. For instance, in my first experience at Fiesta Cornyation, I was a new resident of San Antonio, and the fact that city staff members and the city manager were part of the show felt personally meaningful. Seeing officials dressed in outrageous costumes dancing on stage for an AIDS fundraiser made me feel like the city government supported me as a queer person. I was, from the outset of this study, keenly attentive to the ways that the presence of major

Figure 7.1. The Entrance of Ernest as Queen of Apollo

political and social figures in a city was meaningful. At events like Fiesta San Antonio, where the circulation and attendance of politicians and other major city figures is part of the event, the presence of city officials was extra meaningful.

I had no idea, though, that I would meet so many family members of LGBTQ festival participants. Particularly in cities with more traditionalistic festival cultures, family was an integral part of the festival and LGBTQ people's involvement in it. In Baton Rouge and Mobile, family was supposed to be involved in Mardi Gras balls. I met people's grandparents, parents, uncles, nephews, cousins, and children while conducting fieldwork. Largely, these family members were not "PFLAG parents"[2] or people who identify as strong allies, yet they showed up to publicly support their LGBTQ children. This chapter is about mothers who sew their sons' drag, gay hat parties that are thrown in a father's backyard, fathers who display pictures of their son in drag in their gun rooms, nieces who perform in shows, and mothers who pay for their daughters' royalty gowns. These connections can even be reconciliatory, repairing damage done to parent-child relationships in volatile reactions to coming out, shaming reactions to living openly, and other harms that have cut closest because they came from family.

Moms and mayors alike—their presence and involvement with LGBTQ festival spaces and events, was, time and again, described by my interviewees as profound, meaningful, and symbolically representative of advances in LGBTQ rights. These special participants became symbols of progress, both politically and personally.

Symbolic Progress

In 2010, President Barack Obama joined the It Gets Better Project, an outreach campaign targeted to LGBTQ youth experiencing bullying and harassment. The White House put out a video of Obama telling young LGBTQ people "you are not alone, you didn't do anything wrong . . . And there is a whole world waiting for you, filled with possibilities."[3] Twenty years earlier, I went to my first Pride festival in Long Beach, California. Amidst the dance floors, beer tents, vendors, children's games, and entertainment stages, there was an enthusiastic senior white woman wearing a PFLAG shirt. "Would you like a hug?" she asked loudly. She embraced each of my friends as we smiled, then gave us stickers proclaiming that we had been hugged by a PFLAG Mom.

Thus far, I've written in this book about recognition for LGBTQ communities and festival participation in terms of access, museums, newspaper coverage, popularity, and fundraising prowess. This chapter zooms in, focusing on significant individuals and the way their attendance at events and support of LGBTQ people during festivals becomes symbolic of general progress and acceptance. A note: By referring to this support as "symbolic" of LGBTQ rights, I am not being dismissive or saying it's not real support, but employing a broader definition of symbols as holding meaning beyond the evident and functioning as an important form of socially circulated capital.[4]

LGBTQ progress is replete with symbols, such as rainbow crosswalks in major cities or mayors' declaration of support of Pride.[5] These symbols are reparative, compensating for histories of, and helping create futures without, violence, invisibility, and neglect in the arenas of LGBTQ political and family life. When the mayor stands up and declares "we're one family" at a LGBTQ event, these remarks help compensate for the ways queer folks in the past have been constructed as outside the social body.[6] Political scientist Shane Phelan refers to this as a long history of gay men and lesbians being understood as "strangers" within the national body, considered too different and not a "valid possibility for the conduct of life."[7] Politicians like President Ronald Regan, who refused to acknowledge or discuss the AIDS epidemic for four years, have, of course, been met with activism and public reprobation, but they've also done long-lasting harm by steering national conversations about belonging in distinctly divisive and exclusionary directions. Whether loudly derogatory or committing the violence of silence, leaders have endeavored to exclude queer folks from civic life. They will need to work just as hard to truly and respectfully include them going forward. Symbols help.

More personally, LGBTQ people are often alienated from—made strangers by—their families. Much of the literature on family and queer life focuses on family estrangement and tension after LGBTQ people come out to family members.[8] Scholarship on LGBTQ families in the South is typically dire. In her book *Pray the Gay Away*, Bernadette Barton documents patterns of abuse and neglect inflicted by parents of Bible Belt gay men and lesbians, including physical violence and religious condemnation.[9] Scholars like Katie Acosta have shown how Black and Latinx LGBTQ people negotiate family expectations that LGBTQ people will cover or downplay their sexuality.[10] It is no wonder that LGBTQ people have, seemingly forever, created chosen families or alternative kinship to compensate for damaging negative experiences with families of origin.[11]

LGBTQ people often have to work to accommodate themselves in family rituals and celebrations like weddings, funerals, and holiday celebrations due to the heterosexism in these events.[12] Ramona Oswald argues that when gay and lesbian adults attend family weddings, especially religious wedding rituals, they are often "outsiders within"; indeed, gay men and lesbians from religious families frequently described themselves to Oswald as living outside the ritual, religion, and family.[13]

Less is understood about the inverse: how (predominately heterosexual) parents of adult children navigate their presence in *LGBTQ* spaces and events.[14] Steven Hopkins mentions that Southern mothers occasionally attend their sons' drag performances.[15] Gay and lesbian people who are having a same-sex wedding report that some parents refuse or resist invitations, and also that family members' attendance at the ritual leads to increased familial support for the relationship.[16]

The ease of this participation and the meaningfulness of it depended on the cultural structures not just of the city's event but of the type of festival. I focus in this chapter on family member and politician involvement in LGBTQ events, thus I do not cover Fiesta de Santa Fe (which has no LGBTQ-specific events) in this chapter. In Fiesta San Antonio, there was a strong expectation that royalty and public officials would circulate among major festival events, such that a lack of attendance signaled a problem. Within the traditions of Mardi Gras, there are more opportunities and expectations for family members to attend Carnival balls. In the Carnival culture of Mobile, family members often invested deeply in LGBTQ family members' involvement in Carnival balls.

Baton Rouge: The Daddy Cried, We All Cried

I knew it was Aubrey's mother at the ball without her even introducing herself. Aubrey is a slender young Black man with soft brown eyes that look perpetually marked with eyeliner. One of the newer associate members of the Krewe of Apollo, he does drag as his costuming at the ball every year. Aubrey's mom sports a fur vest and makes a grand entrance into the Krewe of Apollo ball by hugging and kissing many members of the group. It seems Aubrey's love of performing for an appreciative crowd is at least partially handed down.

According to Aubrey, his mom had always been invested in him "looking good" in drag and helped him dress from time to time. She came early to the ball to have her makeup done by a krewe member, then ran around asking, "Where's my son? Where's my son? Oh, I mean, where's my 'daughter'?" At the ball, she is pleased each time someone asks her if she's Aubrey's mother—they share the same smile, an undeniable family resemblance. Aubrey comes to her at the end of the ball, tears streaming down his face, telling her how her presence meant the world to him.

Family participation has been a part of Carnival balls for ages; it is ritualized as part of the cultural structure of Mardi Gras. Members of high-status krewes often debut their daughters at Carnival balls, and partners and family members attend the event. When krewe members are royalty, extended family, even minor children, often attend the ball or come up on stage during "call-outs." Carnival royalty rituals and cultural traditions are familiar to Gulf South families, and there is an expectation that naturally, if one of their own is crowned, the family *will* attend. When Ernest, elaborately festooned with drag, was crowned the Queen of Apollo, relatives came from rural corners of Louisiana to attend the ball in their own crowns and krewe insignia. During his pre-entrance video, more than a thousand attendees cheered when he described how meaningful it was that his father was attending the Krewe of Apollo Ball for the first time.

That participation is a cultural expectation may ease the involvement of family members. I met a lot of family members at the Mardi Gras events I attended. My fieldnotes are full of stories: people inviting their adult son to the Spanish Town Ball and reminding him that he might get hit on by other men, elderly fathers from rural Louisiana attending drag balls, mothers instructing their sons to start shaving several days before their big performances. They were just as present in the actual shows. Jayce, a slender white man who performed drag regularly, was Queen of the Apollo in the second year that I attended the ball. When the Queen appeared as the grand finale, her entourage of pages walking ahead of her or carrying her train included her mother, who, having recently recovered from a broken hip, was guided and supported by a krewe member, as well as Jayce's childhood friends and Black gay roommate. Jayce described his father as supportive, an important figure in his life who passed several years earlier. In his memory, Jayce embedded his father's initials in the sparkling, expensive crown that he wore as queen.

Some of the Krewe of Apollo members described the attendance of family members, their family or others' family, as reconciliatory and as symbolizing the progress of gay rights. The most dramatic story came from James, a younger white gay krewe member. James had an ambivalent relationship with his mother. When he came out at age eighteen, she kicked him out of the house. A tumultuous decade later, James was costuming for the first time and invited his mother to attend the Apollo Ball. Knowing she was concerned about him performing drag at the ball and intimidated by the event's formality, James bought her a ball gown, had her come early so that the krewe could do her hair

Figure 7.2. Initials of the Queen of Apollo and her deceased father on her crown

and makeup, and made sure her favorite cocktail was on hand. "She had a day, it was nice," James told me. James reported that after the ball she was immediately enthusiastic and told him, "You did amazing, it was awesome. Next year we're gonna do this, this, and this; me and your aunt are gonna make all the food, so you're not gonna have to spend any money." James's mother became more involved in his krewe events—and his life in general. She met his friends and attended his mostly LGBTQ house party during the Spanish Town Parade. His mother hung out in his kitchen during the party, making gumbo, and insisted later that James's friends refer to her as "Mama Zee."

After I shared these anecdotes about James during a presentation at an academic conference, two gay men approached me with tears in their eyes. The story, they said, was beautiful and touching, and indeed, I can see several elements of James's story that could evoke these emotions. James was vulnerable in asking his mother to attend the ball after a history of alienation from her. He did what I have termed "comfort work" to make attendance at the ball comfortable for her.[17] His mother came to the ball even though she was nervous, because she wanted to support her adult gay son. Mama Zee was so taken with the event that she worked to become closer with him: She learned about his life, met his friends, and found a place for herself in his social life. She committed time and energy to supporting him doing activities with other gay men. This story was not about the morality of homosexuality, gay sex lives, or romantic relationships. It was the integration of (presumed heterosexual) parents into gay spaces and cultural events that was so symbolic—itself a marker of progress.

LGBTQ krewe members understood other people's supportive parents' involvement in this way. It seemed to them like a sign that social progress was in motion. Leonard, an older gay man in Baton Rouge, described a meaningful moment ten years earlier when that year's Queen learned his father had decided at the last moment to attend. The krewe was anxious; it was still uncommon for fathers, let alone the Queen's "Daddy," to come to the event. Both of the Queen's parents ended up being there, and they came to the krewe member brunch the morning after the ball. The Queen's father asked to say a few words:

> I just want to say . . . I am blown away by this weekend. The thought, before I came here, of watching two men kiss each other would've been, "Why do I have to see that? Not that there's anything wrong with it, but why do I have to see it?" I have to say now, after seeing it all weekend, I've never seen people love each other the way y'all do; the friendship—the *friendship*—that y'all have. Gentlemen, I just want to tell y'all, y'all hold on to this brotherhood. I've never witnessed anything like this in my life.

Leonard remembers that "the daddy cried, and we all cried." The father's acceptance of their Queen was socially significant for the entire krewe, and his understanding and comprehension of queer culture and the importance of friendship and fraternal bonds after being immersed in their group's traditions made them all tearful. Some of the men in the Krewe of Apollo had been bullied for their male femininity and for performing drag throughout their lives, had even been thrown out of their family homes when they came out. And so many expected their parents, fathers in particular, to hate every moment of these balls, where men wore drag and openly kissed and performances could get racy. When parents like the Daddy or Mama Zee above start with involvement, move to acceptance, and get all the way to enthusiasm about the Carnival events, that emerging recognition and support of their gay and lesbian adult children's lives is a watershed moment.

Mobile Mardi Gras: It's Like Our Wedding

Like the Krewe of Apollo Ball, the Mobile Order of Osiris Ball is often attended by the city's mayor and school superintendent. A few Osiris krewe members, all white lesbians, explained the tradition as we set up tables before the Ball and clued me in on why the school superintendent was a big deal. It turned out that many of the women involved in this Mobile krewe were teachers, and their state has no nondiscrimination protections against being fired for being out. Several krewe members said the superintendent and his wife had wanted to come to the ball for a few years, but were unable to get tickets; in the early years of the LGBTQ balls, teachers in the krewe and their coworker guests even wore masks and left early if they got nervous about being spotted by someone with the power to fire them. But krewe members, including several teachers, told me the superintendent's eventual—and continued—attendance made them more comfortable at work. Since becoming a fan of the Osiris Ball, the superintendent has written sexual orientation protections into school nondiscrimination policies and has done work to support gay and lesbian teachers. The same teachers who used to wear masks to the ball, a gay Osiris member says as if to underscore the change, "now they go over and give [the superintendent] a kiss during the tableau and they're all on film and it's no big deal." Taking part in this high-demand, high-profile event was complicated for teachers in Osiris, but ultimately it led to their increased support and security in their professional lives.

LGBTQ krewes in Mobile had more widespread family involvement than the Krewe of Apollo had in Baton Rouge. Family not only attended but helped with the extensive process of setting up the Ball. During a pre-ball setup for Osiris, I encountered a mother helping her twenty-something lesbian daughter decorate tables for the first time ("my daughter just loves this group," the mother cooed); a resistant adult sibling helped her brother decorate his elaborate tables (complaining, "Brother, aren't we done yet?"); an adult child rolled her eyes and confided that her mother had been making her help set up tables for years, at least now she was finally twenty-one years old and could attend the Ball; and a mother of a thirty-something white lesbian kept an eye on a toddling niece who squealed with delight around her young aunt ("she *loves* her auntie," the mother proclaimed).

Discussions about family involvement in krewe events were the most emotional parts of my interviews. The only time interviewees cried during formal interviews is when they told me about their parents attending the ball or supporting them in their work in the krewe. Sometimes family members cried to me during my research as well. At the second Osiris Ball I attended, I sat at the table of one of the royalty, an enthusiastic and creative white butch woman named Mo, who loved both her chosen family and family of origin so much that her royalty slideshow during the ball featured both prominently. The night before the ball, Mo told me her nephew, who'd never been to a gay event, was going to walk with her in her entourage. There was considerable anxiety about his involvement, but family members told me afterward that the nephew loved it and was so proud to be escorting his butch aunt dressed up like a king in front of an audience of almost two thousand people. Mo and her partner Allison were both heavily involved in the krewe. Allison's sister quilted part of Mo's royalty train, a beautiful tree with complex, interconnected roots that symbolized Mo's family. The sister came up to me, crying, in the middle of the Ball. She leaned against me and whispered over the thrumming bass of the dance music that she was so pleased that I was writing about something so special to her sister.

Krewe members also expressed strong positive emotion, including gleeful crying during interviews and the ball, at their parents' attendance and support. Reportedly, the ball offered some parents a propitious moment to express pride in their adult children's accomplishments and to support them emotionally and/or financially. Joshua, who had been anxious about his rural father seeing him perform in drag, noticed the next time he visited his parents that, "In my dad's gun room, there's an 8 × 10″ of me in drag." He smiled and rolled his eyes a little as he said his dad described it as "a great conversation piece." It may

Figure 7.3. Royal Train quilted by family member

be incongruous, but the gesture helped Joshua see his father's growing understanding that his son is both a product of his rural origins and his urban gayness. The transformation of parents from skeptics to avid supporters of the krewe could be the start of a huge change for krewe members' families.

Parental involvement was most intense when the adult child in question was becoming royalty; parents with time and money to share supported the expensive experience of being a festival Queen (or King) financially, while others volunteered to help gussy up plainer, more economical gowns and tables. To keep costs down on the gown, lengthy train, crown, tiara, and elaborately decorated tables, I noted that many LGBTQ royalty members had a professional sew the basics of their outfit and train, then sewed and glued the décor on by hand with friends and family. One white gay man recalled that his mother was largely ambivalent about the ball until she attended. Then, when her son became royalty, she went all in, even contributing financially:

> I said, "Mom, I've never asked you for money, ever, but I'm coming up a little short. I need some money to get some things I really need to do." She was like, "Tell me how much you need, and it's yours." And then several times during the year after I talked to my mom about the money, she would come up and give me a hug and slip me $200. I would be like, "What is this for?" And she would say, "You have to buy boots, don't you? You have to buy this don't you?" It was so sweet that it made me cry.

This mother had enough personal wealth to help support her son, and he was incredibly grateful for it, but it was his mother's enthusiasm for his term among the royalty that made him cry.

Several lesbian festival Queens and Kings also mentioned receiving money from family to help with costs. described financial support from family to pay for part of their royalty expenses. The mother of one white lesbian in Mobile paid for her royalty gown and train with funds that had originally been put aside for her wedding. Other family members paid for receptions or helped make part of the train. I was conducting this project as same-sex marriage was being legalized statewide, and so many interviewees described family support around their krewe coronations as equivalent to the money and attention they might have lavished on a wedding. It, in many ways, compensated for the ways that LGBTQ people had been unable to fit into heteronormative coming of age rituals like prom or weddings. Rather than being the "outsider within," LGBTQ royalty got the chance to be celebrated by family members within their *own* rituals.

Fiesta San Antonio

In Fiesta San Antonio's LGBTQ events, family member attendance is not routinized at all, but I was surprised at the ways family members became involved. In my attendance at Fiesta Frenzy, the colorful drag show in San Antonio, my fieldnotes are full of surprised comments about how many audience members had their parents in tow. One year, I sat behind a young man seated with his mother, then noted that several drag queens on stage had called out to their parents during their introductions or end of their performances. The Latinx emcee joked that one performer seats his mother in the far back of the theater, presumably so she cannot see his performance, and, when a drag queen cheered that *her* mom is there all the way from California, the emcee yelled out, "Thank you parents for your support! That's fucking fabulous!"

The parents and family members involved in Cornyation, Fiesta Frenzy, and other LGBTQ events were predominately Latina mothers. The Latinx performers who shared a dressing room with my "house" backstage at Cornyation brought in plates of food every evening—often made by their mothers—and they showed me pictures on Facebook of their mothers sewing costumes, even pictures of the show taken *by* their mothers. *Of course* she comes to the show, many fellow performers told me.

Fathers were less prevalent, but still present. Roberto shared the history of the Hat Party, which started as just a group of Latino and Anglo gay men gathering in Roberto's cramped apartment to drink mimosas before heading downtown to the Battle of Flowers Parade on Fiesta Friday (a day when most of the city takes the day off work or school). Each year, the party grew, so, on the fifth year, when Roberto's father was going on a ten-day cruise, he hatched a plan. "[I]t was like high school all over again . . . if we can clean up the backyard, have the party, and clean up the backyard again, he'd be none the wiser." Robert manicured the lawn, pressure washed the house, and hosted fifty gay men in the backyard around the theme Fiesta Hats. Over the course of the party, Roberto's guests took hat decorating to a whole new level. Roberto quickly came clean with his dad about the backyard party, to which he responded, "Oh that's fine, *mijo*, that's fine" and told him he could throw

Figure 7.4. Hat-wearing man at the Fiesta Hat Party

the event the next year, too. That backyard is where, having waded through a sea of people in huge, heavily decorated hats, I met Roberto's dad, an elderly Latino man with a firm handshake. He was surrounded by gay men drinking mimosas in wild hats.

Parental involvement in Fiesta San Antonio events usually took place in these casual ways, and it came up casually in my research, too. An aside here, a mention there, but San Antonio interviewees rarely linked this family involvement to progress such as what I witnessed in Mobile and Baton Rouge. If parental participation was not routinized, however, the intentional circulation of politicians, Fiesta Commission members, major royalty, and performance companies was. It was often evoked by respondents as the sign of progress and acceptance of LGBTQ events into the citywide festival they best recognized.

Attendance of these individuals and groups may be part of how events in San Antonio are integrated and connected with the larger city. While working stage crew for the show Cornyation, I supported the event royalty King Anchovy for that year, Charlie Gonzales, longtime member of the House of Representatives. Unlike other minor royalty, King Anchovy is not typically a long-standing member of the group or even an LGBTQ person. Instead, King Anchovy is often a visible public figure who is supportive of the community. I helped Gonzales with his light-up mariachi pants and the large papier-mâché doobie that was key to his introductory sketch, and I watched the antics of his crew of costumed friends. This crew included two short-statured Latino men performing as well-known South Texas politicians, identical twin brothers Julián and Joaquin Castro. At a critical juncture in each opening number, these men unbuttoned their shirts to reveal homemade t-shirts that pronounced "I am not Joaquin" and "I am not Julian," and later in the evening, during curtain call, they'd toss replica shirts to the crowd. By the Thursday night show, then-mayor Julián Castro had asked that shirts be reserved so that he could pick them up when he attended—as he regularly did, alongside other San Antonio political figures.

Cornyation interviewees were also attentive to whether major royalty attended their events; making it onto the Fiesta schedules of the major royalty was a signal of importance. Interviewees stressed that the royalty who used to sometimes skip Cornyation were now regulars, announced at the start of each show. In San Antonio, royalty figures visit even some unofficial Fiesta events. I was awed to see teen Fiesta royalty at the Fiesta Frenzy, a fundraising drag show headlined by Black and Latinx queens and guest stars putting on epic performances. I reveled in the moment when a teenage Latina Fiesta Queen in her dress, sash, and tiara posed on stage for a photo with the two Latinx drag queen emcees.

The importance of attendance by royalty, politicians, and policymakers may extend to employing entertainment for events. In San Antonio, show-type festival events invite local performers for entertainment. The first year I went to Fiesta Frenzy, the opening entertainment was a group of tween Latinas doing ballet folklórico, stamping their heels and swishing their skirts to the loud pre-recorded Spanish mariachi music. Drunken audience members cheered as they danced. When I told a work colleague about how young the girls were, she commented that they probably had no idea what the event was about and the parents were probably angry that their kids were there. But Fiesta Frenzy frequently has mariachi, flamenco, or ballet folklórico performers. Ballet San Antonio and San Antonio Street Dance & Drum Company, a Latinx arts group, has performed consistently at Cornyation for years. Ballet San Antonio plays with the homoeroticism of ballet as male dancers, topless and in booty shorts, lift and touch each other as a crowd of hundreds cheers rowdily. At a Cornyation cast event in someone's backyard, an award-winning high school mariachi band performs—part of the Fiesta tradition of bringing in popular forms of partying from the city's Latinx community. In San Antonio, in particular, these symbols of support and engagement may be more meaningful for the Latinx LGBTQ participants in these festival events.

Progress and Recognition

Of all the aspects of festival life that LGBTQ interviewees discussed, the involvement of parents was the most emotional and reconciliatory. Family relationships are usually considered private and personal, so it is contradictory that a public event like a Carnival ball would be the site for healing past neglect and mistreatment. Yet, participants' fears about their parents getting involved in their festival events were often allayed. Instead of LGBTQ sexualities being ignored or evaded in family life, parents showed up to these explicitly LGBTQ events and actively supported their children. Parental attendance at the Krewe of Apollo Ball in Baton Rouge was reparative. For LGBTQ participants in the traditionalistic culture of Mobile Carnival, this support often substituted for major heteronormative rituals like weddings and prom. In San Antonio, Fiesta San Antonio was a family affair, and the involvement of Latinx parents was an assumed part of their festival experience.

Similarly, when politicians, major royalty, and festival entertainment were visible and enthusiastic about LGBTQ events, it helped remedy a long history of erasure and hostility to LGBTQ subjectivities and experiences. A mayor clapping for drag queens does not necessarily change existing laws or policies, but it does demonstrate for all residents that LGBTQ people are members of the city, worthy of belonging and support. In San Antonio, this was layered with the circulation, in particular, of Latinx politicians, royalty, and entertainment, a symbolic affirmation of the strength and belonging of the Latinx LGBTQ community in that city.

In both of these instances, recognition and support from key community members—whether that be one's mayor or one's mother—translated into symbolic support and progress. This recognition symbolized something larger than the mere attendance of a parent to a ball, it signaled that LGBTQ people were an important part of the family and community. The moral worth and belonging of LGBTQ people were affirmed by such visible and positive support.

Conclusion

This book addresses questions at the heart of cultural citizenship. Am I valued because of (not in spite of) my difference? How do I build a community in which difference is valued? Am I treated in an equitable way by others? Can I take care of members of my own community? Do I see progress in the acceptance of me and my community? The answers to these questions depend on who is speaking, where they live, and when the question is being asked. This kind of cultural citizenship is constantly being made, undone, and remade in a dynamic process.

I argue in this book that urban festivals are a rich site for understanding cultural citizenship for LGBTQ people in the urban South and Southwest. Within the contested, shifting nature of LGBTQ belonging in citywide festivals, there are consistent signs of increased cultural citizenship and belonging for LGBTQ people in the city. Being a valued contribution to citywide festivals does indeed fill part of the recognition gap described by Lamont in my introduction.[1] During festivals, LGBTQ people are often recognized as contributing cultural aesthetics like fabulousness and drag and throwing the best parties in town. There is public recognition of the ways that many LGBTQ festival events are inclusive, collective parties that buck local cultural traditions of racial exclusivity. LGBTQ festival events also take up new spaces and access venues in the city center. LGBTQ people get recognition for the ways they are devoted to fundraising and benevolent aid for their own communities. Major social and political figures in the city visibly show their support during festival season. And, more intimately, parents and other family members engage in reconciliation by supporting their LGBTQ family members.

This recognition is limited by the racism, classism, heteronormativity, and sexism within city and festival culture. This recognition is dampened by the use of gay culture as a spectacle or as a "tourist" adventure by heterosexual participants, along with pressure to conform to the politics of respectability. In many ways, transgender and non-binary people were invisible in these recognition processes. LGBTQ people face systems of heteronormativity, racism, and classism that prevent their access to elite events. Access to being major royalty and other elite roles was significantly limited for Black LGBTQ, transgender, or non-binary people. Black LGBTQ people in the Gulf South often had to navigate predominately white LGBTQ organizations to participate in LGBTQ festival events. Some members of the LGBTQ community—mostly Latinx or Anglo cisgender men—receive this recognition more easily, often due to the greater familiarity of gay men's culture to heterosexual audiences. This disproportionate recognition of gay men fits within a long history of gay men occupying public spaces with greater facility and allowance than cisgender women, transgender, or non-binary people.[2] The labor and creative contributions of LBQ cisgender women were frequently ignored in these recognition processes.

The study of LGBTQ cultural citizenship during citywide festivals in the urban South and Southwest gives us insight into broader processes of what it means to have citizenship in a city, be valued for one's culture, navigate city tradition, and live in the urban south and southwest.

The City and Citizenship

In her 2010 American Sociological Association (ASA) Presidential Address, Evelyn Nakano Glenn contended that sociology's contribution to the study of citizenship "may lie in its focus on the social processes by which citizenship and its boundaries are formed. In particular, sociologists can highlight how citizenship is constructed through face-to-face interactions and through place-specific practices that occur within larger structural contexts."[3] This book takes up Glenn's charge by focusing on the complexities of cultural citizenship and the cultivation of belonging and acknowledgment through place-specific practices in the city. Put simply, our sense of whether we belong in a community is reinforced daily in the interactions we have and the practices that are common within the place we live. There are moments and interactions in this book that are a rich site for understanding citizenship in the city.

The focus on urban festivals contributes to citizenship studies by refocusing on the city as a site of citizenship, as urban civic festivals are outside the bounds of the state control and national interests and rooted in local practices and culture. According to James Holston and Arjun Appadurai, "cities remain the strategic arena for the development of citizenship . . . But with their concentrations of the nonlocal, the strange, the mixed, and the public, cities engage most palpably the tumult of citizenship."[4] The city is an ideal site to analyze these cultural aspects of citizenship, as claims to citizenship in the city privilege modes of belonging beyond and in addition to formal citizenship, including "the right to the city."[5]

In this study, recognition is local. Although it is influenced by federal and state law and changing societal norms, recognition and cultural citizenship are also deeply embedded within local placemaking practices like urban festivals. Whether or not someone belongs depends on whether they belong to a particular place or community. It is firmly related to that place, and this study is firmly related to the places in which they quite literally "take place."

In the introduction, I noted that festivals are supposed to be events in which the whole city comes together, a place where everyone belongs. Contemporary urban festivals are often rich placemaking practices, so being a part of the festival can be a type of belonging in the city. The importance of the belonging can be seen in the ways that minority groups in cities such as New Orleans, San Antonio, and Mobile have advocated and organized for minority-sponsored events to be visibly included in the larger festival. Having royalty from minority communities becomes symbolically important for belonging in the city. Similarly, for the LGBTQ community, having LGBTQ-run events or visibility during other events signifies LGBTQ people being citizens of the city. In this citizenship, LGBTQ culture is valued and community events are attended by everyone from the mayor to one's mom. These interactions reinforce a sense of cultural citizenship and belonging in the city.

The interactions can also reinforce a sense of second-class citizenship. LGBTQ citizens of this city are acutely aware of the ways that this citizenship is only partial. Interviewees were attentive when their ball was not listed in the local newspaper or their history was not covered in the festival museum display. These denials of recognition reinforced histories of second-class citizenship for LGBTQ people. When only closeted gay, lesbian, and bisexual rich people can be major royalty, this practice reinforces histories of heteronormativity and the glass closet, along with classism and white supremacy. When Black gay men walk into the spaces of white krewes and feel out of place, it reinforces a history of second-class citizenship and racial segregation in the South.

Studying citizenship within a place (the city) and an event (the festival) demonstrates the way cultural citizenship is a dynamic and ongoing process rather than a goal that is clearly, permanently achieved. Cultural citizenship is more challenging to study than legal rights, as it is rarely codified into written law or policy. But the way legal rights are experienced by members of society is often uneven, relational, and contingent. For example, non-discrimination laws in employment do not necessarily end discrimination in employment. These laws are enforced in often haphazard or incomplete ways, and employment discrimination changes and becomes more coded to evade laws.[6] Similarly, cultural citizenship in the city is complicated.

Recognizing Queer Cultural Contributions

This project engages with a critical debate within sociology about multiculturalism and the valuation of cultural differences,[7] specifically the simultaneous right to recognition "as a moral equal treated by the same standards and values and due the same level of respect and dignity as all other members" and the "right to be different."[8] Political scientist Shane Phelan argues that LGBTQ people are "sexual strangers" in relationship to citizenship in the United States, because LGBTQ people are most consistently missing or depicted as a threat in the national imaginary.[9] According to Phelan, to be fully a citizen of the United States "requires that one be recognized not in spite of one's unusual or minority characteristics, but with those characteristics understood as part of a valid possibility for the conduct of life."[10] I have read Phelan's book *Sexual Strangers* many times over the years, and this statement about "valid possibility for the conduct of life" always captivates me. I am writing this at a time when the phrase "you're valid" is socially resonant to LGBTQ youth. My youth research assistants designed a series of Pride stickers about resilience that included one with the phrase "You're valid" on it. To be valid is not just to be tolerated but to be understandable and understood.

One thing that was immediately apparent in this research, as I spent time with Cornyation, Osiris, and Apollo participants, is that these

LGBTQ people felt tremendous pride in the fact that their event was so popular, that their tickets were coveted by the general public. I think this pride was a combination of being recognized as important *and* not having to conform to the politics of respectability. The glittery, gender-bending chaos that is Cornyation was desired just as it was, and no one was asking the event to be any less queer. In the discourse around multiculturalism and diversity, there is much discussion about tolerance and understanding. But how does it feel to be desired after a long history of either hostility or merely being tolerated? There is something reconciliatory about being desired for one's difference.

And indeed there is much that is fun and exciting about LGBTQ culture. The pageantry of drag and cross-dressing. The satire and humor of camp. The creativity of transforming existing materials, meanings, and objects into new forms. The double entendre and politics of vulgarity. The complex way that LGBTQ representations relate to mainstream culture. The costumes and embrace of rhinestones and glitter. The "never too big, never too much" embrace of outrageousness. The openness to various forms of touch and physical connection.

There are limitations to the culture that was embraced during festival time. For example, very little of this study addresses the actual sexual and romantic relationships of LGBTQ people. The cultural citizenship described in this book is not necessarily sexual citizenship. Although LGBTQ people touched, danced with, and kissed each other during festival events depicted in this book, the citizenship cultivated during festivals was not about sex, romance, or the formal recognition of their right to relationships.

There was also a sexist bias within the recognition of LGBTQ culture that fails to see the contributions of LBQ women (and almost always transgender men or non-binary people).[11] Most popular images of LGBTQ culture represent the culture and aesthetics of gay men, such as *Ru Paul's Drag Race* and *Queer Eye for the Straight Guy*. A tweet in July 2019 by scholar Michelle Nolan joked about "*Queer Eye* but with a team of butch lesbians who buy you six pairs of the same jeans because they're comfortable and point out that the reason you have no time for self-care is capitalism." The tweet got over 75,000 likes and 12,000 retweets. When I presented a paper about LBQ women's aesthetics at a conference, I made a slide titled "Devaluing of Lesbian Aesthetics" that included a screenshot from the online game "Lesbian or Redneck?" It showed images of a Birkenstock, *Xena: Warrior Princess*, and a Subaru ad with a white, middle-aged lesbian in it. This slide resonated uncomfortably with many conference attendees. When I posted the slide on Facebook, a friend joked, "Aren't lesbian aesthetics anti-aesthetics?!?" Acceptance of gay culture and gay people does not necessarily extend to bisexual, transgender, non-binary, or lesbian people.[12] I caution readers not to assume that the embrace of gay cultural aesthetics will be applied evenly—and in due time—to trans, lesbian, and queer forms of LGBTQ culture.

Traditions and LGBTQ Life

Beyond LGBTQ culture itself, in this book I take seriously the ways that LGBTQ festival participants interact with festival traditions and city culture more broadly. The ways that LGBTQ people interacted with traditionalism within festivals varied significantly.

It has been far too easy in the study of LGBTQ life to focus on the ways that LGBTQ people resist traditions about gender and sexuality. The study of LGBTQ religiosity has been most engaged with this question, studying the way that religious LGBTQ people mediate between anti-queer religious traditions and their own identities as religious people.[13] I argue that we have not considered deeply enough the way that LGBTQ people *engage* with local traditions that are important to them and their sense of belonging. Not all LGBTQ people are radical queer rebels, bucking their religion, family, home, and social norms about respectability to live as LGBTQ adults. In this study, I was struck by the profound ways that Hispano LGBTQ people I interviewed in Santa Fe related to Our Lady, La Conquistadora. Several interviewees pledged extreme allegiance to her, felt God's love through her, and went to her for guidance. They believed that she encouraged them to come out, that she loved them as drag queens. This Catholic tradition became an affirmation of being unconditionally loved as queer people. In other cities, LGBTQ interviewees similarly expressed the desire to belong to their family, religion, community, and city.

Some festival cultural traditions facilitated the recognition and involvement of LGBTQ people. Similar to Southern traditions of pageantry that facilitate drag traditions in the South, festival cultures often include values of performativity, outrageousness, style, and throwing a fabulous party or event that facilitate the valuation of LGBTQ culture.

Festival culture also contributes to the oppression of LGBTQ people, as part of the broader role of symbolic boundaries in reinforcing social inequality. Historical links between urban festivals and debutante culture, which is steeped in heteronormativity and racial segregation, challenges the participation of LGBTQ people as out and visible royalty. The way social elites reinforce these symbolic boundaries between valued urban citizens and outsiders is a central part of how these boundaries create inequality during festivals.

LGBTQ people also mustered a challenge to some of these symbolic boundaries, following in the footsteps of other marginalized groups in the city who have challenged festival life. In addition to challenging heteronormative culture within festivals, LGBTQ people often also tried to dismantle racial segregation and settler colonialism during festivals. They protested events, bucked traditions of racial segregation, and pushed for an inclusive collective party that captured the festival spirit. This boundary work may cultivate dissident citizenship within festival events.[14] These practices are an excellent example of the "bottom-up" aspects of festival life that I document in chapter 1, that festivals are a space in which marginalized communities can push for more recognition and attempt to remedy existing social inequalities in the city.

Rethinking the Queer Urban South and Southwest

I stated in the introduction that we know preciously little about the urban South and Southwest compared to some of the great cities that are often the focus of research on LGBTQ urban life, such as New York, San Francisco, Los Angeles, and Chicago. The cities that are featured in this book are not the LGBTQ-friendly stars of the South, such as Atlanta, New Orleans, or Austin. Santa Fe, however, is often considered a LGBTQ haven in the Southwest, and of the festivals in this study was the one that was the most religious.

When theories about how gay neighborhoods or bars are written based on these great cities, scholars run the risk of ignoring different forms of LGBTQ community, visibility, and organization-building. For example, in Mobile and Baton Rouge, a LGBTQ krewe and the MCC were the oldest LGBTQ organizations in the city, suggesting the importance of both religious institutions and festival organizations in the Gulf South. Krewes are not a LGBTQ organization found in the great cities, and this absence may explain the paucity of research on LGBTQ festival organizations.

The prominence of these new LGBTQ organization types challenges a history of scholarship that assumes urban life outside the great cities just mimics LGBTQ life in these cities. Geographers Larry Knopp and Michael Brown argue that most queer studies assume that a few key metropolitan areas are where the "most exciting and innovative forms of subjectivity, culture, and political resistance on the parts of queer people originate" and that these innovations diffuse their way to more peripheral locations.[15] This approach creates hierarchies between LGBTQ urban life in different cities, positioning some places and practices as more queer than others.[16] In her work on "ordinary cities," Jennifer Robinson argues that creating theories about cities based on these hierarchical relationships engenders prescriptive notions about what cities should be based on a small group of major metropolitan areas.[17] This theory implies that LGBTQ people in Mobile, Alabama, are simply imitating or mimicking practices that are developed in cities like New York or San Francisco.

But LGBTQ participants in festivals in Mobile and other cities discussed in this book are innovative with their own practices. They draw on the cultural influences of their region, city, festival, and LGBTQ community, along with their own imagination. In San Antonio, the event Cornyation combines the pageantry of the South and Southwest with festival traditions satirizing social elites with a Latinx-majority LGBTQ community that has a rich history of drag. This innovativeness may be part of urban South and Southwestern LGBTQ life. In *Queering the Redneck Riviera*, historian Jerry Watkins III describes the Emma Jones Society and its Independence Day festivities in the 1960s on the beaches of Pensacola, Florida, just across the causeway from Mobile. The society's Independence Day party attracted thousands of sexually and racially diverse attendees and in 1971 became a full-fledged convention instead of a public beach party, making it one of the largest gay-organized events in the country at the time. In 1972, almost three thousand LGBTQ people from eight Southern states attended the Independence Day event.[18] The event combined patriotism, camp, and a push for visibility in the South.

There is much to learn about the nature and quality of LGBTQ urban life by studying the South and Southwest further. This approach to studying urban life moves beyond seeing the South and Southwest as inherently welcoming or hostile but rather embraces the complexity of LGBTQ life. This work also pushes scholars to consider LGBTQ life outside of LGBTQ-organized spaces and events, such as bars, activist organizations, neighborhoods, churches, and Pride parades. These spaces are important and understanding them is critical to understanding LGBTQ life. However, they do not tell the full story of LGBTQ urban life. The story of LGBTQ urban life must include Carnival organizations, grandiose balls, mothers who sew drag, pink floats in parades, glass closets, campy costumes, and glitter—lots of glitter.

ACKNOWLEDGMENTS

I put the finishing touches on my full manuscript during the summer of 2020, a time of protest, rioting, the great coronacoaster of quarantine and emotions, and the Supreme Court case to outlaw discrimination against LGBTQ people. I finalized the manuscript during the great Texas winter catastrophe of February 2021. At times it felt bizarre to be writing about festival research I conducted almost four years prior at a time that seemed distinctly unfestive. For the first year since World War II, most of the festival events in this book have been canceled. However, this book feels even more important to write now, at a time when people are reconsidering the ways we do community, the city, health, family, gender, race, and sexuality.

This book was a long time in the making, and although I was present at every interview and event, this research could not have been completed without a network of supportive friends and colleagues. First and foremost, this book would not have happened without strong support from Trinity University, including internal funding for undergraduate research assistants, faculty summer stipends, and support for grant writing. My undergraduate research assistants were indispensable company and support during my summer research trips. Caitlin Gallagher and Jady Domingue dug through piles of archival material and tracked down octogenarian Cornyation participants from the 1950s and 1960s. Analicia Garcia helped with the remainder of Fiesta San Antonio research, interviewing Cornyation fans and accompanying me on my first trip through the Gulf South. Elizabeth Gilbert and Danielle Hoard were stalwart and professional researchers who endured often back-to-back interviews with few breaks. I told you we'd have a day off on the trip, and we never did. Rosa Perales and Beatrice Roman helped with research on fundraising and photography issues, respectively. Georgina Continas and María Olalde practically adopted my dogs during our several-week stay in a condo in Santa Fe, along with being incredible sources of company and research help. I frequently brought friends and colleagues to events, so I thank Analicia Garcia, Alfred Montoya, Tahir Naqvi, Habiba Noor, Angela Tarango, Rose Spire, Jason Johnson, D'Lane Compton, and Michaele Haynes. You are the best research wing people I could have asked for.

Mark Brodl and Claudia Scholz looked at this project in its early years and encouraged me to see it as fundable and to chase grants for the first time in my academic career. Claudia and Peggy Sundermeyer helped me with endless grant applications. The research for this project was funded by the American Sociological Association, National Geographic Society, and the Society for the Psychological Study of Social Issues. I was in the middle of a new team research project on LGBTQ resilience during the writing of this book, and a yearlong research leave was funded by the Robert Wood Johnson Foundation Interdisciplinary Research Leaders program that helped me finish my writing.

So many informants and interviewees made this book possible. I especially thank Mel and Angie for their hospitality, Ernest and Corey for teaching me all about Mardi Gras, and everyone who allowed me to sit as a guest at their Carnival ball tables. Lori Hall, John McBurney, Elaine Wolff, and Jesse Mata were critical to the Cornyation part of my project.

Several people who were interviewed or assisted with this project passed away before the book was written. Lauryn Farris, a truly outstanding woman and photographer who had so much to give. Your courage is unmatched. Jim, the best interview surprise, who allowed me into his world of secrets. Thelonius, who could charm a ballroom full of people. Larry Freemin, the last surviving original member of the Krewe of Apollo. Danny Spear, who told me all about the Cornyation of the 1980s. Mark Steckly, my Cornyation designer who recruited me to join his team even though my dancing and acting skills were questionable. I have fond memories of sewing his Cornyation costumes in my living room. Robert Rehm, who taught me much about the history of Cornyation and how to be creative with limitations. Tim, who was in my Cornyation team and did both my hair and makeup. I hope you and Mark are doing some tacky drag in the afterlife. Pat Wells, who was kind to me even though I was a questionable stagehand. Michael Marmontello, who always impressed me with his kindness and sense of humor. Gene Elder, the cut and file master of haphazard archives and art cars, who sat with me for hours in the backroom archive of the Bonham Exchange. I can't imagine this book without any of you, and your loss breaks my heart.

Some of my ideas from this book have been developed in other publications. My concept of "comfort work" was develop in a *Journal of Family Issues* article, "When My Parents Came to the Gay Ball: Comfort Work in Adult Child-Parent Relationships." My analysis of LBQ women's aesthetics during festival events was developed in a special issue of *Journal of Lesbian Studies* focused on lesbian spaces, in my article, "'You out-gayed the gays': Gay Aesthetic Power and Lesbian, Bisexual, and Queer Women in LGBTQ Spaces."

Many colleagues read through drafts of this manuscript or gave me feedback on developing my ideas. This includes Michaele Haynes, Dana Berkowitz, Melissa Gohlke, Japonica Brown-Saracino, Laura Hernandez-Ehrisman, Tina Fetner, Rin Reczek, stef shuster, Brandon Robinson, Catherine Connell, KL Broad, Greggor Matson, Theo Greene, Emily Kazyak. Friends who gave me feedback on my introduction include Foula D., Marla G., Kelli Wilder, Dara Bryant, Cassidy Laurens, and Robert Salcido Jr. Christine Williams and the Feminist Ethnography group at UT Austin workshopped a rough draft of this book and helped move the analysis forward. My Covid writing group of D'Lane Compton, CJ Pascoe, S Crawley, Lisa Wade, and Tey Meadow helped me workshop one of my chapters. Letta Page and Kate Schubert were indispensable copyeditors in the last months of manuscript writing. Ilene Kalish at New York University Press had enthusiasm about this book from the beginning. The staff at NYU Press has made this process smooth and delightful.

As always, I am grateful for my chosen fae—Grin, Slick, Neon, Crow, Kotori, Albatross, and Firefly. Thank you, Angela Tarango, for the household sharing and dog sitting that aided with the research for this project, and Brandon Robinson for house sitting during one particularly long research trip. Thanks to my quarantine germ squad and supporters who helped me make it through the pandemic mostly in one piece, including Grin, Tarango, Jason, Colleen, Jim, Holly, Alex, Dusty, and Vivien. My heart circle people of Ananda, Yossie, B.T., Smiles, Annie, Gabby, and Michael helped me with the worst of it. Niki and Hex deserve a special thanks for tolerating my coronangst. There were many swiss rolls, pandemic baked goods, distance walks, Tik Tok videos, FaceTime chats, heart circles, cookie dropoffs, barbeque swims, card games, and candy-fed cuddles (Reese's Pieces!) that were a critical part of the completion of this book. Kris was the best surprise of quarantine, and the kayaking, love, and partnership was an important part of my experience revising this manuscript. My parents—Karen and Tom Stone—drove to Texas in the middle of a pandemic to help me move into my new home a few weeks before this manuscript was due. As always, my dogs Lucy and Penny are my most enthusiastic writing supporters. Finn also did his best to help with emotional dog support. His help was indeed helpful. Dogs are the real winners of quarantine.

APPENDIX

This huge project began as a summer research project studying the history of the event Cornyation as it was performed in the 1950s and 1960s. I originally was interested in completing a case study of the show Cornyation, which I did do, in the form of a public sociology book with more than one hundred pictures. As I shopped this idea around to friends who were book editors, one of them suggested that a comparative study would be more interesting. And thus, the project grew considerably.

SELECTING CASES

My first thought was that I should find a more traditional version of the Fiesta festivities celebrated in San Antonio. I initially was going to compare Fiesta San Antonio to the historical pageantry of the George Washington Birthday celebrations in Laredo, Texas. I encountered two issues: one being that these celebrations happened at almost the same time as Fiesta San Antonio, and the other, bigger issue being that there were border safety and security issues when I began this research. A colleague studying border cities strongly recommended I seek a new field site. I chose Fiesta de Santa Fe as a long-running and traditional fiesta celebration that offered some parallels to Fiesta San Antonio.

I also considered comparing the festivities of Fiesta to other kinds of urban festivals in the South. I was initially resistant to studying Mardi Gras, as my only imagery of the festival was the debauchery of the French Quarter. I'm not prudish, just not interested in the sexual antics and drunken revelry of American college students. However, a short reading of works on Mardi Gras suggested to me that the experience of Mardi Gras might be rich and interesting. I also never imagined myself spending time doing research in the Deep South, as I had never been to the states of Louisiana, Mississippi, or Alabama before doing this research.

It was important to me to study cities that are not typically included in studies of LGBTQ urban life, thus I ruled out studying Atlanta, Austin, and New Orleans. I also knew of a historian doing research on gay men's involvement in New Orleans Mardi Gras, and I wanted to include cities that were not typically studied. I read about Mardi Gras throughout the Gulf South and seriously considered the cities of Lafayette, Baton Rouge, Biloxi, Mobile, and Pensacola. Mobile seemed parallel to Fiesta de Santa Fe in many ways, particularly in city marketing claims for being the origins of Mardi Gras and having more traditional, family-friendly Carnival festivities. The size and racial diversity of Baton Rouge and laissez-faire organization of Mardi Gras in the city made it an appealing comparison case to Fiesta San Antonio.

OVERVIEW OF THE PROJECT

I entered this project with few pre-existing social networks in any of these cities. I had been living in San Antonio for six years but was not well networked in the LGBTQ Fiesta community. I was fortunate that my co-worker Christine Drennon hosted a St. Patrick's Day party that was attended by Lori Hall, a member of the Cornyation board. I attended the party at Christine's invite and that was my "in" to working backstage (and being on stage) at Cornyation for four Fiesta seasons. For other events, I bought tickets and met people when I attended.

I knew no one—I mean, no one—in the other three cities. My first year of doing this project was devoted to creating connections and getting a sense of the scope of the project. My first road trip through the Gulf South was entirely devoted to this endeavor. I collected no formal interviews, but instead I sat with my research assistant Analicia in archives in New Orleans looking at old LGBTQ newspaper coverage of Carnival balls, sat in the living rooms of Krewe of Apollo members and watched a video of a ball with them while they explained the components of it, had drinks with members of the Order of Osiris, and attended a pool party with the Krewe of Phoenix. We went to local bars and watched drag shows, went to museums devoted to Carnival, and got invitations to as many Carnival events for the next year as we could. These early meetings were about building trust and getting consent to be involved in krewe events while I was in town. Backstage access is complicated at Mardi Gras events; many private LGBT events are run by krewes with a secret membership, and thus entrée into the group and trust by participants is critical to the success of this research.[1]

From 2012 to 2016, I traveled a lot to do festival research. All festivals took place during the academic year, so I frequently would teach Monday through Thursday and then rush out of town for festival events from Thursday night to Sunday night. Cornyation happened on three weeknights in a row, often the last full week of classes at Trinity. I have (fond?) memories of sleeping on the floor of my office between classes. In the summer, I built my summer research around a three-week trip in June to either the Gulf South or Santa Fe. During these trips I would conduct formal interviews along with going to museums, archives, gay bars, and other local places of interest. These trips were an attempt to get to know the city better outside of festival time and to conduct recorded interviews, which were nearly impossible during festival time. Before festival time, I worked to gain backstage access and a good, diverse vantage point from which to view events, which is important for conducting ethnography of ephemeral events like festivals.[2]

I worked with undergraduate research assistants for this project and often recruited students who complemented my own knowledge. So, for example, I recruited a Spanish-speaking student during my summer fieldwork in Santa Fe, and I worked with a student who was born and raised in Lafayette during one of my Gulf South trips.

ETHNOGRAPHY

I spent more than one hundred days doing fieldwork at festival events. Every time someone suggested I was doing this project in order to party hardy, I rolled my eyes. All of these festivals took place during the school year, so I frequently flew away for the weekend to attend events and then taught my courses during the week. To study festival events, I followed strategies for the ethnography of ephemeral events, which included getting good backstage access and experiencing events from multiple vantage points.[3] When possible, I brought undergraduate research assistants and friends to events to get another perspective on the event. I walked the route of parades, chatted with parade lineups, came to ball dress rehearsals, and went to pre-parties.

In each city, I attended the major popular events (e.g., the largest parades, big coronations, etc.), visibly LGBTQ events, and events that were known for being LGBTQ- friendly. When possible, I attended events run by social elites. For the major LGBTQ events, I had deeper involvement, including working backstage at Cornyation and attending each of the major krewe balls at least twice. I also attended a few parades and events outside of my case studies to understand either New Mexico Catholicism or Mardi Gras. My students and I attended rituals at Chimayó, a pilgrimage site. I went to parades in which gay men or LBQ women visibly paraded in Lafayette and New Orleans, respectively. There were a few events I missed due to physical limitations, particularly ones late at night or on the last day of a long weekend of festivities. In such instances, I examined coverage of them in the newspaper, asked questions about them on interviews, or watched social media coverage of the events.

If I had more time, bandwidth, and funding, I would have extended my research to better investigate Black gay men and white LBQ women who were part of men's and women's krewes. I was able to talk to a few lesbians both in interviews and informally who were involved in women's krewes. I also spoke to a white straight woman who shared a float with Black gay men in her all-inclusive krewe. There are some krewes—like the Krewe of Mutts, about fundraising for animal rescue—that I had heard had strong participation by LBQ women, but I was unable to make the event.

INTERVIEWS

I conducted formal interviews with 101 people for this book. These were interviews in which interviewees signed a consent form, filled out a demographic sheet, and were either recorded or had notes taken during the interview. I also interviewed other participants, including Cornyation fans and participants in the earlier years of Cornyation, due to my work on the Cornyation book. I did substantially more interviews in Mobile (35) and San Antonio (34) because of the size and scale of their festival events. Almost all the formal interviews were conducted in the summer, in a series of road trips—three to the Gulf South in 2013–2015 and one to Santa Fe in 2016.

Many of my interview participants are white, modestly middle-class lesbian and gay men who were born and raised in the city or state of the interview. Only about a dozen interviewees identified as bisexual, queer, or transgender, but I made inquiries in every city about who I should speak to who identified as bisexual or transgender. Almost all interviewees worked in occupations such as gym teachers, artists, bus drivers, nurses, real estate agents, funeral directors, FedEx drivers, and high school teachers.

Twenty-seven of my formal interviews were with someone who identified as Black, Latino, Latina, Hispanic, or Chicana. Many of my interview respondents in San Antonio and Santa Fe identified as Latino, Latina, Hispanic, or Chicana, reflecting the demographics of both cities. It was challenging getting formal interviews with Black men and women involved in Mardi Gras in Mobile and Baton Rouge, particularly in Baton Rouge. I made a point of informally talking with Black residents of both Mobile and Baton Rouge whenever possible. In each interaction, I informed the person that I was writing a book on the local festival and curious about their experience. Thus, I intentionally chatted with more Black participants at events and parades, including at the Baton Rouge Pride Festival, in their employment as service personnel at balls, and as guests at events. I spent a lot of time in local gay bars talking with drag queens.

Sixty-seven interviewees were men, thirty-four were women. However, men were much more likely to be informants about other types of festival life, so some of this disparity is that many museum historians, leaders of other organizations, and major festival figures were men. I don't think I represent very well the experiences of LGBTQ people who do not like festivals. I conducted semi-structured interviews that were tailored to each event and city but included general questions about the person's involvement in and feelings about their festival, sense of the festival in relation to the city, and experience with family members.

Almost every interviewee here was given a pseudonym and has had identifying features blurred. A few people insisted that I use their real name or that their identity be easily discoverable with an Internet search. For example, only one man has ever run for Don Diego de Vargas as an out gay man, and he was written up in the newspaper. For a few people, I have split them into two or three people, so that I would not "out" them as members of elite or secret societies.

ARCHIVES

I am a sociologist with a strong historical orientation. I did archival research in each city on the history of the festival and specific events. All four festivals have well-archived histories at collections like the Carnival Collection at Tulane University, the Baton Rouge history room, the Fiesta Commission Records at the University of Texas San Antonio, and the Santa Fe Fiesta Council collections at the Museum of New Mexico. I spent dozens of hours in the Happy Foundation, a haphazard archive run by the belated Gene Elder in the backroom of the Bonham Exchange. I also looked at documents in the living rooms and storage rooms of individuals and organizations, a quest that I have written about elsewhere.[4]

BEING MYSELF

In this study, some parts of my identity became more salient that others—my race, history of lesbianism, residence in Texas, and how partnered I was. My queerness and Texas residence helped me access otherwise secretive groups that were suspicious of outsiders coming in to study them. I was asked constantly about whether I was partnered, particularly by LBQ women. All of the young women who were my research assistants were asked at some point if they were my partner, and after that happened the first time, I prepared my research assistants in advance for this question. "Just let me answer it," I would tell them, "or say that I'm your teacher." But there was always a moment of palpable awkwardness when that moment came.

There are some aspects of my personal history that helped me relate to the people I met writing this book. Although I no longer identify as Christian, my experience in evangelical Christian churches as a child helped me relate to the many Christian informants I spent time with. I am Anglo, but I grew up in a neighborhood in which Spanish was spoken at home by most of my friends. I can speak what I've always referred to as "Schoolyard Spanish" with a relatively high listening comprehension of Spanish. And I lived for ten years in San Antonio, a very bilingual and bicultural city. These experiences brought me some facility and familiarity to aspects of Southwestern Latinx culture. There were other moments in which I was acutely aware that I was working within a racially segregated festival in the Gulf South. I could feel this tension about race and segregation during my attempts to approach young Black gay and bisexual men to chat at events.

There is a part of me that grew to love festivals and that misses the rhythm of festival events, the hurried and dramatic setup, the excitement of the evening, the post-event exhaustion. Although I do not miss the travel this project required, I miss the people who became part of my research experience, along with the adventure of exploring the food and history of a new place. I miss searching for the best char-grilled oysters across the Gulf South and finding my favorite restaurant in Baton Rouge that served the best barbecued shrimp and grits. This project involved a lot of exploration for me and being outside of my comfort zone. And so much glitter that still, years later, I find glitter stuck to the boots I used to perform in Cornyation. So. Much. Glitter.

NOTES

INTRODUCTION

1 Stone, *Cornyation.*

2 Lindsay Kastner, "A Super Cornyation," *San Antonio Express-News*, April 22, 2009, 01B.

3 Nancy Preyor-Johnson, "Fiesta's Cornyation Gives Charities a Reason to Celebrate," *San Antonio Express-News*, July 26, 2009, 03B.

4 Ibid.

5 Holston and Appadurai, *Cities and Citizenship Public Culture*, 200.

6 Ward, "Producing Pride'; Kates and Belk, "The Meanings of Lesbian and Gay Pride Day; Vogler, "Welcoming Diversity?"

7 Delanty, Giorgi, and Sassatelli, *Festivals and the Cultural Public Sphere*. However, there is a lively sociological literature on festivals that is part of the study of symbolic interaction and ethnography. Cobb, "'For a While They Live a Few Feet Off the Ground'"; Denzin, "Cowboys and Indians"; Eder, Staggenborg, and Sudderth, "The National Women's Music Festival; Gardner, "The Portable Community"; Holyfield et al., "Musical Ties That Bind"; Irvin, "Constructing Hybridized Authenticities"; Newmahr, "Eroticism as Embodied Emotion."

8 Delanty et al., *Festivals and the Cultural Public Sphere.*

9 Cobb, "'For a While They Live a Few Feet Off the Ground'"; Davis, "Experiential Places or Places of Experience?"; Wynn, *Music/City.*

10 Ibid., 4.

11 Davis, *Parades and Power*; Marston, "Public Rituals and Community Power"; Rinaldo, "Space of Resistance."

12 Gill, *Lords of Misrule*; Skipper and Wharton, "Diasporic Kings and Queens"; Stillman and Villmoare, "Democracy Despite Government."

13 Dawkins, "Race Relations and the Sport of Golf."

14 The literature on LGBTQ people in public spaces is vast. Here are a few examples within urban spaces. Chauncey, *Gay New York*; Watkins III, *Queering the Redneck Riviera*; Doan, "Queers in the American City"; Thompson, *The Un-Natural State*; Bruce, *Pride Parades.*

15 Alaa Elassar and Isabelle Lee, "Miss Staten Island Was Banned from Taking Part in the St. Patrick's Day Parade after Coming Out as Bisexual," CNN, 03, https://www.cnn.com.

16 Seidman, "From Identity to Queer Politics"; Volpp, "Feminist, Sexual, and Queer Citizenship."

17 Bakhtin, *Rabelais and His World*; Stallybrass and White, *The Politics and Poetics of Transgression*.

18 Gamson, *Freaks Talk Back*; Taylor, Rupp, and Gamson, "Performing Protest"; Thumma and Gray, *Gay Religion*.

19 Cresswell, *In Place–Out of Place*, vol. 2, p. 8.

20 I acquired the concept of democracy without government from Stillman and Villmoare, "Democracy Despite Government."

21 Glenn, "Settler Colonialism as Structure"; Morgensen, "Settler Homonationalism."

22 Bourdieu, *Distinction*; Lamont and Fournier, *Cultivating Differences*.

23 Hall, "Cultural Meanings and Cultural Structures."

24 Kinser, *Carnival, American Style*, 113–14.

25 Suttles, "The Cumulative Texture of Local Urban Culture."

26 Fraser and Honneth, *Redistribution or Recognition*; Honneth, "Recognition or Redistribution?"; Carter, *American While Black*; Roberts, *Welfare and the Problem of Black Citizenship*; Shklar, *American Citizenship*.

27 In his classic work, T. H. Marshall divided citizenship into two types: formal and substantive citizenship. Formal citizenship encompasses the legal rights and responsibilities that are most familiar when we hear the term "citizenship": the passport symbolizes belonging to a nation, the laws that treat all citizens equally. Substantive citizenship is more ambiguous and harder to measure, as it captures belonging to a social entity larger than oneself and being acknowledged by that entity as a member, including the "right to share to the full in the social heritage." Polanyi and MacIver, *The Great Transformation*; Marshall, *Citizenship and Social Class*, 8; Somers, *Genealogies of Citizenship*. Studies of substantive citizenship are often narrowly focused on the study of economic rights and social welfare, and Marshall himself gave short shrift to cultural aspects of substantive citizenship. Stevenson, "Cultural Citizenship."

28 Phelan, *Sexual Strangers*; Spade, *Normal Life*; Walters, *The Tolerance Trap*; Eisner, *Bi: Notes for a Bisexual Revolution*; Sumerau and Mathers, *America through Transgender Eyes*.

29 Most notably, Ong, "Cultural Citizenship as Subject-Making"; Rosaldo, "Cultural Citizenship and Educational Democracy"; Somers, *Genealogies of Citizenship*; Stevenson, "Cultural Citizenship"; Young, *Justice and the Politics of Difference*.

30 Somers, *Genealogies of Citizenship*, 6. See also Nancy Fraser, "Rethinking Recognition."

31 Lamont, "Addressing Recognition Gaps."

32 Lamont et al., *Getting Respect*.

33 Phelan, *Sexual Strangers*.

34 Barton, *Pray the Gay Away*; Mucciaroni, *Same Sex, Different Politics*.

35 Bloemraad, Korteweg, and Yurdakul, "Citizenship and Immigration"; Kasinitz et al., *Inheriting the City*; Waters and Jiménez, "Assessing Immigrant Assimilation"; Lister, "Citizenship"; Yuval-Davis, "Women, Citizenship and Difference"; Berlant, *The Queen of America Goes to Washington City*.

36 Glenn, "Settler Colonialism as Structure"; Canaday, *The Straight State.*

37 Cohen, *The Boundaries of Blackness*; Skeggs, "Uneasy Alignments, Resourcing Respectable Subjectivity"; White, *Dark Continent of Our Bodies*; Higginbotham, *Righteous Discontent.*

38 Joshi, "Respectable Queerness"; Skeggs, "Uneasy Alignments, Resourcing Respectable Subjectivity"; Stryker, "Transgender History, Homonormativity, and Disciplinarity"; Warner, *The Trouble with Normal*; Weiss, "Gay Shame and BDSM Pride."

39 Berlant, *The Queen of America Goes to Washington City*; Rupp and Taylor, *Drag Queens at the 801 Cabaret.*

40 Rosaldo, "Cultural Citizenship and Educational Democracy."

41 Ferguson, *One-Dimensional Queer*, 29–30.

42 Bruce, *Pride Parades*, 32.

43 Ibid., 162.

44 Walters, *The Tolerance Trap*, 13.

45 Lister, "Citizenship"; Yuval-Davis, "Women, Citizenship and Difference"; Chauncey, *Gay New York*, 2008; Stryker, "Transgender History, Homonormativity, and Disciplinarity"; Rust, *Bisexuality and the Challenge to Lesbian Politics*; Stone, "More than Adding a T"; Sumerau and Cragun, *Christianity.*

46 Ong, "Cultural Citizenship as Subject-Making."

47 Lamont, "Addressing Recognition Gaps," 419.

48 Cultural structures are institutionalized cultural repertoires. Dobbin, "Cultural Models of Organization"; Hall, "Cultural Meanings and Cultural Structures"; William H. Sewell, "A Theory of Structure."

49 I am not the only scholar who gets this kind of response. See the perspectives of D'Lane Compton in Compton, Meadow, and Schilt, *Other, Please Specify.*

50 Williams Institute, "Adult LGBT Population in the United States." https://williamsinstitute.law.ucla.edu.

51 Richard Lloyd, "Urbanization."

52 Bernard and Rice, *Sunbelt Cities*; Hollander, *Sunburnt Cities*; Shermer, *Sunbelt Capitalism.*

53 However, there is some amazing new work by Baker Rogers, Bernadette Barton, J. Sumerau, Theo Greene, Miriam Abelson, and Kathleen Bruce.

54 Johnson, *Sweet Tea*, 5.

55 Stone, "The Geography of Research on LGBTQ Life."

56 Brown-Saracino, "Aligning Our Maps."

57 Stone, "The Geography of Research on LGBTQ Life"; Mattson, "Small-City Gay Bars."

58 Brown-Saracino, "Aligning Our Maps," 37.

59 Brown, "Urban (Homo) Sexualities."

60 McQueeney, "We Are God's Children, Y'all"; Sumerau, "'Some of Us Are Good, God-Fearing Folks'"; Howard, *Men Like That*; Johnson, *Sweet Tea*; Harker, *The Lesbian South.*

61 Brown-Saracino, *How Places Make Us*; Rogers, "'Contrary to All the Other Shit I've Said'"; Abelson, *Men in Place.*
62 Bruce, *Pride Parades.*
63 Stone, "Queer 13 Persistence in the Archive."
64 Reyes, "Three Models of Transparency" ; Walford, "The Impossibility of Anonymity."
65 Orne, *Boystown.*

CHAPTER 1. THINKING ABOUT THE SOUTH, THE SOUTHWEST, AND FESTIVALS

1 Ward, Bone, and Link, "Preface."
2 Griffin, "The American South and the Self"; Hernández-Ehrisman, *Inventing the Fiesta City*, 12; Ward et al., "Preface"; Jansson, "Internal Orientalism."
3 Dews and Law, *Out in the South*, 3.
4 Smith, "Queering the South," 378.
5 Abraham, "The Homosexuality of Cities."
6 Hunter and Robinson, *Chocolate Cities.*
7 Rice, McLean, and Larsen, "Southern Distinctiveness"; Degler, *Place over Time*; Hurlbert, "The Southern Region"; White, "The Heterogeneity of Southern White Distinctiveness"; Lang, "Locating the Civil Rights Movement."
8 Lassiter and Crespino, *The Myth*, 14. See also McPherson, *Reconstructing Dixie.*
9 Kinser, *Carnival, American Style*; Watkins III, *Queering the Redneck Riviera.*
10 Hunter and Robinson, *Chocolate Cities.*
11 Hernández-Ehrisman, *Inventing the Fiesta City.*
12 Rodríguez, "Art, Tourism"; Babcock, "'A New Mexican Rebecca.'"
13 Weigle, "Southwest Lures."
14 Riley, "Constituting the Southwest"; Mullin, *Culture in the Marketplace*; Hinsley, "Authoring Authenticity."
15 Abelson, *Men in Place.*
16 Capous-Desyllas and Johnson-Rhodes, "Collecting Visual Voices"; Ford, "Becoming the West"; Compton, "Queer Eye on the Gay Rodeo."
17 Johnson, *Sweet Tea*, 2–3.
18 Compton, "Queer Eye on the Gay Rodeo."
19 Thompson, *The Un-Natural State.*
20 Ashley A. Baker and Kimberly Kelly, "Live Like a King."
21 Harker, *The Lesbian South.*
22 Mikhail Bakhtin, *Rabelais and His World.*
23 Stallybrass and White, *The Politics and Poetics of Transgression.*
24 Turner, Abrahams, and Harris, *The Ritual Process*; Rosaldo, "Grief."
25 Ehrenreich, *Dancing in the Streets*, 89.
26 Falassi, *Time Out of Time.*
27 Ehrenreich, *Dancing in the Streets*, 9.
28 Ibid., p. 103. According to scholars Stallybrass and White, "It is in fact striking how frequently violent social clashes apparently 'coincided' with carnival . . . to

call it a 'coincidence' of social revolt and carnival is deeply misleading, for . . . it was only in the late 18th and early 19th centuries—and then only in certain areas—that one can reasonably talk of popular politics *dissociated* from the carnivalesque at all." Stallybrass and White, *The Politics and Poetics of Transgression*, 14.

29 Guss, *The Festive State*.
30 Picard and Robinson, "Remaking Worlds."
31 For example, Milhausen, Reece, and Perera, "A Theory-based Approach."
32 Rogers, *Halloween*.
33 Aching, "Carnival Time," 418.
34 Ibid., 416.
35 Riggio, *Carnival*, 15.
36 Gotham, "Theorizing Urban Spectacles."
37 Guss, *The Festive State*; Picard and Robinson, "Remaking Worlds"; Riggio, *Carnival*.
38 There's a whole literature on festival management in organizations.
39 Gill, *Lords of Misrule*, 4.
40 Guss, *The Festive State*, 3.
41 Picard and Robinson, "Remaking Worlds."
42 They may be like the "cowbirds" described in work by Wendy Griswold. Griswold and Wright, "Cowbirds."
43 Gotham, "Theorizing Urban Spectacles."
44 Ibid., 226.
45 Picard and Robinson, "Remaking Worlds," 20.
46 Riggio, *Carnival*, 14.
47 Picard and Robinson, "Remaking Worlds."
48 Ehrenreich, *Dancing in the Streets*, 112.
49 Ibid., 167.
50 Gill, *Lords of Misrule*.
51 Dawkins, "Race Relations and the Sport of Golf."
52 This personal freedom includes "bodily self-mastery that externalizes itself as 'exaggeration,' 'overdetermination,' and 'hypervisibility.'" Aching, "Carnival Time," 418.
53 Wilcox, *Queer Nuns*.
54 Picard and Robinson, "Remaking Worlds," 19.
55 Palmer and Jankowiak, "Performance and Imagination."
56 Picard and Robinson, "Remaking Worlds."
57 Delanty et al., *Festivals and the Cultural Public Sphere*.
58 Aching, "Carnival Time," 425; Gotham, "Theorizing Urban Spectacles," 226.
59 Gill, *Lords of Misrule*, 239.
60 Ehrenreich, *Dancing in the Streets*, 88.
61 James N. Green, *Beyond Carnival*, 3.
62 Smith, *Unveiling the Muse*.

CHAPTER 2. MARDI GRAS AND FIESTA IN THE AMERICAN GULF SOUTH AND SOUTHWEST

1 Griswold and Wright, "Cowbirds."
2 Wynn, *Music/City*.
3 Shrum, "Ceremonial Disrobement," 39–58; Shrum and Kilburn, "Ritual Disrobement"; Redmon, "Examining Low Self-Control Theory"; Redmon, "Playful Deviance"; Milhausen et al., "A Theory-based Approach"; Jankowiak and White, "Carnival on the Clipboard."
4 Stanonis, "Through a Purple (Green and Gold) Haze."
5 Ibid., 118.
6 Grams, "Freedom and Cultural Consciousness"; Stanonis, "Through a Purple (Green and Gold) Haze."
7 Edmonson, "Carnival in New Orleans"; Pond, *The Ritualized Construction of Status*.
8 Kinser, *Carnival, American Style*.
9 Gill, *Lords of Misrule*, 280.
10 Dawkins, "Race Relations and the Sport of Golf."
11 Gill, *Lords of Misrule*.
12 Roberts, *Mardi Gras in Mobile*.
13 Lohman, "'It Can't Rain Every Day.'"
14 Atkins, *New Orleans Carnival Balls*.
15 Edmonson, "Carnival in New Orleans."
16 Carey, "New Orleans Mardi Gras Krewes"; Smith, *Unveiling the Muse*. Wayne Dean, personal communication and draft of book on Mobile Carnival.
17 For example, the Krewe of Muses in New Orleans has this reputation. For a history of Muses, see Roberts, "New Orleans Mardi Gras ."
18 In the Gulf South (Mississippi, Louisiana, Alabama), the average Municipal Equality Index score in 2012 was 18, and only New Orleans scored above 25 points. Baton Rouge (7) and Mobile (21) are thus typical cities in the Gulf South in terms of municipal LGBT rights. The Municipal Equality Index was developed by the Human Rights Campaign.
19 "Mardi Gras : City of Mobile." www.cityofmobile.org.
20 Roberts, *Mardi Gras in Mobile*.
21 Delaney and Whistler, *Remember Mobile*, 225–27; Kinser, *Carnival, American Style*, 170.
22 Roberts, *Mardi Gras in Mobile*.
23 Ibid.
24 Bonilla-Silva, *Racism Without Racists*, 28.
25 Kinser, *Carnival, American Style*, 98–99.
26 "Joe Cain," in *Wikipedia*. https://en.wikipedia.org.
27 Roberts, *Mardi Gras in Mobile*, 73.
28 Wayne Dean, Wayne Dean, personal communication and draft of book on Mobile Carnival.

29 Machado, "Never Too Big."
30 "16 Most Segregated Cities in America—24/7 Wall St." https://247wallst.com.
31 Ibid.
32 Costello, *Carnival in Louisiana*, 146.
33 Pam Bordelon, "What Is a Krewe? *** Understanding the BR Area's Growing Celebration of Mardi Gras," *The Advocate* (Baton Rouge, LA), January 17, 2010: 01D.
34 Costello, *Carnival in Louisiana*, 147.
35 Ibid.
36 "Mardi Gras | The Advocate | Theadvocate.Com." www.theadvocate.com.
37 Costello, *Carnival in Louisiana*, 148.
38 Ibid., 148–49.
39 Ibid., 149.
40 "Krewe of Divas." http://kreweofdivas.blogspot.com.
41 Montaño, *Tradiciones Nuevomexicanas*; Rodríguez, "Fiesta Time"; Rodríguez, "The Taos Fiesta"; Rehberger, "Visions"; Sklar, *Dancing with the Virgin*.
42 Rodríguez, "The Taos Fiesta"; Horton, *The Santa Fe Fiesta*.
43 Hernández-Ehrisman, *Inventing the Fiesta City*, 10.
44 McWilliams, *Southern California Country*. For a more recent analysis of the Spanish Fantasy Past, see Kropp, "Citizens of the Past?"
45 Deverell, *Whitewashed Adobe*.
46 Dennis, "Washington's Birthday"; Young, "Red Men"; Cantú, "Dos Mundos [Two Worlds]."
47 Mitchell, *Coyote Nation*.
48 Wolfe, "Settler Colonialism and the Elimination of the Native"; Veracini, *Settler Colonialism*; Wolfe, *Settler Colonialism*; Morgensen, *Spaces between Us*.
49 Glenn, "Settler Colonialism as Structure."
50 Trujillo, *Land of Disenchantment*.
51 "Census Data from New Mexico Tribal Communities | NMEDD." https://gonm.biz/site-selection/tribal-profiles.
52 Hernández-Ehrisman, *Inventing the Fiesta City*; Wilson, *The Myth of Santa Fe*.
53 Rodríguez, "The Taos Fiesta."
54 "2019 Fiestas Schedule." www.visitlasvegasnm.com.
55 Wilson, *The Myth of Santa Fe*, 3.
56 Ibid., 8.
57 Chávez, *The Lost Land*; Rodríguez, "Art, Tourism."
58 Deutsch, *No Separate Refuge*.
59 Rodríguez, "Art, Tourism."
60 Ibid., 78.
61 Ibid.
62 Weigle and Fiore, *Santa Fe and Taos*.
63 Horton, *The Santa Fe Fiesta*; Wilson, *The Myth of Santa Fe*.
64 Wilson, *The Myth of Santa Fe*.
65 Ibid.

66 Ibid., 192.
67 Ibid., 196.
68 Wenger, *We Have a Religion*.
69 Weigle and Fiore, *Santa Fe and Taos*, 26.
70 Gibson, *The Santa Fe and Taos Colonies*, 253.
71 Horton, *The Santa Fe Fiesta*, 43; Wilson, *The Myth of Santa Fe*, 213.
72 Horton, *The Santa Fe Fiesta*, 43.
73 Ibid., 42.
74 Horton, *The Santa Fe Fiesta*.
75 Megan Bennett, "Caballeros Explain Decision to End Entrada Re-Enactment," *Albuquerque Journal*, July 31, 2018. www.abqjournal.com.
76 Williams Institute, "Same-Sex Couple Data & Demographics." https://williamsinstitute.law.ucla.edu.
77 Daniel Reynolds, "Why Are There No Gay Bars in Santa Fe?" *The Advocate*, February 22, 2018. www.advocate.com.
78 Reynolds, "Why Are There No Gay Bars in Santa Fe?"
79 Brown-Saracino, *How Places Make Us*. This has not been historically true in New Mexico. See Franzen, "Differences and Identities."
80 "Everything Gay in Santa Fe" website. Details regarding this event may be found In "Gay Santa Fe," *Everything Gay in Santa Fe* (blog), March 7, 2010. http://gaysantafe.com.
81 Hernández-Ehrisman, *Inventing the Fiesta City*.
82 Ibid.
83 "Our Story," Rey Feo Scholarship Foundation, www.reyfeoscholarship.com.
84 Stone, *Cornyation*; Stone, "Crowning King Anchovy."

CHAPTER 3. THE HOTTEST TICKET IN TOWN IS A GAY BALL

1 Michael Quintanilla, "Best of the Best; Risque Business; Cornyation Too Big for One King," *San Antonio Express-News* (TX), April 15, 2016: M6. http://infoweb.newsbank.com.
2 "FAQs," *The Burning of Will Shuster's Zozobra* (blog). https://burnzozobra.com.
3 "Azalea Gay Old Time at the Order of Osiris Ball," *Press-Register* (Mobile, AL), January 19, 2010.
4 "Well, the Good Times Have Already Started Rolling in The Port City, And I've Been Catching," *Lagniappe* (Mobile, AL), June 1, 2009.
5 Pam Bordelon, "Apollo Turns 30," *The Advocate* (Baton Rouge, LA), January 20, 2011, 01D.
6 Walters, *The Tolerance Trap*, 3:13.
7 Halperin, *How To Be Gay*.
8 Ibid., 209; Clum, *Something for the Boys*; Clum, *Staging Gay Lives*.
9 Moore, *Fabulous*, vii.
10 Halperin, *How To Be Gay*, 140.
11 Ward, *Respectably Queer*; Newton, "Dick (Less) Tracy."

12 Newton, "Dick (Less) Tracy."

13 Baker and Kelly, "Live Like a King"; Thompson, *The Un-Natural State*; Rupp and Taylor, *Drag Queens at the 801 Cabaret*, 2015.

14 Hemmings, "Rescuing Lesbian Camp"; Nielsen, "Lesbian Camp: An Unearthing."

15 Chauncey, *Gay New York*; d'Emilio, "Capitalism and Gay Identity."

16 Diamond, "'I'm Straight, but I Kissed a Girl'"; Inness and Lloyd, "'G.I. Joes in Barbie Land'"; Jackson and Gilbertson, "'Hot Lesbians.'"

17 Pam Bordelon, "Apollo Mardi Gras Celebration, 'Runway' Win Top Busy Week," *The Advocate* (Baton Rouge, LA), January 27, 2013: 03D. http://infoweb.newsbank.com.

18 Bordelon, "Apollo Turns 30."

19 Pam Bordelon, "First Balls Open Door to Mardi Gras Madness," *The Advocate* (Baton Rouge, LA), February 6, 2011: 03D. http://infoweb.newsbank.com.

20 "Apollo Celebrates 35th Ball," *The Advocate* (Baton Rouge, LA), January 24, 2016: 09D. http://infoweb.newsbank.com.

21 Report, Advocate Staff, "Local Krewe of Apollo Spins 'The Disco Ball,'" *The Advocate* (Baton Rouge, LA), January 15, 2012: 06D. http://infoweb.newsbank.com.

22 Boozie Beer Nues, "Mobile's Reality TV Show Cup Runneth Over," *Lagniappe* (Mobile, AL), September 24, 2014. http://infoweb.newsbank.com.

23 "Azalea Gay Old Time at the Order of Osiris Ball."

24 The Masked Observer, "Masked One Gets Fabulous," *Press-Register* (Mobile, AL), February 14, 2011: 01. http://infoweb.newsbank.com.

25 "Azalea Gay Old Time at the Order of Osiris Ball." o

26 "Well, the Good Times Have Already Started Rolling."

27 "Inca, Osiris and Maskers," *Mobile Register* (AL), February 15, 2004.

28 "Well the Insanity Has Begun. Man, It's Just Too Early This Year. Oh Well, I'm a Troop," *Lagniappe* (Mobile, AL), June 1, 2009. http://infoweb.newsbank.com.

29 The Masked Observer, "Masked One Gets Fabulous."

30 Boozie Beer Nues, "Osiris and the Land of Oz, 'Prostidude' and Pitt Stains," *Lagniappe* (Mobile, AL), January 26, 2010. http://infoweb.newsbank.com.

31 Hart, "We're Here, We're Queer"; Papacharissi and Fernback, "The Aesthetic Power of the Fab 5."

32 Nues, "Osiris and the Land of Oz. "

33 Casey, "De-Dyking Queer Space(s"; Hartless, "They're Gay Bars,"; Hartless, "Questionably Queer."

34 Roberts, *Mardi Gras in Mobile.*

35 Halperin, *How To Be Gay*; Clum, *Something for the Boys.*

36 Michael Quintanilla, "Viva Fiesta Style; Fun Trends Punch Up the Party Spirit," *San Antonio Express-News* (TX), April 3, 2014: 1D. http://infoweb.newsbank.com.

37 Richard A. Marini, "Fiesta; Cornyation Draws Laughter, Charity Funds," *San Antonio Express-News* (TX), April 26, 2012: 08B. http://infoweb.newsbank.com.

38 Vianna Davila, "Coronation's Dazzling Court; Cornyation Breaks 'a Few Rules,'" *San Antonio Express-News* (TX), April 22, 2010: 01B. http://infoweb.newsbank.com.

39 Nancy Preyor-Johnson, "Fiesta's Cornyation Gives Charities a Reason to Celebrate," *San Antonio Express-News* (TX), July 26, 2009: 03B. http://infoweb.newsbank.com.

40 "Tip Sheet; Our Critics' Picks on What to Do in S.A.," *San Antonio Express-News* (TX), April 19, 2013: 10M. http://infoweb.newsbank.com.

41 Melissa Ludwig, "Cornyation Lampoons Pageants, Palins," *San Antonio Express-News* (TX), April 14, 2011: 08B. http://infoweb.newsbank.com.

42 Robert Crowe, "Cornyation Is as Corny, Fun as Ever," *San Antonio Express-News* (TX), April 24, 2008: 08B. http://infoweb.newsbank.com.

43 Deborah Martin, "Fiesta's Cornyation Shines Again," *San Antonio Express-News* (TX), April 24, 2013: 6A. http://infoweb.newsbank.com.

44 "Fiesta 2016 Preview; 125 Reasons We Love Fiesta," *San Antonio Express-News* (TX), April 10, 2016: T3. http://infoweb.newsbank.com.

45 Stone, *Cornyation*.

46 Moreman and McIntosh, "Brown Scriptings"; Muñoz, *Disidentifications*.

47 Moore, *Fabulous*, 8.

48 Stokes, "The Glass Runway."

49 Lister, "Citizenship"; Lister and Campling, *Citizenship*; Yuval-Davis, "Women, Citizenship and Difference"; Chauncey, *Gay New York*, 1994; "Self-Made Men: Identity and Embodiment Among Transsexual Men—Henry Rubin—Google Books," https://books.google.com; Rust, *Bisexuality and the Challenge to Lesbian Politics*; Stone, "More than Adding a T."

50 McKenzie, *Perform Or Else*.

51 Jonece Starr Dunigan, "Alabama Sees Hundreds of Same-Sex Marriages Each Year, Despite Eight Holdout Counties," October 16, 2018, www.al.com.

CHAPTER 4. INCLUSIVE COLLECTIVE PARTYING

1 The politics of vulgarity was developed as a theory by Rupp and Taylor, *Drag Queens at the 801 Cabaret*.

2 Dino Foxx, "Tencha La Jefa's Alternative Approach to Drag—Out in SA," May 25, 2016. https://outinsa.com.

3 Hall, "The Spectacle of the Other"; Debord, *Society of the Spectacle*; Crary, *Suspensions of Perception*.

4 Chauncey, *Gay New York*, 1994; Heap, *Slumming*.

5 Orne, *Boystown*.

6 Gotham, "Theorizing Urban Spectacles," 226.

7 Ibid., 243.

8 Debord, *Society of the Spectacle*, ch. 1 paragraph 4.

9 Picard and Robinson, "Remaking Worlds," 19.

10 Bernstein, "Celebration and Suppression."

11 Gamson, *Freaks Talk Back*; Rupp and Taylor, *Drag Queens at the 801 Cabaret*, 2003.

12 Taylor et al., "Performing Protest."

13 Delanty et al., *Festivals and the Cultural Public Sphere*.

14 Browne, "A Party with Politics?"
15 Bruce, *Pride Parades*, 24.
16 Moore, *Fabulous*, vii.
17 Browne, "A Party with Politics?" 75.
18 Braunstein, Fulton, and Wood, "The Role of Bridging Cultural Practices."
19 Berrey, *The Enigma of Diversity*, 26.
20 Summers, *Black in Place*.
21 I'm building on ideas about colorblind racist ideologies by scholars like Bonilla-Silva, *Racism Without Racists*.
22 Bonilla-Silva, *Racism Without Racists*, 28.
23 Bell and Hartmann, "Diversity in Everyday Discourse."
24 Bernstein, "Celebration and Suppression."
25 Ibid., 538.
26 The City Key, "The City Key :: Demographics :: Parish :: East Baton Rouge." www.brcitykey.com.
27 Greene, "Gay Neighborhoods."
28 Isch, *Capitol Park and Spanish Town*.
29 Amy Stone, "Wearing Pink in Fairy Town: The Spanish Town Parade in the Baton Rouge Gayborhood." In *The Rise and Decline of Gay Neighborhoods*, 139–58. Springer, 2021.
30 Bowman, Kitchens, and Shkreli, "FEMAture," 299.
31 Hall, "In the Pink."
32 Carey, "New Orleans Mardi Gras Krewes"; Green and Green, *Beyond Carnival*; Smith, *Unveiling the Muse*.
33 Edelman, *No Future*.
34 Bruce, *Pride Parades*, 186.
35 Bowman et al., "FEMAture Evacuation," 300.
36 Katelyn Gardner, "A Look Inside Mobile's 'Alternative Lifestyle' Mardi Gras," *Lagniappe* (Mobile, AL), January 23, 2013. http://infoweb.newsbank.com.
37 "Masked One Gets Fabulous."
38 Kevin Lee, " 'This Is It, the Night of Nights,'" *Lagniappe* (Mobile, AL), January 12, 2010. http://infoweb.newsbank.com.
39 Bernstein, "Celebration and Suppression."
40 Barrios, "You Found Us Doing This, "; Stillman and Villmoare, "Democracy Despite Government."
41 Kinser, *Carnival, American Style*; Roberts, *Mardi Gras in Mobile*.
42 Kinser, *Carnival, American Style*; Roberts, *Mardi Gras in Mobile*.
43 Dumas, "'People's Parade.'"
44 Harress, "LGBTQ Mardi Gras Groups."
45 Ibid.
46 Hunter et al., "Black Placemaking."
47 Moore, *Invisible Families*.
48 Skipper and Wharton, "Diasporic Kings and Queens."

49 For a good definition of camp, see Sontag, "Notes on Camp," Also Newton, *Mother Camp*.
50 Siede, "20 Years Ago, But I'm A Cheerleader Reclaimed Camp for Queer Women," The A.V. Club. www.avclub.com.
51 Moore, *Fabulous*, 14.
52 Staff, "Resurrected Cornyation Pokes Fun at Rival," *Express News*, April 21, 1982, 1-C.
53 Esther Wu, "Cornyation Proves Some Like It Haute," *Express News*, April 20, 1983, 1-C.
54 Chacon, "Protesters."
55 Chacon, "Fiesta."
56 "De Vargas Statue Removed; Overnight Attempt to Move Plaza Obelisk Fails | Local News | Santafenewmexican.Com." www.santafenewmexican.com.
57 Alicia Inez Guzman, "Burn Whom?" *Santa Fe Reporter*, August 29, 2017. www.sfreporter.com.
58 Rodriguez, "Tourism," 203–4.
59 Horton, *The Santa Fe Fiesta*, 37.
60 Asenap, "Confronting Colonialism."
61 And this tension between diversity and building identity during festivals may be common. See Eder et al., "The National Women's Music Festival."

CHAPTER 5. SOCIAL ELITES, GLASS CLOSETS, AND CONTESTED SPACES

1 Nigel Duara and Copy Link, "Great Read: A Drag Queen's Final Tribute to the Grandmother Who Loved and Accepted Him," Los Angeles Times, July 3, 2015, sec. World & Nation. www.latimes.com.
2 Wilcox, *Queer Nuns*.
3 Somers, *Genealogies of Citizenship*, 6; Rosaldo, "Cultural Citizenship and Educational Democracy."
4 Titchkosky, *The Question of Access*.
5 Ibid., 3.
6 Kitchin, "Out of Place"; Puwar, *Space Invaders*; Eaves, "Black Geographic Possibilities"; Bledsoe, Eaves, and Williams, "Introduction."
7 Cresswell, *In Place–Out of Place*.
8 Ibid., 2:12.
9 Mohanram, *Black Body*, 3.
10 Cresswell, *In Place–Out of Place*.
11 Karp, *Exhibiting Cultures*; Hooper-Greenhill, "Museums"; Sandell, *Museums*.
12 Alderman and Inwood, "Street Naming "; Dunn, "Using Cultural Geography."
13 Karp, "On Civil Society and Social Identity."
14 Schein, "Belonging."
15 Bourdieu, *Distinction*; Carnoy, *Education*; Lamont and Fournier, *Cultivating Differences*; Lamont and Molnár, "The Study of Boundaries"; Tomlinson, "Cultural Imperialism"; Young, *Justice and the Politics of Difference*.

16 Sedgwick, *Epistemology of the Closet*; Snorton, *Black on Both Sides*; Snorton, "Trapped"; McGlotten, "On Glass Closets."
17 Acosta, "The Language of (in) Visibility."
18 Decena, "Tacit Subjects"; Fisher, "Immigrant Closets"; King, Roberts, and White, "Remixing the Closet."
19 Decena, "Tacit Subjects," 340.
20 Ibid., 349.
21 Collins, *Black Sexual Politics*; Garcia, "'Now Why Do You Want to Know about That?'"; Smith and Shin, "Negotiating the Intersection."
22 Morgensen, "Settler Homonationalism."
23 Rifkin, *When Did Indians Become Straight?*
24 Knowles, *Race and Social Analysis*, 80; Neely and Samura, "Social Geographies of Race."
25 Eaves, "Black Geographic Possibilities," 87.
26 Deluney, "The Boundaries of Responsibility Interpretations."
27 Bailey and Shabazz, *Gender*.
28 Dowd, "From Access to Outcome Equity"; Posselt et al., "Access without Equity"; Rizvi and Lingard, "Disability."
29 Culyer and Wagstaff, "Equity and Equality"; Oliver and Mossialos, "Equity of Access to Health Care"; Gulliford et al., "What Does 'Access to Health Care' Mean?"
30 Talen and Anselin, "Assessing Spatial Equity."
31 Lievrouw and Farb, "Information and Equity."
32 Ownby, *Manners and Southern History*.
33 Kitchin, "Out of Place"; Puwar, *Space Invaders*; Ruddick, "Constructing Difference."
34 Holston, *Cities and Citizenship*; Smith and McQuarrie, *Remaking Urban Citizenship*.
35 "Op-Ed: I Am Jewish. I Wear Glasses. I Am Bisexual—and I'm the Rose Queen," *Los Angeles Times*, December 31, 2018 www.latimes.com.
36 King-O'Riain, "Making the Perfect Queen"; Cohen, *Beauty Queens on the Global Stage*; Greene, *Drag Queens and Beauty Queens*.
37 Greene, *Drag Queens and Beauty Queens*, 29; Cohen, *Beauty Queens on the Global Stage*.
38 Blum, "Review Essay"; Harrison, "It's a Nice Day for a White Wedding"; King-O'Riain, "Making the Perfect Queen."
39 Haynes, *Dressing Up Debutantes*.
40 Berkowitz and Padavic, "Getting a Man or Getting Ahead."
41 Westbrook and Schilt, "Doing Gender, Determining Gender."
42 Gupta and Ferguson, "Beyond 'Culture'"; Puwar, *Space Invaders*; Ruddick, "Constructing Difference"; Duncan, *Bodyspace*.
43 Horton, *The Santa Fe Fiesta*, 42.
44 Horton, *The Santa Fe Fiesta*.
45 Bennett, "Caballeros Explain Decision."

46 Morgensen, "Settler Homonationalism"; Smith, "Queer Theory and Native Studies."
47 Pascoe, *Dude, You're a Fag.*
48 Hardin, "Altering Masculinities."
49 Collins, *Black Sexual Politics*; Snorton, *Black on Both Sides.*
50 Somerville, "Scientific Racism."
51 Pascoe, *Dude, You're a Fag.*
52 Carnaghi and Maass, "In-Group and Out-Group Perspectives."
53 Lepore, *The Name of War.*
54 "Our Story," Rey Feo Scholarship Foundation, www.reyfeoscholarship.com.
55 "Chili Queens Chili Cook Off." https://fiestasanantonio.org.
56 Elaine Ayala, "Finally, the Cavaliers Elect a Mexican-American King Antonio," June 27, 2016, www.expressnews.com.
57 Stone, *Cornyation.*
58 Chauncey, *Gay New York*, 1994; Heap, *Slumming.*
59 Puar, "Mapping US Homonormativities"; Montegary, "Militarizing US Homonormativities."
60 Brown, "Homonormativity"; Gorman-Murray, "Que (e) Rying Homonormativity." *Sexuality and Gender at Home: Experience, Politics, Transgression*, 2017, 149–62.
61 Lamont, "Addressing Recognition Gaps."

CHAPTER 6. FUNDRAISING AND BENEVOLENT AID

1 "Fiesta San Antonio," Fiesta SA Org, www.fiesta-sa.org.
2 Greene, *Drag Queens and Beauty Queens*; Gould, *Moving Politics.*
3 Spade, *Mutual Aid.*
4 Kidd, "Philanthropy and the 'Social History Paradigm.'"
5 Ibid.
6 Peiss, "'Charity Girls' and City Pleasures"; Cohen, *The Boundaries of Blackness*; Lamont, *The Dignity of Working Men*; Skeggs, *Formations of Class & Gender*; Skeggs, "Uneasy Alignments, Resourcing Respectable Subjectivity"; White, *Dark Continent of Our Bodies*; Higginbotham, *Righteous Discontent.*
7 Goffman, *Stigma.*
8 Yoshino, *Covering.*
9 Walters, *The Tolerance Trap.*
10 Charity work can make one respectable but can also reinforce the politics of respectability on the subject of charitable giving. Wolcott, *Remaking Respectability*; Friedman and McGarvie, *Charity, Philanthropy, and Civility.*
11 Lamont, *The Dignity of Working Men.*
12 Ibid.
13 Mucciaroni, *Same Sex, Different Politics*; Phelan, *Sexual Strangers*; Barton, *Pray the Gay Away*, 2012; Johnson, *Sweet Tea.*
14 Loseke, "'The Whole Spirit of Modern Philanthropy.'"
15 Ibid.

16 Dinerstein, "Second Lining Post-Katrina"; Regis, "Blackness and the Politics of Memory." Also, more generally, there is a lot of fundraising during Mardi Gras. See examples of this fundraising at www.makechange.aspiration.com.

17 "History," Krewe of Zulu, www.kreweofzulu.com.

18 Vaz, *The "Baby Dolls."*

19 Personal communication with Pride Center Executive Director, Robert Salcido, Jr., December 5, 2019.

20 Sam Sanchez, "LGBT Community Cheers Rosie Gonzalez's Victorious Campaign for Judge," *Out in SA* (blog), November 7, 2018. https://outinsa.com.

21 Jeffrey Sullivan, "Fundraising Goal Reached for Rainbow Crosswalk in San Antonio," *San Antonio Report*, May 29, 2018. https://sanantonioreport.org.

22 See also the Boystown pylons. Reed, "We're from Oz."

23 Joey Palacios, "Profits Prep to 'Party With a Purpose,'" *Texas Public Radio*, March 28, 2018. www.tpr.org.

24 See Steven Sanchez, "Community Creating Change: WEBB Party's Past, Present, and Future," *San Antonio Report*, April 3, 2015. https://sanantonioreport.org.

25 Stone, *Cornyation.*

26 Hernández-Ehrisman, *Inventing the Fiesta City.*

27 Stone, "Crowning King Anchovy."

28 Shilts, *And the Band Played On*; Gould, *Moving Politics.*

29 Shilts, *And the Band Played On*; Román, *Acts of Intervention*; Gitterman and Schulman, *Mutual Aid Groups*; Bennett and West, "'United We Stand, Divided We Fall'"; Greene, *Drag Queens and Beauty Queens.*

30 Carey, "New Orleans Mardi Gras Krewes."

CHAPTER 7. PARTYING WITH THE MAYOR AND YOUR MOM

1 McQueeney, "We Are God's Children, Y'all."

2 I.e., Parents, Families, and Friends of Lesbians and Gays.

3 Alex Eichler, "Obama Joins the 'It Gets Better' Project," *The Atlantic*, October 22, 2010. www.theatlantic.com.

4 Bourdieu and Wacquant, "Symbolic Capital and Social Classes."

5 Bitterman, "Rainbow Diaspora."

6 Phelan, *Sexual Strangers*; Berlant, *The Queen of America Goes to Washington City.*

7 Phelan, *Sexual Strangers*, 16.

8 LaSala, "Lesbians, Gay Men, and Their Parents"; Reczek, "Ambivalence"; Robinson, "Conditional Families"; Savin-Williams and Dubé, "Parental Reactions to Their Child's Disclosure of a Gay/Lesbian Identity"; Scherrer, Kazyak, and Schmitz, "Getting 'Bi' in the Family"; Schmitz and Tyler, "The Complexity of Family Reactions."

9 Barton, *Pray the Gay Away.*

10 Acosta, "'How Could You Do This to Me?'"; Glass, "'We Are with Family.'"

11 Weston, *Families We Choose*; Arnold and Bailey, "Constructing Home and Family"; Bailey, *Butch Queens Up in Pumps.*

12 Oswald, "A Member of the Wedding?"
13 Oswald, "Religion, Family, and Ritual"; Collins, "Learning from the Outsider Within."
14 Oswald, "Resilience within the Family Networks."
15 Hopkins, "'Let the Drag Race Begin.'"
16 Fetner and Heath, "Editor's Pick"; Ocobock, "The Power and Limits of Marriage."
17 Stone, "When My Parents Came to the Gay Ball."

CONCLUSION

1 Lamont, "Addressing Recognition Gaps."
2 Binnie, "Trading Places; Casey, "De-Dyking Queer Space(s)"; Doan, "Queers in the American City"; Ruddick, "Constructing Difference in Public Spaces"; Sumerau and Mathers, *America through Transgender Eyes.*
3 Glenn, "Constructing Citizenship."
4 J. Holston, "Appadurai, (2003) Cities and Citizenship," 188.
5 Smith and McQuarrie, *Remaking Urban Citizenship*; Harvey, "The Right to the City"; Lefebvre, Kofman, and Lebas, *Writings on Cities.*
6 This has been documented widely. In terms of queer life, see Spade, *Normal Life.*
7 Kymlicka, *Multicultural Citizenship*; Benhabib, *The Claims of Culture*; Young, *Justice and the Politics of Difference.*
8 Rosaldo, "Cultural Citizenship and Educational Democracy"; Somers, *Genealogies of Citizenship*, 6.
9 Phelan, *Sexual Strangers*, 7.
10 Ibid., 15–16.
11 Sumerau, Padavic, and Schrock, "'Little Girls Unwilling to Do What's Best for Them.'"
12 Sumerau and Cragun, *Christianity*; Stone, "'You Out-Gayed the Gays.'"
13 Woodell, Kazyak, and Compton, "Reconciling LGB and Christian Identities in the Rural South"; Sumerau, "'Some of Us Are Good, God-Fearing Folks.'"
14 Bell and Binnie, *The Sexual Citizen.*
15 Knopp and Brown, "Queer Diffusions."
16 This epistemological blind spot normalizes and naturalizes queer practices in a few cities, which implicitly frames queer practices elsewhere as exceptional, different, or a form of mimicry. Knopp and Brown, "Queer Diffusions"; Brown, "Urban (Homo) Sexualities"; Myrdahl, "Ordinary (Small) Cities and LGBQ Lives."
17 Robinson, *Ordinary Cities.*
18 Watkins III, *Queering the Redneck Riviera*, 123.

APPENDIX

1 Brown-Saracino, "From Methodological Stumbles to Substantive Insights."
2 Paulsen, "Ethnography of the Ephemeral."
3 Bruce, *Pride Parades*; Paulsen, "Ethnography of the Ephemeral."
4 Stone, "Queer Persistence in the Archive," 216.

BIBLIOGRAPHY

Abelson, Miriam J. *Men in Place: Trans Masculinity, Race, and Sexuality in America.* University of Minnesota Press, 2019.

Abraham, Julie. "The Homosexuality of Cities." *The New Blackwell Companion to the City*, edited by Gary Bridge and Sophie Watson, John Wiley & Sons, 2011, pp. 586–95.

Aching, Gerard. "Carnival Time versus Modern Social Life: A False Distinction." *Social Identities* 16, no. 4 (July 2010): 415–25. https://doi.org/10.1080/13504630.2010.497699.

Acosta, Katie. "'How Could You Do This to Me?': How Lesbian, Bisexual, and Queer Latinas Negotiate Sexual Identity with Their Families." *Black Women, Gender + Families* 4, no. 1 (2010): 63–85. https://doi.org/10.5406/blacwomegendfami.4.1.0063.

Acosta, Katie L. "The Language of (in) Visibility: Using in-between Spaces as a Vehicle for Empowerment in the Family." *Journal of Homosexuality* 58, no. 6–7 (2011): 883–900.

Alderman, Derek H., and Joshua Inwood. "Street Naming and the Politics of Belonging: Spatial Injustices in the Toponymic Commemoration of Martin Luther King Jr." *Social & Cultural Geography* 14, no. 2 (March 2013): 211–33. https://doi.org/10.1080/14649365.2012.754488.

Arnold, Emily A., and Marlon M. Bailey. "Constructing Home and Family: How the Ballroom Community Supports African American GLBTQ Youth in the Face of HIV/AIDS." *Journal of Gay & Lesbian Social Services* 21, no. 2–3 (May 20, 2009): 171–88. https://doi.org/10.1080/10538720902772006.

Asenap, Jason. "Confronting Colonialism While Others Celebrate It." *High Country News*, May 24, 2018. www.indianz.com.

Atkins, Jennifer. *New Orleans Carnival Balls: The Secret Side of Mardi Gras, 1870–1920.* Louisiana State University Press, 2017.

Babcock, Barbara A. "'A New Mexican Rebecca': Imaging Pueblo Women." *Journal of the Southwest*, 1990, 400–437.

Bailey, Marlon M. *Butch Queens Up in Pumps: Gender, Performance, and Ballroom Culture in Detroit.* University of Michigan Press, 2013.

Bailey, Marlon M., and Rashad Shabazz. *Gender and Sexual Geographies of Blackness: Anti-Black Heterotopias (Part 1).* Taylor & Francis, 2014.

Baker, Ashley A., and Kimberly Kelly. "Live Like a King, Y'all: Gender Negotiation and the Performance of Masculinity among Southern Drag Kings." *Sexualities* 19, no. 1–2 (2016): 46–63.

Bakhtin, Mikhail. *Rabelais and His World.* Indiana University Press, 1984.

Barrios, Roberto E. "You Found Us Doing This, This Is Our Way: Criminalizing Second Lines, Super Sunday, and Habitus in Post-Katrina New Orleans." *Identities* 17, no. 6 (December 15, 2010): 586–612. https://doi.org/10.1080/1070289X.2010.533522.

Barton, Bernadette. *Pray the Gay Away: The Extraordinary Lives of Bible Belt Gays*. New York University Press, 2012.

Bell, David, and Jon Binnie. *The Sexual Citizen: Queer Politics and Beyond*. Polity Cambridge, 2000.

Bell, Joyce M., and Douglas Hartmann. "Diversity in Everyday Discourse: The Cultural Ambiguities and Consequences of 'Happy Talk.'" *American Sociological Review*, June 24, 2016. https://doi.org/10.1177/000312240707200603.

Benhabib, Seyla. *The Claims of Culture: Equality and Diversity in the Global Era*. Princeton University Press, 2002.

Bennett, Jeffrey, and Isaac West. "'United We Stand, Divided We Fall': AIDS, Armorettes, and the Tactical Repertoires of Drag." *Southern Communication Journal* 74, no. 3 (2009): 300–313.

Berkowitz, Alexandra, and Irene Padavic. "Getting a Man or Getting Ahead: A Comparison of White and Black Sororities." *Journal of Contemporary Ethnography* 27, no. 4 (January 1, 1999): 530–57. https://doi.org/10.1177/089124199129023325.

Berlant, Lauren Gail. *The Queen of America Goes to Washington City: Essays on Sex and Citizenship*. Duke University Press, 1997.

Bernard, Richard M., and Bradley R. Rice. *Sunbelt Cities: Politics and Growth since World War II*. University of Texas Press, 2014.

Bernstein, Mary. "Celebration and Suppression: The Strategic Uses of Identity by the Lesbian and Gay Movement." *American Journal of Sociology* 103, no. 3 (1997): 531–65.

Berrey, Ellen. *The Enigma of Diversity: The Language of Race and the Limits of Racial Justice*. University of Chicago Press, 2015.

Binnie, Jon. "Trading Places: Consumption, Sexuality and the Production of Queer Space." *Mapping Desire: Geographies of Sexualities*, 1995, 182–99.

Bitterman, Alex. "Rainbow Diaspora: The Emerging Renaissance of Gay Neighbourhoods." *Town Planning Review* 91, no. 2 (2020): 99–108.

Bledsoe, Adam, Latoya E. Eaves, and Brian Williams. "Introduction: Black Geographies In and Of the United States South." *Southeastern Geographer* 57, no. 1 (2017): 6–11.

Bloemraad, Irene, Anna Korteweg, and Gökçe Yurdakul. "Citizenship and Immigration: Multiculturalism, Assimilation, and Challenges to the Nation-State." *Annual Review of Sociology* 34, no. 1 (August 2008): 153–79. https://doi.org/10.1146/annurev.soc.34.040507.134608.

Blum, Linda M. "Review Essay: Body Wars, the Clash of the Paradigms." *Qualitative Sociology* 25, no. 2 (June 1, 2002): 305–14. https://doi.org/10.1023/A:1015427003600.

Bonilla-Silva, Eduardo. *Racism Without Racists: Color-Blind Racism and the Persistence of Racial Inequality in the United States*. Rowman & Littlefield, 2010.

Bourdieu, Pierre. *Distinction: A Social Critique of the Judgement of Taste*. Harvard University Press, 1984.

Bourdieu, Pierre, and Loïc Wacquant. "Symbolic Capital and Social Classes." *Journal of Classical Sociology* 13, no. 2 (2013): 292–302.

Bowman, Ruth Laurion, Melanie Kitchens, and Linda Shkreli. "FEMAture Evacuation: A Parade." *Text and Performance Quarterly* 27, no. 4 (October 1, 2007): 277–301. https://doi.org/10.1080/10462930701573329.

Braunstein, Ruth, Brad R. Fulton, and Richard L. Wood. "The Role of Bridging Cultural Practices in Racially and Socioeconomically Diverse Civic Organizations." *American Sociological Review* 79, no. 4 (2014): 705–25.

Brown, Gavin. "Homonormativity: A Metropolitan Concept That Denigrates 'Ordinary' Gay Lives." *Journal of Homosexuality* 59, no. 7 (2012): 1065–72.

———. "Urban (Homo) Sexualities: Ordinary Cities and Ordinary Sexualities." *Geography Compass* 2, no. 4 (2008): 1215–31.

Browne, Kath. "A Party with Politics? (Re)Making LGBTQ Pride Spaces in Dublin and Brighton." *Social & Cultural Geography* 8, no. 1 (February 1, 2007): 63–87. https://doi.org/10.1080/14649360701251817.

Brown-Saracino, Japonica. "Aligning Our Maps: A Call to Reconcile Distinct Visions of Literatures on Sexualities, Space, and Place." *City & Community* 18, no. 1 (2019): 37–43. https://doi.org/10.1111/cico.12378.

———. *How Places Make Us: Novel LBQ Identities in Four Small Cities*. University of Chicago Press, 2018.

———. "From Methodological Stumbles to Substantive Insights: Gaining Ethnographic Access in Queer Communities." *Qualitative Sociology* 37, no. 1 (March 2014): 43–68. https://doi.org/10.1007/s11133-013-9271-7.

Bruce, Katherine McFarland. *Pride Parades: How a Parade Changed the World*. New York University Press, 2016.

Canaday, Margot. *The Straight State: Sexuality and Citizenship in Twentieth-Century America*. Vol. 64. Princeton University Press, 2009.

Cantú, Norma E. "Dos Mundos [Two Worlds]: Two Celebrations in Laredo, Texas—Los Matachines de La Santa Cruz and The Pocahontas Pageant of the George Washington's Birthday Celebration." In *Global Mexican Cultural Productions*, 61–74. Springer, 2011.

Capous-Desyllas, Moshoula, and Marina Johnson-Rhodes. "Collecting Visual Voices: Understanding Identity, Community, and the Meaning of Participation within Gay Rodeos." *Sexualities* 21, no. 3 (2018): 446–75.

Carey, Albert. "New Orleans Mardi Gras Krewes." *Glbtq: An Encyclopedia of Gay, Lesbian, Bisexual, Transgender and Queer Culture*. Reference Reviews, 2006.

Carnaghi, Andrea, and Anne Maass. "In-Group and Out-Group Perspectives in the Use of Derogatory Group Labels: Gay Versus Fag." *Journal of Language and Social Psychology* 26, no. 2 (June 1, 2007): 142–56. https://doi.org/10.1177/0261927X07300077.

Carnoy, Martin. *Education as Cultural Imperialism*. Longman New York, 1974.

Carter, Niambi Michele. *American While Black: African Americans, Immigration, and the Limits of Citizenship*. Oxford University Press, USA, 2019.

Casey, Mark. "De-Dyking Queer Space(s): Heterosexual Female Visibility in Gay and Lesbian Spaces:" *Sexualities*, November 6, 2016. https://doi.org/10.1177/1363460704047062.

Chacon, Daniel. "Fiesta Drops Divisive Entrada Pageant in Santa Fe." *Santa Fe New Mexican*, July 24, 2018. www.santafenewmexican.com.

———. "Protesters at Annual Fiesta Entrada Aim to Expose City's Uneasy History." *Santa Fe New Mexican*, September 11, 2015. www.santafenewmexican.com.

Chauncey, George. *Gay New York: Gender, Urban Culture, and the Making of the Gay Male World, 1890–1940*. Hachette UK, 2008.

———. *Gay New York: Gender, Urban Culture, and the Makings of the Gay Male World, 1890–1940*. Basic Books, 1994.

Chávez, John R. *The Lost Land: The Chicano Image of the Southwest*. University of New Mexico Press, 1984.

Clum, John M. *Staging Gay Lives: An Anthology of Contemporary Gay Theater*. Routledge, 2018.

———. *Something for the Boys: Musical Theater and Gay Culture*. St. Martin's Press, 1999.

Cobb, Maggie C. "'For a While They Live a Few Feet Off the Ground': Place and Cultural Performance at the Walnut Valley Festival." *Journal of Contemporary Ethnography* 45, no. 4 (August 1, 2016): 367–95. https://doi.org/10.1177/0891241614568192.

Cohen, Alfred M. *Beauty Queens on the Global Stage: Gender, Contests, and Power*. Psychology Press, 1996.

Cohen, Cathy J. *The Boundaries of Blackness: AIDS and the Breakdown of Black Politics*. University of Chicago Press, 1999.

Collins, Patricia Hill. *Black Sexual Politics: African Americans, Gender, and the New Racism*. Routledge, 2004. https://doi.org/10.4324/9780203309506.

———. "Learning from the Outsider Within: The Sociological Significance of Black Feminist Thought." *Social Problems* 33, no. 6 (1986): s14–32.

Compton, D'Lane. "Queer Eye on the Gay Rodeo." In *Gender in the Twenty-First Century*, 222–38. University of California Press, 2017.

Compton, D'Lane, Tey Meadow, and Kristen Schilt. *Other, Please Specify: Queer Methods in Sociology*. University of California Press, 2018.

Costello, Brian J. *Carnival in Louisiana: Celebrating Mardi Gras from the French Quarter to the Red River*. Louisiana State University Press, 2017.

Crary, Jonathan. *Suspensions of Perception: Attention, Spectacle, and Modern Culture*. MIT Press, 2001.

Cresswell, Tim. *In Place–Out of Place: Geography, Ideology, and Transgression*. Vol. 2. University of Minnesota Press, 1992.

Culyer, Anthony J., and Adam Wagstaff. "Equity and Equality in Health and Health Care." *Journal of Health Economics* 12, no. 4 (1993): 431–57.

Davis, Andrew. "Experiential Places or Places of Experience? Place Identity and Place Attachment as Mechanisms for Creating Festival Environment." *Tourism Management* 55 (2016): 49–61.

Davis, Susan G. *Parades and Power: Street Theatre in Nineteenth-Century Philadelphia.* Temple University Press, 1986.

Dawkins, Marvin P. "Race Relations and the Sport of Golf: The African American Golf Legacy." *Western Journal of Black Studies* 28, no. 1 (2004): 327.

Debord, Guy. *Society of the Spectacle.* Bread and Circuses Publishing, 2012.

Decena, Carlos Ulises. "Tacit Subjects." *GLQ: A Journal of Lesbian and Gay Studies* 14, no. 2–3 (2008): 339–59.

Degler, Carl N. *Place over Time: The Continuity of Southern Distinctiveness.* Taylor & Francis, 1997.

Delaney, Caldwell, and Clark S. Whistler. *Remember Mobile.* Haunted Book Shop, 1980.

Delanty, Gerard, Liana Giorgi, and Monica Sassatelli. *Festivals and the Cultural Public Sphere.* Taylor & Francis, 2011.

Deluney, Davd. "The Boundaries of Responsibility Interpretations of Geography in School Desegregation Cases." *Urban Geography* 15, no. 5 (1994): 470–86.

d'Emilio, John. "Capitalism and Gay Identity." *Families in the US: Kinship and Domestic Politics*, 131–41. Temple University Press, 1983.

Dennis, Dion. "Washington's Birthday on the Texas Border." *Ctheory*, 2015, 2–17.

Denzin, Norman K. "Cowboys and Indians." *Symbolic Interaction* 25, no. 2 (2002): 251–61.

Deutsch, Sarah. *No Separate Refuge: Culture, Class, and Gender on an Anglo-Hispanic Frontier in the American Southwest, 1880–1940.* Oxford University Press on Demand, 1989.

Deverell, William. *Whitewashed Adobe: The Rise of Los Angeles and the Remaking of Its Mexican Past.* University of California Press, 2004.

Dews, Carlos Lee Barney, and Carolyn Leste Law. *Out in the South.* Temple University Press, 2001.

Diamond, Lisa M. "'I'm Straight, but I Kissed a Girl': The Trouble with American Media Representations of Female-Female Sexuality." *Feminism & Psychology* 15, no. 1 (February 1, 2005): 104–10. https://doi.org/10.1177/0959353505049712.

Dinerstein, Joel. "Second Lining Post-Katrina: Learning Community from the Prince of Wales Social Aid and Pleasure Club." *American Quarterly* 61, no. 3 (2009): 615–37.

Doan, Petra L. "Queers in the American City: Transgendered Perceptions of Urban Space." *Gender, Place & Culture* 14, no. 1 (February 2007): 57–74. https://doi.org/10.1080/09663690601122309.

Dobbin, Frank. "Cultural Models of Organization: The Social Construction of Rational Organizing Principles." SSRN Scholarly Paper. Rochester, NY: Social Science Research Network, 1994. https://papers.ssrn.com.

Dowd, Alicia C. "From Access to Outcome Equity: Revitalizing the Democratic Mission of the Community College." *The ANNALS of the American Academy of Political and Social Science* 586, no. 1 (2003): 92–119.

Dumas, Michael. "'People's Parade' Proves Why Joe Cain Day May Very Well Be the Most Popular Day of the Mardi Gras Calendar—al.Com." *Al.Com*, March 6, 2019. www.al.com.

Duncan, Nancy. *Bodyspace: Destabilizing Geographies of Gender and Sexuality*. Psychology Press, 1996.

Dunn, Kevin M. "Using Cultural Geography to Engage Contested Constructions of Ethnicity and Citizenship in Sydney." *Social & Cultural Geography* 4, no. 2 (June 2003): 153–65. https://doi.org/10.1080/14649360309057.

Eaves, Latoya E. "Black Geographic Possibilities: On a Queer Black South." *Southeastern Geographer* 57, no. 1 (2017): 80–95.

Edelman, Lee. *No Future: Queer Theory and the Death Drive*. Duke University Press, 2004.

Eder, Donna, Suzanne Staggenborg, and LORI Sudderth. "The National Women's Music Festival: Collective Identity and Diversity in a Lesbian-Feminist Community." *Journal of Contemporary Ethnography* 23, no. 4 (January 1, 1995): 485–515. https://doi.org/10.1177/089124195023004004.

Edmonson, Munro S. "Carnival in New Orleans." *Caribbean Quarterly* 4, no. 3–4 (1956): 233–45.

Ehrenreich, Barbara. *Dancing in the Streets: A History of Collective Joy*. Macmillan, 2007.

Eisner, Shiri. *Bi: Notes for a Bisexual Revolution*. Basic Books, 2013.

Falassi, Alessandro. *Time Out of Time: Essays on the Festival*. University of New Mexico Press, 1987.

Ferguson, Roderick A. *One-Dimensional Queer*. John Wiley & Sons, 2018.

Fetner, Tina, and Melanie Heath. "Editor's Pick: Do Same-Sex and Straight Weddings Aspire to the Fairytale? Women's Conformity and Resistance to Traditional Weddings." *Sociological Perspectives* 59, no. 4 (2016): 721–42.

Fisher, Diana. "Immigrant Closets: Tactical-Micro-Practices-in-the-Hyphen." *Journal of Homosexuality* 45, no. 2–4 (2003): 171–92.

Ford, Elyssa. "Becoming the West: Cowboys as Icons of Masculine Style for Gay Men." *Critical Studies in Men's Fashion* 5, no. 1–2 (2018): 41–53.

Franzen, Trisha. "Differences and Identities: Feminism and the Albuquerque Lesbian Community." *Signs: Journal of Women in Culture and Society* 18, no. 4 (July 1, 1993): 891–906. https://doi.org/10.1086/494847.

Fraser, Nancy. "Rethinking Recognition." *New Left Review* 3 (2000): 107.

Fraser, Nancy, and Axel Honneth. *Redistribution or Recognition?: A Political-Philosophical Exchange*. Verso, 2003.

Friedman, Lawrence J., and Mark D. McGarvie. *Charity, Philanthropy, and Civility in American History*. Cambridge University Press, 2003.

Gamson, Joshua. *Freaks Talk Back: Tabloid Talk Shows and Sexual Nonconformity*. University of Chicago Press, 1998.

Garcia, Lorena. "'Now Why Do You Want to Know about That?' Heteronormativity, Sexism, and Racism in the Sexual (Mis) Education of Latina Youth." *Gender & Society* 23, no. 4 (2009): 520–41.

Gardner, Robert Owen. "The Portable Community: Mobility and Modernization in Bluegrass Festival Life." *Symbolic Interaction* 27, no. 2 (2004): 155–78.

Gibson, Arrell Morgan. *The Santa Fe and Taos Colonies: Age of the Muses, 1900–1942.* University of Oklahoma Press, 1983.

Gill, James. *Lords of Misrule: Mardi Gras and the Politics of Race in New Orleans.* University Press of Mississippi, 1997.

Gitterman, Alex, and Lawrence Schulman. *Mutual Aid Groups, Vulnerable and Resilient Populations, and the Life Cycle.* Columbia University Press, 2005.

Glass, Valerie Q. "'We Are with Family': Black Lesbian Couples Negotiate Rituals with Extended Families." *Journal of GLBT Family Studies* 10, no. 1–2 (January 1, 2014): 79–100. https://doi.org/10.1080/1550428X.2014.857242.

Glenn, Evelyn Nakano. "Settler Colonialism as Structure: A Framework for Comparative Studies of U.S. Race and Gender Formation." *Sociology of Race and Ethnicity*, January 1, 2015. https://doi.org/10.1177/2332649214560440.

———. "Constructing Citizenship: Exclusion, Subordination, and Resistance." *American Sociological Review* 76, no. 1 (February 1, 2011): 1–24. https://doi.org/10.1177/0003122411398443.

Goffman, Erving. *Stigma: Notes on the Management of Spoiled Identity.* Simon & Schuster, 2009.

Gorman-Murray, Andrew. "Que (e) Rying Homonormativity: The Everyday Politics of Lesbian and Gay Homemaking." *Sexuality and Gender at Home: Experience, Politics, Transgression*, 149–62. Bloomsbury Publishing, 2017.

Gotham, Kevin Fox. "Theorizing Urban Spectacles." *City* 9, no. 2 (2005): 225–46.

Gould, Deborah B. *Moving Politics: Emotion and ACT UP's Fight against AIDS.* University of Chicago Press, 2009.

Grams, Diane M. "Freedom and Cultural Consciousness: Black Working-Class Parades in Post-Katrina New Orleans." *Journal of Urban Affairs* 35, no. 5 (2013): 501–29.

Green, James N. *Beyond Carnival: Male Homosexuality in Twentieth-Century Brazil.* University of Chicago Press, 1999.

Greene, Laurie. *Drag Queens and Beauty Queens: Contesting Femininity in the World's Playground.* Rutgers University Press, 2020.

Greene, Theodore. "Gay Neighborhoods and the Rights of the Vicarious Citizen." *City & Community* 13, no. 2 (2014): 99–118. https://doi.org/10.1111/cico.12059.

Griffin, Larry J. "The American South and the Self." *Southern Cultures* 12, no. 3 (2006): 6–28.

Griswold, Wendy, and Nathan Wright. "Cowbirds, Locals, and the Dynamic Endurance of Regionalism." *American Journal of Sociology* 109, no. 6 (2004): 1411–51.

Gulliford, Martin, Jose Figueroa-Munoz, Myfanwy Morgan, David Hughes, Barry Gibson, Roger Beech, and Meryl Hudson. "What Does 'Access to Health Care' Mean?" *Journal of Health Services Research & Policy* 7, no. 3 (2002): 186–88.

Gupta, Akhil, and James Ferguson. "Beyond 'Culture': Space, Identity, and the Politics of Difference." *Cultural Anthropology* 7, no. 1 (1992): 6–23.

Guss, David M. *The Festive State: Race, Ethnicity, and Nationalism as Cultural Performance.* University of California Press, 2001.

Hall, Christie. "In the Pink: The Origins of the Spanish Town Mardi Gras Parade." Country Road Magazine, January 25, 2016. https://countryroadsmagazine.com.

Hall, John R. "Cultural Meanings and Cultural Structures in Historical Explanation." *History and Theory* 39, no. 3 (2000): 331–47. https://doi.org/10.1111/0018-2656.00134.

Hall, Stuart. "The Spectacle of the Other." *Discourse Theory and Practice: A Reader*, 324–44. Sage, 2001.

Halperin, David M. *How To Be Gay*. Harvard University Press, 2012.

Hardin, Michael. "Altering Masculinities: The Spanish Conquest and the Evolution of the Latin American Machismo." *International Journal of Sexuality and Gender Studies* 7, no. 1 (January 1, 2002): 1–22. https://doi.org/10.1023/A:1013050829597.

Harker, Jaime. *The Lesbian South: Southern Feminists, the Women in Print Movement, and the Queer Literary Canon*. University of North Carolina Press, 2018.

Harress, Christopher. "LGBTQ Mardi Gras Groups Cut through the Racial Divide." *Al.Com*, February 8, 2018. www.al.com.

Harrison, Lyn. "'It's a Nice Day for a White Wedding': The Debutante Ball and Constructions of Femininity." *Feminism & Psychology* 7, no. 4 (November 1, 1997): 495–516. https://doi.org/10.1177/0959353597074004.

Hart, Kylo-Patrick R. "We're Here, We're Queer—and We're Better Than You: The Representational Superiority of Gay Men to Heterosexuals on Queer Eye for the Straight Guy." *The Journal of Men's Studies* 12, no. 3 (June 1, 2004): 241–53. https://doi.org/10.3149/jms.1203.241.

Hartless, Jaime. "Questionably Queer: Understanding Straight Presence in the Post-Gay Bar." *Journal of Homosexuality* 66, no. 8 (2019): 1035–57.

———. "'They're Gay Bars, but They're Men Bars': Gendering Questionably Queer Spaces in a Southeastern US University Town." *Gender, Place & Culture* 25, no. 12 (2018): 1781–1800.

Harvey, David. "The Right to the City." *International Journal of Urban and Regional Research*. John Wiley & Sons, Ltd., December 1, 2003. https://onlinelibrary.wiley.com/doi/abs/10.1111/j.0309-1317.2003.00492.x.

Haynes, Michaele Thurgood. *Dressing Up Debutantes: Pageantry and Glitz in Texas*. Berg, 1998.

Heap, Chad. *Slumming: Sexual and Racial Encounters in American Nightlife, 1885–1940*. University of Chicago Press, 2008.

Hemmings, Clare. "Rescuing Lesbian Camp." *Journal of Lesbian Studies* 11, no. 1–2 (August 2007): 159–66. https://doi.org/10.1300/J155v11n01_12.

Hernández-Ehrisman, Laura. *Inventing the Fiesta City: Heritage and Carnival in San Antonio*. University of New Mexico Press, 2008.

Higginbotham, Evelyn Brooks. *Righteous Discontent: The Women's Movement in the Black Baptist Church, 1880–1920*. Harvard University Press, 1994.

Hinsley, Curtis M. "Authoring Authenticity." *Journal of the Southwest*, 1990, 462–78.

Hollander, Justin B. *Sunburnt Cities: The Great Recession, Depopulation and Urban Planning in the American Sunbelt*. Routledge, 2011.

Holston, James. *Cities and Citizenship*. Duke University Press, 1999.

Holston, James, and Arjun Appadurai. *Cities and Citizenship Public Culture*. University of Chicago Press, 1996.

Holyfield, Lori, Maggie Cobb, Kimberly Murray, and Ashleigh McKinzie. "Musical Ties That Bind: Nostalgia, Affect, and Heritage in Festival Narratives." *Symbolic Interaction* 36, no. 4 (2013): 457–77.

Honneth, Axel. "Recognition or Redistribution?" *Theory, Culture & Society* 18, no. 2–3 (2001): 43–55.

Hooper-Greenhill, Eilean. "Museums and the Interpretation of Visual Culture / Eilean Hooper-Greenhill." *Library Books*, October 15, 2018. http://onesearch.museumsiam.org.

Hopkins, Steven J. "'Let the Drag Race Begin': The Rewards of Becoming a Queen." *Journal of Homosexuality* 46, no. 3–4 (2004): 135–49.

Horton, Sarah Bronwen. *The Santa Fe Fiesta, Reinvented: Staking Ethno-Nationalist Claims to a Disappearing Homeland*. School for Advanced Research Press, 2010.

Howard, John. *Men Like That: A Southern Queer History*. University of Chicago Press, 2001.

Hunter, Marcus Anthony, Mary Pattillo, Zandria F. Robinson, and Keeanga-Yamahtta Taylor. "Black Placemaking: Celebration, Play, and Poetry." *Theory, Culture & Society* 33, no. 7–8 (December 1, 2016): 31–56. https://doi.org/10.1177/0263276416635259.

Hunter, Marcus Anthony, and Zandria Robinson. *Chocolate Cities: The Black Map of American Life*. University of California Press, 2018.

Hurlbert, Jeanne S. "The Southern Region: A Test of the Hypothesis of Cultural Distinctiveness." *Sociological Quarterly* 30, no. 2 (1989): 245–66.

Inez Guzman, Alicia. "Burn Whom?" *Santa Fe Reporter*, August 29, 2017. www.sfreporter.com.

Inness, Sherrie A., and Michele Lloyd. "'G.I. Joes in Barbie Land': Recontextualizing Butch in Twentieth-Century Lesbian Culture." *NWSA Journal* 7, no. 3 (1995): 1–23.

Irvin, Cate. "Constructing Hybridized Authenticities in the Gourmet Food Truck Scene." *Symbolic Interaction* 40, no. 1 (2017): 43–62.

Isch, Matt. *Capitol Park and Spanish Town*. Arcadia Publishing, 2016.

Jackson, Sue, and Tamsyn Gilbertson. "'Hot Lesbians': Young People's Talk About Representations of Lesbianism." *Sexualities*, 2009. https://journals.sagepub.com/doi/abs/10.1177/1363460708100919.

Jankowiak, William, and C. Todd White. "Carnival on the Clipboard: An Ethnological Study of New Orleans Mardi Gras." *Ethnology* (1999): 335–49.

Jansson, David R. "Internal Orientalism in America: WJ Cash's *The Mind of the South* and the Spatial Construction of American National Identity." *Political Geography* 22, no. 3 (2003): 293–316.

Johnson, E. Patrick. *Sweet Tea: Black Gay Men of the South*. University of North Carolina Press, 2011.

Joshi, Yuvraj. "Respectable Queerness." *Columbia Human Rights Law Review* 43 (2012): 415–67.

Karp, Ivan. "On Civil Society and Social Identity." *Museums and Communities: The Politics of Public Culture* (1992): 19–33.

———. *Exhibiting Cultures: The Poetics and Politics of Museum Display*. Smithsonian Institution, 1991.

Kasinitz, Philip, John H. Mollenkopf, Mary C. Waters, and Jennifer Holdaway. *Inheriting the City: The Children of Immigrants Come of Age*. Russell Sage Foundation, 2009.

Kates, Steven M., and Russell W. Belk. "The Meanings of Lesbian and Gay Pride Day: Resistance through Consumption and Resistance to Consumption." *Journal of Contemporary Ethnography* 30, no. 4 (August 1, 2001): 392–429. https://doi.org/10.1177/089124101030004003.

Kidd, Alan J. "Philanthropy and the 'Social History Paradigm.'" *Social History* 21, no. 2 (May 1, 1996): 180–92. https://doi.org/10.1080/03071029608567968.

King, Jason, Frank León Roberts, and Marvin K. White. "Remixing the Closet." *If We Have to Take Tomorrow: HIV, Black Men & Same Sex Desire*. Institute for Gay Men's Health, 2006, 65–68.

King-O'Riain, Rebecca Chiyoko. "Making the Perfect Queen: The Cultural Production of Identities in Beauty Pageants." *Sociology Compass*. John Wiley & Sons, Ltd, January 1, 2008. https://onlinelibrary.wiley.com/doi/abs/10.1111/j.1751-9020.2007.00056.x.

Kinser, Samuel. *Carnival, American Style: Mardi Gras at New Orleans and Mobile*. University of Chicago Press, 1990.

Kitchin, Rob. "'Out of Place,' 'Knowing One's Place': Space, Power and the Exclusion of Disabled People." *Disability & Society* 13, no. 3 (June 1998): 343–56. https://doi.org/10.1080/09687599826678.

Knopp, Larry, and Michael Brown. "Queer Diffusions." *Environment and Planning D: Society and Space* 21, no. 4 (August 1, 2003): 409–24. https://doi.org/10.1068/d360.

Knowles, Caroline. *Race and Social Analysis*. Sage, 2003.

Kropp, Phoebe S. "Citizens of the Past?: Olvera Street and the Construction of Race and Memory in 1930s Los Angeles." *Radical History Review* 81, no. 1 (October 1, 2001): 35–60.

Kymlicka, Will. *Multicultural Citizenship: A Liberal Theory of Minority Rights*. Clarendon Press, 1995.

Lamont, Michèle. "Addressing Recognition Gaps: Destigmatization and the Reduction of Inequality." *American Sociological Review* 83, no. 3 (2018): 419–44.

Lamont, Michèle, and Marcel Fournier. *Cultivating Differences: Symbolic Boundaries and the Making of Inequality*. University of Chicago Press, 1992.

Lamont, Michèle. *The Dignity of Working Men: Morality and the Boundaries of Race, Class, and Immigration*. Harvard University Press, 2009.

Lamont, Michèle, and Virág Molnár. "The Study of Boundaries in the Social Sciences." *Annual Review of Sociology* 28, no. 1 (2002): 167–95.

Lamont, Michèle, Graziella Moraes Silva, Jessica Welburn, Joshua Guetzkow, Nissim Mizrachi, Hanna Herzog, and Elisa Reis. *Getting Respect: Responding to Stigma and Discrimination in the United States, Brazil, and Israel.* Princeton University Press, 2016.

Lang, Clarence. "Locating the Civil Rights Movement: An Essay on the Deep South, Midwest, and Border South in Black Freedom Studies." *Journal of Social History* 47, no. 2 (2013): 371–400.

LaSala, Michael C. "Lesbians, Gay Men, and Their Parents: Family Therapy for the Coming-Out Crisis*." *Family Process* 39, no. 1 (2000): 67–81. https://doi.org/10.1111/j.1545-5300.2000.39108.x.

Lassiter, Matthew D., and Joseph Crespino. *The Myth of Southern Exceptionalism.* Oxford University Press, 2009.

Lefebvre, Henri, Eleonore Kofman, and Elizabeth Lebas. *Writings on Cities.* Vol. 63. Blackwell Oxford, 1996.

Lepore, Jill. *The Name of War: King Philip's War and the Origins of American Identity.* Knopf Doubleday, 2009.

Lievrouw, Leah A., and Sharon E. Farb. "Information and Equity." *Annual Review of Information Science and Technology* 37, no. 1 (2003): 499–540.

Lister, Ruth. "Citizenship: Towards a Feminist Synthesis." *Feminist Review* 57, no. 1 (September 1, 1997): 28–48. https://doi.org/10.1080/014177897339641.

Lister, Ruth, and Jo Campling. *Citizenship: Feminist Perspectives.* Macmillan International Higher Education, 2017.

Lloyd, Richard. "Urbanization and the Southern United States." *Annual Review of Sociology* 38 (2012): 483–506.

Lohman, Jon. "'It Can't Rain Every Day': The Year-Round Experience of Carnival." *Western Folklore* 58, no. 3/4 (1999): 279–98. https://doi.org/10.2307/1500462.

Loseke, Donileen R. "'The Whole Spirit of Modern Philanthropy': The Construction of the Idea of Charity, 1912–1992." *Social Problems* 44, no. 4 (November 1, 1997): 425–44. https://doi.org/10.2307/3097216.

Machado, Isabel. "Never Too Big, Never Too Much: The Order of Osiris and the LGBTQ Community in Mobile, Alabama." *Oral History* 46, no. 1 (2018): 78–90.

Marshall, Thomas Humphrey. *Citizenship and Social Class: And Other Essays.* Cambridge University Press, 1950.

Marston, Sallie A. "Public Rituals and Community Power: St. Patrick's Day Parades in Lowell, Massachusetts, 1841–1874." *Political Geography Quarterly* 8, no. 3 (1989): 255–69.

Mattson, Greggor. "Small-City Gay Bars, Big-City Urbanism." *City & Community* 19, no. 1 (2020): 76–97. https://doi.org/10.1111/cico.12443.

McGlotten, Shaka. "On Glass Closets and Not-Gay Gay Sex." *GLQ: A Journal of Lesbian and Gay Studies* 23, no. 4 (2017): 589–97.

McKenzie, Jon. *Perform Or Else: From Discipline to Performance.* Routledge, 2002.

McPherson, Tara. *Reconstructing Dixie: Race, Gender, and Nostalgia in the Imagined South.* Duke University Press, 2003.

McQueeney, Krista. "We Are God's Children, Y'all: Race, Gender, and Sexuality in Lesbian- and Gay-Affirming Congregations." *Social Problems* 56, no. 1 (February 1, 2009): 151–73. https://doi.org/10.1525/sp.2009.56.1.151.

McWilliams, Carey. *Southern California Country: An Island on the Land*. New York: Duell, 1946.

Milhausen, Robin R., Michael Reece, and Bilesha Perera. "A Theory-based Approach to Understanding Sexual Behavior at Mardi Gras." *Journal of Sex Research* 43, no. 2 (May 2006): 97–106. https://doi.org/10.1080/00224490609552304.

Mitchell, Pablo. *Coyote Nation: Sexuality, Race, and Conquest in Modernizing New Mexico, 1880–1920*. University of Chicago Press, 2008.

Mohanram, Radhika. *Black Body: Women, Colonialism, and Space*. Vol. 6. University of Minnesota Press, 1999.

Montaño, Mary Caroline. *Tradiciones Nuevomexicanas: Hispano Arts and Culture of New Mexico*. University of New Mexico Press, 2001.

Montegary, Liz. "Militarizing US Homonormativities: The Making of 'Ready, Willing, and Able' Gay Citizens." *Signs: Journal of Women in Culture and Society* 40, no. 4 (2015): 891–915.

Moore, Madison. *Fabulous: The Rise of the Beautiful Eccentric*. Yale University Press, 2018.

Moore, Mignon. *Invisible Families: Gay Identities, Relationships, and Motherhood Among Black Women*. University of California Press, 2011.

Moreman, Shane T., and Dawn Marie McIntosh. "Brown Scriptings and Rescriptings: A Critical Performance Ethnography of Latina Drag Queens." *Communication and Critical/Cultural Studies* 7, no. 2 (June 2010): 115–35. https://doi.org/10.1080/14791421003767912.

Morgensen, Scott Lauria. *Spaces between Us: Queer Settler Colonialism and Indigenous Decolonization*. University of Minnesota Press, 2011.

———. "Settler Homonationalism: Theorizing Settler Colonialism within Queer Modernities." *GLQ: A Journal of Lesbian and Gay Studies* 16, no. 1–2 (April 1, 2010): 105–31. https://doi.org/10.1215/10642684-2009-015.

Mucciaroni, Gary. *Same Sex, Different Politics: Success and Failure in the Struggles over Gay Rights*. University of Chicago Press, 2009.

Mullin, Molly H. *Culture in the Marketplace: Gender, Art, and Value in the American Southwest*. Duke University Press, 2001.

Muñoz, José Esteban. *Disidentifications: Queers of Color and the Performance of Politics*. University of Minnesota Press, 1999.

Myrdahl, Tiffany Muller. "Ordinary (Small) Cities and LGBQ Lives." *ACME: An International Journal for Critical Geographies* 12, no. 2 (2013): 279–304.

Neely, Brooke, and Michelle Samura. "Social Geographies of Race: Connecting Race and Space." *Ethnic and Racial Studies* 34, no. 11 (2011): 1933–52.

Newmahr, Staci. "Eroticism as Embodied Emotion: The Erotics of Renaissance Faire." *Symbolic Interaction* 37, no. 2 (2014): 209–25.

Newton, Esther. *Mother Camp: Female Impersonators in America*. University of Chicago Press, 1972.

———. "Dick (Less) Tracy and the Homecoming Queen: Lesbian Power and Representation in Gay Male Cherry Grove." In *Inventing Lesbian Cultures in America*, edited by Ellen Lewin, 161–93. Beacon Press, 1996.

Nielsen, Elly-Jean. "Lesbian Camp: An Unearthing." *Journal of Lesbian Studies* 20, no. 1 (January 2, 2016): 116–35. https://doi.org/10.1080/10894160.2015.1046040.

Ocobock, Abigail. "The Power and Limits of Marriage: Married Gay Men's Family Relationships." *Journal of Marriage and Family* 75, no. 1 (2013): 191–205.

Oliver, Adam, and Elias Mossialos. "Equity of Access to Health Care: Outlining the Foundations for Action." *Journal of Epidemiology & Community Health* 58, no. 8 (2004): 655–58.

Ong, Aihwa. "Cultural Citizenship as Subject-Making: Immigrants Negotiate Racial and Cultural Boundaries in the United States [and Comments and Reply]." *Current Anthropology* 37, no. 5 (December 1, 1996): 737–62. https://doi.org/10.1086/204560.

Orne, Jason. *Boystown: Sex and Community in Chicago*. University of Chicago Press, 2017.

Oswald, Ramona Faith. "A Member of the Wedding? Heterosexism and Family Ritual." *Journal of Lesbian Studies* 7, no. 2 (March 1, 2003): 107–31. https://doi.org/10.1300/J155v07n02_08.

———. "Resilience within the Family Networks of Lesbians and Gay Men: Intentionality and Redefinition." *Journal of Marriage and Family* 64, no. 2 (2002): 374–83.

———. "Religion, Family, and Ritual: The Production of Gay, Lesbian, Bisexual, and Transgender Outsiders-Within." *Review of Religious Research*, 2001, 39–50.

Ownby, Ted. *Manners and Southern History*. University Press of Mississippi, 2007.

Palmer, Gary B., and William R. Jankowiak. "Performance and Imagination: Toward an Anthropology of the Spectacular and the Mundane." *Cultural Anthropology* 11, no. 2 (1996): 225–58.

Papacharissi, Zizi, and Jan Fernback. "The Aesthetic Power of the Fab 5: Discursive Themes of Homonormativity in Queer Eye for the Straight Guy." *Journal of Communication Inquiry* 32, no. 4 (October 1, 2008): 348–67. https://doi.org/10.1177/0196859908320301.

Pascoe, C. J. *Dude, You're a Fag: Masculinity and Sexuality in High School*. University of California Press, 2011.

Paulsen, Krista E. "Ethnography of the Ephemeral: Studying Temporary Scenes through Individual and Collective Approaches." *Social Identities* 15, no. 4 (July 2009): 509–24. https://doi.org/10.1080/13504630903043865.

Peiss, Kathy. "'Charity Girls' and City Pleasures: Historical Notes on Working-Class Sexuality, 1880–1920." In *Powers of Desire*, edited by Snitow, Stansell, and Thompson, 74–87. New York University Press, 1983.

Phelan, Shane. *Sexual Strangers: Gays, Lesbians, and Dilemmas of Citizenship*. Temple University Press, 2010.

Picard, David, and Mike Robinson. "Remaking Worlds: Festivals, Tourism and Change." *Festivals, Tourism and Social Change: Remaking Worlds*, 2006, 1–31.

Polanyi, Karl, and Robert Morrison MacIver. *The Great Transformation*. Vol. 2. Beacon Press, 1944.

Pond, Ann Janine Jurgens. *The Ritualized Construction of Status: The Men Who Made Mardi Gras, 1830–1900*. University of Southern Mississippi, 2006.

Posselt, Julie Renee, Ozan Jaquette, Rob Bielby, and Michael N. Bastedo. "Access without Equity: Longitudinal Analyses of Institutional Stratification by Race and Ethnicity, 1972–2004." *American Educational Research Journal* 49, no. 6 (2012): 1074–1111.

Puar, Jasbir K. "Mapping US Homonormativities." *Gender, Place & Culture* 13, no. 1 (2006): 67–88.

Puwar, Nirmal. *Space Invaders: Race, Gender and Bodies out of Place*. Berg, 2004. http://research.gold.ac.uk/2017/.

Reczek, Corinne. "Ambivalence in Gay and Lesbian Family Relationships." *Journal of Marriage and Family* 78, no. 3 (2016): 644–59. https://doi.org/10.1111/jomf.12308.

Redmon, David. "Playful Deviance as an Urban Leisure Activity: Secret Selves, Self-Validation, and Entertaining Performances." *Deviant Behavior* 24, no. 1 (2003): 27–51.

Redmon, David. "Examining Low Self-Control Theory at Mardi Gras: Critiquing the General Theory of Crime within the Framework of Normative Deviance." *Deviant Behavior* 24, no. 4 (2003): 373–92.

Reed, Christopher. "We're from Oz: Marking Ethnic and Sexual Identity in Chicago." *Environment and Planning D: Society and Space* 21, no. 4 (August 1, 2003): 425–40. https://doi.org/10.1068/d372.

Regis, Helen A. "Blackness and the Politics of Memory in the New Orleans Second Line." *American Ethnologist* 28, no. 4 (2001): 752–77.

Rehberger, Dean. "Visions of the New Mexican in Public Pageants and Dramas of Santa Fe and Taos, 1918–1940." *Journal of the Southwest* 37, no. 3 (1995): 450–69.

Reyes, Victoria. "Three Models of Transparency in Ethnographic Research: Naming Places, Naming People, and Sharing Data." *Ethnography* 19, no. 2 (June 1, 2018): 204–26. https://doi.org/10.1177/1466138117733754.

Rice, Tom W., William P. McLean, and Amy J. Larsen. "Southern Distinctiveness over Time, 1972–2000." *American Review of Politics* 23 (2002): 193–220.

Rifkin, Mark. *When Did Indians Become Straight?: Kinship, the History of Sexuality, and Native Sovereignty*. Oxford University Press, 2010.

Riggio, Milla Cozart. *Carnival: Culture in Action–the Trinidad Experience*. Routledge, 2004.

Riley, Michael J. "Constituting the Southwest Contesting the Southwest Re-Inventing the Southwest." *Journal of the Southwest*, 1994, 221–41.

Rinaldo, Rachel. "Space of Resistance: The Puerto Rican Cultural Center and Humboldt Park." *Cultural Critique*, no. 50 (2002): 135–74.

Rizvi, F., and B. Lingard. "Disability, Education and the Discourses of Justice." In *Disability and the Dilemmas of Education and Justice*, edited by Carol Christensen and Fazal Rizvi, 9–26. Open University Press, 1996.

Roberts, Dorothy E. *Welfare and the Problem of Black Citizenship*. HeinOnline, 1995.

Roberts, L. Craig. *Mardi Gras in Mobile*. Arcadia Publishing, 2015.

Roberts, Robin. "New Orleans Mardi Gras and Gender in Three Krewes: Rex, the Truck Parades, and Muses." *Western Folklore* 65, no. 3 (2006): 303–28.

Robinson, Brandon Andrew. "Conditional Families and Lesbian, Gay, Bisexual, Transgender, and Queer Youth Homelessness: Gender, Sexuality, Family Instability, and Rejection." *Journal of Marriage and Family* 80, no. 2 (2018): 383–96. https://doi.org/10.1111/jomf.12466.

Robinson, Jennifer. *Ordinary Cities: Between Modernity and Development*. Psychology Press, 2006.

Rodríguez, Sylvia. "Tourism, Whiteness, and the Vanishing Anglo." In *Seeing and Being Seen: Tourism in the American West*, 194–210. University Press of Kansas, 2001.

———. "Fiesta Time and Plaza Space: Resistance and Accommodation in a Tourist Town." *Journal of American Folklore* 111, no. 439 (1998): 39–56. https://doi.org/10.2307/541319.

———. "The Taos Fiesta: Invented Tradition and the Infrapolitics of Symbolic Reclamation." *Journal of the Southwest* 39, no. 1 (1997): 33–57.

———. "Art, Tourism, and Race Relations in Taos: Toward a Sociology of the Art Colony." *Journal of Anthropological Research* 45, no. 1 (1989): 77–99.

Rogers, Baker A. "'Contrary to All the Other Shit I've Said': Trans Men Passing in the South." *Qualitative Sociology*, August 26, 2019. https://doi.org/10.1007/s11133-019-09436-w.

Rogers, Nicholas. *Halloween: From Pagan Ritual to Party Night*. Oxford University Press, 2002.

Román, David. *Acts of Intervention: Performance, Gay Culture, and AIDS*. Indiana University Press, 1998.

Rosaldo, Renato. "Cultural Citizenship and Educational Democracy." *Cultural Anthropology* 9, no. 3 (1994): 402–11.

———. "Grief and a Headhunter's Rage: On the Cultural Construction of Emotions." *Text, Play and Story* (1983): 78–195.

Rubin, Henry. *Self-Made Men: Identity and Embodiment Among Transsexual Men*. Vanderbilt University Press, 2003.

Ruddick, Susan. "Constructing Difference in Public Spaces: Race, Class, and Gender as Interlocking Systems." *Urban Geography* 17, no. 2 (February 1996): 132–51. https://doi.org/10.2747/0272-3638.17.2.132.

Rupp, Leila J., and Verta A. Taylor. *Drag Queens at the 801 Cabaret*. University of Chicago Press, 2003.

Rust, Paula C. *Bisexuality and the Challenge to Lesbian Politics: Sex, Loyalty, and Revolution*. New York University Press, 1995.

Sandell, Richard. *Museums, Society, Inequality*. Routledge, 2003.

Savin-Williams, Ritch C., and Eric M. Dubé. "Parental Reactions to Their Child's Disclosure of a Gay/Lesbian Identity." *Family Relations* 47, no. 1 (1998): 7–13. https://doi.org/10.2307/584845.

Schein, Richard H. "Belonging through Land/Scape." *Environment and Planning A: Economy and Space* 41, no. 4 (April 1, 2009): 811–26. https://doi.org/10.1068/a41125.

Scherrer, Kristin S., Emily Kazyak, and Rachel Schmitz. "Getting 'Bi' in the Family: Bisexual People's Disclosure Experiences." *Journal of Marriage and Family* 77, no. 3 (2015): 680–96. https://doi.org/10.1111/jomf.12190.

Schmitz, Rachel M., and Kimberly A. Tyler. "The Complexity of Family Reactions to Identity among Homeless and College Lesbian, Gay, Bisexual, Transgender, and Queer Young Adults." *Archives of Sexual Behavior* 47, no. 4 (May 1, 2018): 1195–1207. https://doi.org/10.1007/s10508-017-1014-5.

Sedgwick, Eve Kosofsky. *Epistemology of the Closet*. University of California Press, 2008.

Seidman, Steven. "From Identity to Queer Politics: Shifts in Normative Heterosexuality and the Meaning of Citizenship." *Citizenship Studies* 5, no. 3 (2001): 321–28.

Sewell, William H. "A Theory of Structure: Duality, Agency, and Transformation." *American Journal of Sociology* 98, no. 1 (July 1992): 1–29. https://doi.org/10.1086/229967.

Shermer, Elizabeth Tandy. *Sunbelt Capitalism: Phoenix and the Transformation of American Politics*. University of Pennsylvania Press, 2013.

Shilts, Randy. *And the Band Played On: Politics, People, and the AIDS Epidemic, 20th-Anniversary Edition*. St. Martin's, 2007.

Shklar, Judith N. *American Citizenship: The Quest for Inclusion*. Harvard University Press, 1991.

Shrum, Wesley. "Ceremonial Disrobement and Moral Choice: Consumption Rituals at Mardi Gras." *Contemporary Consumption Rituals: A Research Anthology*, Lawrence Erlbaum Associates, 2004, 39–58.

Shrum, Wesley, and John Kilburn. "Ritual Disrobement at Mardi Gras: Ceremonial Exchange and Moral Order." *Social Forces* 75, no. 2 (1996): 423–58.

Skeggs, Beverley. *Formations of Class & Gender: Becoming Respectable*. Sage, 1997.

———. "Uneasy Alignments, Resourcing Respectable Subjectivity." *GLQ: A Journal of Lesbian and Gay Studies* 10, no. 2 (2004): 291–98.

Skipper, Jodi, and David Wharton. "Diasporic Kings and Queens: Lafayette's Black Mardi Gras Performances in Historical and Hemispheric Contexts." *Southern Quarterly* 52, no. 4 (Summer 2015): 133–54.

Sklar, Deidre. *Dancing with the Virgin: Body and Faith in the Fiesta of Tortugas, New Mexico*. University of California Press, 2001.

Smith, Andrea. "Queer Theory and Native Studies: The Heteronormativity of Settler Colonialism." *GLQ: A Journal of Lesbian and Gay Studies* 16, no. 1–2 (April 1, 2010): 41–68. https://doi.org/10.1215/10642684-2009-012.

Smith, Donna Jo. "Queering the South: Constructions of Southern/Queer Identity." *Carryin' On in the Lesbian and Gay South*, edited by John Howard, 370–85. New York University Press, 1997.

Smith, Howard Philips. *Unveiling the Muse: The Lost History of Gay Carnival in New Orleans*. University Press of Mississippi, 2017.

Smith, Lance C., and Richard Q. Shin. "Negotiating the Intersection of Racial Oppression and Heteronormativity." *Journal of Homosexuality* 62, no. 11 (2015): 1459–84.

Smith, Michael Peter, and Michael McQuarrie. *Remaking Urban Citizenship: Organizations, Institutions, and the Right to the City*. Transaction, 2011.

Snorton, C. Riley. *Black on Both Sides: A Racial History of Trans Identity*. University of Minnesota Press, 2017.

———. "Trapped in the Epistemological Closet: Black Sexuality and the 'Ghettocentric Imagination.'" *Souls* 11, no. 2 (2009): 94–111.

Somers, Margaret. *Genealogies of Citizenship: Knowledge, Markets, and the Right to Have Rights*. Cambridge University Press, 2008.

Somerville, Siobhan. "Scientific Racism and the Emergence of the Homosexual Body." *Journal of the History of Sexuality* 5, no. 2 (1994): 243–66.

Sontag, Susan. "Notes on Camp." *Camp: Queer Aesthetics and the Performing Subject* (1964): 53–65.

Spade, Dean. *Mutual Aid: Building Solidarity during This Crisis (and the Next)*. Verso Books, 2020.

———. *Normal Life: Administrative Violence, Critical Trans Politics, and the Limits of Law*. Duke University Press, 2015.

Stallybrass, Peter, and Allon White. *The Politics and Poetics of Transgression*. Cornell University Press, 1986.

Stanonis, Anthony J. "Through a Purple (Green and Gold) Haze: New Orleans Mardi Gras in the American Imagination." *Southern Cultures* 14, no. 2 (2008): 109–31.

Stevenson, Nick. "Cultural Citizenship." *The Blackwell Encyclopedia of Sociology*, 2007, 1–4.

Stillman, Peter G., and Adelaide H. Villmoare. "Democracy Despite Government: African American Parading and Democratic Theory." *New Political Science* 32, no. 4 (December 1, 2010): 485–99. https://doi.org/10.1080/07393148.2010.520436.

Stokes, Allyson. "The Glass Runway: How Gender and Sexuality Shape the Spotlight in Fashion Design." *Gender & Society* 29, no. 2 (April 1, 2015): 219–43. https://doi.org/10.1177/0891243214563327.

Stone, Amy L. "When My Parents Came to the Gay Ball: Comfort Work in Adult Child–Parent Relationships." *Journal of Family Issues*, 2020, 0192513X20935497.

———. "'You Out-Gayed the Gays': Gay Aesthetic Power and Lesbian, Bisexual, and Queer Women in LGBTQ Spaces." *Journal of Lesbian Studies*, 2019, 1–12.

———. *Cornyation: San Antonio's Outrageous Fiesta Tradition*. Trinity University Press, 2017.

———. "Crowning King Anchovy: Cold War Gay Visibility in San Antonio's Urban Festival." *Journal of the History of Sexuality* 25, no. 2 (2016): 297–322.

———. "Queer Persistence in the Archive." *Other, Please Specify: Queer Methods in Sociology*, edited by D'Lane Compton, Tey Meadow, and Kristin Schilt, 216–29. University of California Press, 2018.

———. "The Geography of Research on LGBTQ Life: Why Sociologists Should Study the South, Rural Queers, and Ordinary Cities." *Sociology Compass* 12, no. 11 (2018): e12638.

———. "More than Adding a T: American Lesbian and Gay Activists' Attitudes towards Transgender Inclusion." *Sexualities* 12, no. 3 (June 1, 2009): 334–54. https://doi.org/10.1177/1363460709103894.

Stryker, Susan. "Transgender History, Homonormativity, and Disciplinarity." *Radical History Review* 2008, no. 100 (January 1, 2008): 145–57. https://doi.org/10.1215/01636545-2007-026.

Sumerau, J. E., and Ryan T. Cragun. *Christianity and the Limits of Minority Acceptance in America: God Loves (Almost) Everyone*. Rowman & Littlefield, 2018.

Sumerau, J. E., and Lain A. B. Mathers. *America through Transgender Eyes*. Rowman & Littlefield, 2019.

Sumerau, J. Edward. "'Some of Us Are Good, God-Fearing Folks': Justifying Religious Participation in an LGBT Christian Church." *Journal of Contemporary Ethnography* 46, no. 1 (February 1, 2017): 3–29. https://doi.org/10.1177/0891241614559142.

Sumerau, J. Edward, Irene Padavic, and Douglas P. Schrock. "'Little Girls Unwilling to Do What's Best for Them': Resurrecting Patriarchy in an LGBT Christian Church." *Journal of Contemporary Ethnography* 44, no. 3 (June 1, 2015): 306–34. https://doi.org/10.1177/0891241614530160.

Summers, Brandi Thompson. *Black in Place: The Spatial Aesthetics of Race in a Post-Chocolate City*. University of North Carolina Press Books, 2019.

Suttles, Gerald D. "The Cumulative Texture of Local Urban Culture." *American Journal of Sociology* 90, no. 2 (September 1, 1984): 283–304. https://doi.org/10.1086/228080.

Talen, Emily, and Luc Anselin. "Assessing Spatial Equity: An Evaluation of Measures of Accessibility to Public Playgrounds." *Environment and Planning A* 30, no. 4 (1998): 595–613.

Taylor, Verta, Leila J. Rupp, and Joshua Gamson. "Performing Protest: Drag Shows as Tactical Repertoire of the Gay and Lesbian Movement." In *Authority in Contention*, edited by Daniel M. Cress and Daniel J. Myers. Emerald Group Publishing Limited, 2004.

Thompson, Brock. *The Un-Natural State: Arkansas and the Queer South*. University of Arkansas Press, 2010.

Thumma, Scott, and Edward R. Gray. *Gay Religion*. Rowman Altamira, 2004.

Titchkosky, Tanya. *The Question of Access: Disability, Space, Meaning*. University of Toronto Press, 2011.

Tomlinson, John. "Cultural Imperialism." *The Wiley-Blackwell Encyclopedia of Globalization*, 2012.

Trujillo, Michael L. *Land of Disenchantment: Latina/o Identities and Transformations in Northern New Mexico*. University of New Mexico Press, 2010.

Turner, Victor, Roger D. Abrahams, and Alfred Harris. *The Ritual Process: Structure and Anti-Structure*. Routledge, 2017.

Vaz, Kim Marie. *The "Baby Dolls": Breaking the Race and Gender Barriers of the New Orleans Mardi Gras Tradition*. Louisiana State University Press, 2013.

Veracini, Lorenzo. *Settler Colonialism*. Palgrave Macmillan, 2010.

Vogler, Stefan. "Welcoming Diversity? Symbolic Boundaries and the Politics of Normativity in Kansas City's LGBTQ Communities." *Journal of Homosexuality* 63, no. 2 (February 2016): 169–92. https://doi.org/10.1080/00918369.2015.1083781.

Volpp, Leti. "Feminist, Sexual, and Queer Citizenship." *The Oxford Handbook of Citizenship*, 2017, 153.

Walford, Geoffrey. "The Impossibility of Anonymity in Ethnographic Research." *Qualitative Research* 18, no. 5 (October 1, 2018): 516–25. https://doi.org/10.1177/1468794118778606.

Walters, Suzanna Danuta. *The Tolerance Trap: How God, Genes, and Good Intentions Are Sabotaging Gay Equality*. Vol. 3. New York University Press, 2016.

Ward, Brian, Martyn Bone, and William Link. "Preface: Understanding the South." *Creating and Consuming the American South*, 2015, ix–x.

Ward, Jane. *Respectably Queer: Diversity Culture in LGBT Activist Organizations*. Vanderbilt University Press, 2008. https://muse.jhu.edu.

———. "Producing 'Pride' in West Hollywood: A Queer Cultural Capital for Queers with Cultural Capital." *Sexualities* 6, no. 1 (2003): 65–94.

Warner, Michael. *The Trouble with Normal: Sex, Politics, and the Ethics of Queer Life*. Harvard University Press, 2000.

Waters, Mary C., and Tomás R. Jiménez. "Assessing Immigrant Assimilation: New Empirical and Theoretical Challenges." *Annual Review of Sociology* 31, no. 1 (August 2005): 105–25. https://doi.org/10.1146/annurev.soc.29.010202.100026.

Watkins III, Jerry T. *Queering the Redneck Riviera: Sexuality and the Rise of Florida Tourism*. University Press of Florida, 2018.

Weigle, Marta. "Southwest Lures: Innocents Detoured, Incensed Determined." *Journal of the Southwest*, 1990, 499–540.

Weigle, Marta, and Kyle Fiore. *Santa Fe and Taos: The Writer's Era, 1916–1941*. Sunstone Press, 2008.

Weiss, Margot D. "Gay Shame and BDSM Pride: Neoliberalism, Privacy, and Sexual Politics." *Radical History Review* 2008, no. 100 (January 1, 2008): 87–101. https://doi.org/10.1215/01636545-2007-023.

Wenger, Tisa. *We Have a Religion: The 1920s Pueblo Indian Dance Controversy and American Religious Freedom*. University of North Carolina Press, 2009.

Westbrook, Laurel, and Kristen Schilt. "Doing Gender, Determining Gender: Transgender People, Gender Panics, and the Maintenance of the Sex/Gender/Sexuality System." *Gender & Society* 28, no. 1 (February 1, 2014): 32–57. https://doi.org/10.1177/0891243213503203.

Weston, Kath. *Families We Choose: Lesbians, Gays, Kinship*. Columbia University Press, 1997.

White, E. Frances. *Dark Continent of Our Bodies: Black Feminism & Politics of Respectability*. Temple University Press, 2010.

White, Steven. "The Heterogeneity of Southern White Distinctiveness." *American Politics Research* 42, no. 4 (2014): 551–78.

Wilcox, Melissa M. *Queer Nuns: Religion, Activism, and Serious Parody*. Vol. 33. New York University Press, 2018.

Wilson, Chris. *The Myth of Santa Fe: Creating a Modern Regional Tradition*. University of New Mexico Press, 1997.

Wolcott, Victoria W. *Remaking Respectability: African American Women in Interwar Detroit*. University of North Carolina Press Books, 2013.

Wolfe, Patrick. "Settler Colonialism and the Elimination of the Native," *Journal of Genocide Research* 8, no. 4 (2006): 387–409.

———. *Settler Colonialism*. A&C Black, 1999.

Woodell, Brandi, Emily Kazyak, and D'Lane Compton. "Reconciling LGB and Christian Identities in the Rural South." *Social Sciences* 4, no. 3 (September 2015): 859–78. https://doi.org/10.3390/socsci4030859.

Wynn, Jonathan R. *Music/City: American Festivals and Placemaking in Austin, Nashville, and Newport*. University of Chicago Press, 2015.

Yoshino, Kenji. *Covering: The Hidden Assault on Our Civil Rights*. Random House Trade Paperbacks, 2007.

Young, Elliott. "Red Men, Princess Pocahontas, and George Washington: Harmonizing Race Relations in Laredo at the Turn of the Century." *Western Historical Quarterly* 29, no. 1 (February 1, 1998): 48–85. https://doi.org/10.2307/970806.

Young, Iris Marion. *Justice and the Politics of Difference*. Princeton University Press, 2011.

Yuval-Davis, Nira. "Women, Citizenship and Difference." *Feminist Review* 57, no. 1 (September 1, 1997): 4–27. https://doi.org/10.1080/014177897339632.

INDEX

ABOUT THE AUTHOR

Amy L. Stone (they/them) is Professor of Sociology and Anthropology at Trinity University, a liberal arts college in San Antonio, Texas. Their research includes the study of lesbian, gay, bisexual, transgender, and queer (LGBTQ) health, family life, politics, and the incorporation of LGBT individuals into communities, cities, and the law. Their book, *Gay Rights at the Ballot Box* (2012) is the first systematic analysis of how activists in political campaigns fight anti-gay initiatives. They are also the author of *Cornyation: San Antonio's Outrageous Fiesta Tradition*, and co-editor of *Out of the Closet, Into the Archives: Researching Sexual Histories*. They have published in journals such as the *Annual Review of Sociology*, *Social Forces*, *Sexualities*, *Journal of Homosexuality*, *GLQ*, and the *Journal of the History of Sexuality*.